Adversarial Justice and Victims' Rights

The rights, status and treatment of sexual assault victims has emerged as a significant 21st-century concern, occupying the forefront of legal commentary on international policy agendas. This book explores the extent to which reforms that offer victims enhanced rights to information and participation across England and Wales, Ireland and South Australia can address sexual assault victims' procedural and substantive justice concerns. Informed by the voices of 26 high-level criminal justice professionals, legal stakeholders and victim support workers, and a quantitative dataset, this book also considers whether legal representation can address some of the problems of the prosecution process for sexual assault victims in Victoria and, indeed, in other adversarial jurisdictions that employ similar legislative frameworks. While acknowledging the value of victim-focused reforms, this book contends that cultural changes to the ways in which sexual assault victims are perceived and treated are necessary in order to improve victims' experiences of the legal process. Reconceptualising the role of sexual assault victims from 'witnesses' to 'participants' will also increase the likelihood that victims' rights and interests will be considered alongside those of the state and the accused. This book situates its findings within broader debates about the role, rights and treatment of sexual assault victims in adversarial justice systems and outlines prospects for the transfer of policy and practice between jurisdictions. *Adversarial Justice and Victims' Rights* will interest academic and policy stakeholders engaged in criminology, law and socio-legal studies, as well as undergraduate and postgraduate students researching sexual violence and victims' access to justice.

Mary Iliadis is a lecturer in criminology at Deakin University in Melbourne, Australia, and the newsletter editor for the Australian and New Zealand Society of Criminology. Mary's research adopts a socio-legal framework to examine, critique and impact legal policy concerning sexual assault victims' rights and role in adversarial systems of justice. Informed by international and comparative contexts, Mary's work explores how access to justice is negotiated by victims of gendered violence, with a particular focus on mechanisms for victim participation in criminal trials.

Victims, Culture and Society

Edited by:
Sandra Walklate, *University of Liverpool, UK and Monash University, Australia*
Kerry Carrington, *Queensland University of Technology, Australia*

Concerns about victimisation have multiplied over the last 50 years. *Victims, Culture and Society* explores the major concepts, debates and controversies that these concerns have generated across a range of disciplines, but particularly within criminology and victimology. As the impacts of globalisation, the movement of peoples and the divergences between the global North and global South have become ever more apparent, this series provides an authoritative space for original contributions in making sense of these far-reaching changes on individuals, localities and nationalities. These issues by their very nature demand an interdisciplinary approach and an interdisciplinary voice outside conventional conceptual boundaries. *Victims, Culture and Society* offers the space for that voice.

Each author adopts a strong personal view and offers a lively and agenda-setting treatment of their subject matter. The monographs encompass a transnational, global or comparative approach to the issues they address. Examining new areas of both empirical and theoretical enquiry, the series offers the opportunity for innovative and progressing thinking about the relationship between victims, culture and society. The books will be useful and thought-provoking resources for the international community of undergraduates, postgraduates, researchers and policymakers working within the broad field of victimisation.

Victim Support and the Welfare State
Carina Gallo and Kerstin Svensson

Towards a Global Femicide Index
Counting the Costs
Sandra Walklate, Kate Fitz-Gibbon, Jude McCulloch and JaneMaree Maher

Adversarial Justice and Victims' Rights
Reconceptualising the Role of Sexual Assault Victims
Mary Iliadis

For more information about this series, please visit: www.routledge.com/Victims-Culture-and-Society/book-series/VICS

Adversarial Justice and Victims' Rights

Reconceptualising the Role of Sexual Assault Victims

Mary Iliadis

Routledge
Taylor & Francis Group
LONDON AND NEW YORK

First published 2020
by Routledge
2 Park Square, Milton Park, Abingdon, Oxon OX14 4RN

and by Routledge
605 Third Avenue, New York, NY 10017

First issued in paperback 2022

Routledge is an imprint of the Taylor & Francis Group, an informa business

Publisher's Note
The publisher has gone to great lengths to ensure the quality of this reprint but points out that some imperfections in the original copies may be apparent.

British Library Cataloguing-in-Publication Data
A catalogue record for this book is available from the British Library

Library of Congress Cataloging-in-Publication Data
A catalog record has been requested for this book

ISBN: 978-0-367-20418-1 (hbk)
ISBN: 978-0-367-49152-9 (pbk)
ISBN: 978-0-429-26136-7 (ebk)

DOI: 10.4324/9780429261367

Typeset in Times New Roman
by Wearset Ltd, Boldon, Tyne and Wear

Contents

	List of illustrations	vi
	Foreword	vii
	Acknowledgements	x
	List of abbreviations	xii
1	Introduction	1
2	Tracing the interest in victims, victims' rights and sexual assault law reform	27
3	Procedural justice	56
4	Providing a check on prosecutorial decision-making: an analysis of the VRR reform	73
5	Separate legal representation for victims under section 34 of the *Sex Offenders Act 2001* (Irl)	97
6	Victim participation through the SACVR	112
7	The prospect of ILR for sexual assault victims within Victoria's criminal prosecution process	126
8	Concluding comments	152
	Appendices	168
	References	188
	Index	204

Illustrations

Figure

4.1 Letter from the CPS to a victim regarding their review 85

Tables

1.1 Participant groups 18
1.2 Distribution of participant groups across the focus jurisdictions 18
1.3 Participants' pseudonym, role and jurisdiction 19
4.1 Stages of the VRR process 76
8.1 The potential for victim-focused reforms to meet victims' procedural justice needs 158

Foreword

Over the past six decades, there has been a gradual, yet dramatic, reconsideration of the plight of victims of crime. Contemporaneous to this, victimology has evolved, albeit unresolved as to whether it is a unique social science or a sub-discipline of criminology. Notwithstanding, developments in the measurement of criminal victimisation, awareness of the shortcomings in criminal justice responses to victims, and knowledge of what works, what does not and what is showing promise in relation to assisting victims to deal with the effects of crime have driven an array of law reforms and procedural changes in Australia, England and Wales, and Ireland. The once common cliché that victims are 'the forgotten people' in criminal justice systems is no longer valid in any of these countries.

Despite the burgeoning victims' rights legislation, too many victims are not receiving the rights to which they are entitled under law. For instance, although the feminist campaign has been an important impetus to improve understanding of the nature, extent and impact of sexual violence against women, as Mary Iliadis reveals, outdated myths about such violence continue to fuel biases that influence the fairness of decision-making throughout the criminal justice process. Thus, improving access to justice for women who are victims of sexual violence remains a victimological priority.

The issue of victim participation in criminal justice systems is also a priority. Significant gains have been made in favour of victims that challenge the dualism of the state as prosecutor and the accused as defendant, which is deeply embedded in adversarial systems of justice. In general, public support for greater victim participation has been melded with a tougher attitude towards crime, which is not necessarily congruent with the intentions of those who have urged that victims should be genuine participants, even a party, in the administration of criminal justice.

A paucity of empirically sound research has meant that progress on victim participation has been fragmented and at times controversial. Therefore, key questions on changes to the legal status of victims in Australia, England and Wales, and Ireland remain largely unanswered. Does the victim's role as a witness in criminal proceedings constrain the efficacy of their participation? Does giving victims a voice result in commensurate voice recognition? What rights mechanisms enhance the participation of victims of sexual violence? Do these rights counteract the causes of secondary victimisation, such as prosecutors' ambivalence and defence counsel's aggressive cross-examination? Does victim participation improve sexual violence victims' procedural justice experiences? Do stronger victims' participatory rights jeopardise the victim-to-survivor transition?

Mary Iliadis makes an important and timely contribution to the development of more evidence-informed policy making. Her comprehensive review of literature and comparative study on sexual violence victims' interactions with adversarial criminal justice systems advances understandings on how access to justice can be better negotiated for victims of these significant social and legal harms.

Moreover, her conclusions and recommendations should inform future steps towards a 'modern' criminal justice system that operates according to a triangulation of interests – victim, defendant and state – and should be used as a springboard for further research.

Michael O'Connell AM APM
Former Commissioner for Victims' Rights, South Australia

Victims of sexual violence experience the most severe violations, suffering the depths of degradation and humiliation. These are crimes of alarming prevalence, largely (though not exclusively) perpetrated against women, striking at their bodily integrity and autonomy.

The sad and chilling truth is that, more often than not, victims of sexual violence fail to report these crimes to the police; and if they do report, they may resile midway through the legal process. This happens not because they are defeatist, complacent or complicit, but rather it is at least in part due to their tainted perception of the adversarial criminal justice process, and the humiliating and frightening culture that it fosters.

In a scholarly but thoroughly accessible manner, this book shines a bright light on the need for victim-focused reform within adversarial legal systems. Highlighting the shibboleths that potentially impede the steep climb to meaningful change, it provides a recipe for reform.

Our adversarial system of justice is based on the fundamental premise that criminal trials engage only two parties – namely, the state acting in the public interest and the defendant with an inalienable right to a fair trial. Against this context, Dr Iliadis sets out to identify reforms that might secure the rights and interests of the victim so that victims may become valued stakeholders and genuine participants in the process rather than mere witnesses to the proceedings.

To achieve procedural and substantive justice ideals, the system must enhance support and protection to victims. Notwithstanding the constraints imposed on the victim's role as a witness to proceedings, Dr Iliadis identifies merit in advancing sexual assault victims' rights and interests through victim review schemes and measures designed to enhance participatory rights, including through independent legal representation in cases where victims' privacy and interests may become compromised.

The author's arguments are strengthened by her invocation of precedents drawn from comparative law found in transnational directives and the gathering momentum of victim-focused reforms in England and Wales, Ireland and Australia.

In measured and incisive terms, this book recognises that not only must these reforms be incremental and introduced with strategic patience, but they must also be accompanied by a change in culture within the legal system itself.

Anyone interested in this troubling and vexed area of justice for victims should ensure that they are not further than an arm's length from this innovative and arresting text.

The Right Honourable Sir John Gillen

Acknowledgements

This book would not have been possible without the support, guidance and encouragement of a number of people to whom I am greatly indebted.

First, I would like to thank the participants of this research upon which this book is based; without you, this book would not have been possible. The positions, status and expertise of the participants contributed to a rich dataset, resulting in deeply textured research findings. In particular, I would like to thank the Crown Prosecution Service in London for offering unique insights into this research, especially in relation to the Victims' Right to Review reform. I would also like to thank the Victim Commissioners who participated in this research – your insights and expertise are tremendously valuable. To the members of the Victorian judiciary, thank you for your enthusiasm and interest in this research.

I am also fortunate to have the support of many wonderful colleagues.

To Professor Sandra Walklate, thank you for your mentorship, encouragement and insights from the initial stages of this book's inception. Words cannot express how truly grateful I am for your support and for always offering candid feedback. Dr Kate Fitz-Gibbon, I am greatly indebted to you for your support, assurance and generous advice while I wrote this book. To Dr Kate Burns, thank you for your encouragement. I am very grateful for your continual support and friendship over the years. I am also very appreciative of the consistent encouragement and support of Michael O'Connell, who is the former South Australian Commissioner for Victims' Rights. Thank you for your belief in my ability to make a difference to victims' rights and experiences within the criminal justice system. I would also like to extend my sincerest appreciation to The Right Honourable Sir John Gillen for supporting this research and engaging with my findings to help to inform sexual assault law reform in Northern Ireland.

This book is based on the findings of my doctoral research conducted at Monash University, which was supervised by Professor Jude McCulloch and Associate Professor Asher Flynn. Jude, thank you for dedicating your time to provide valuable feedback on my research. I feel very fortunate to have worked under your guidance and your words of wisdom helped to shape my research immensely.

Asher, words cannot express the profound impact you had on my doctoral candidature and academic development. I am forever grateful for your mentorship. You have continued to motivate, educate and inspire me through your academic success, and I feel honoured to have experienced this journey with your guidance.

I would like to extend my appreciation to a number of journals for granting me permission to include the findings of some of my prior publications in this book. Earlier versions of this work were published in the following journals:

- Iliadis, M. (2019), 'Victim representation for sexual history evidence in Ireland: a step towards or away from meeting victims' procedural justice needs?', *Criminology & Criminal Justice*, https://doi.org/10.1177/1748895819851848.
- Iliadis, M., Fitz-Gibbon, K. & Walklate, S. (2019), 'Improving justice responses for victims of intimate partner violence: examining the merits of the provision of independent legal representation', *International Journal of Comparative and Applied Criminal Justice*, https://doi.org/10.1080/01924036.2019.1695639.
- Iliadis, M. & Flynn, A. (2018), 'Providing a check on prosecutorial decision-making: an analysis of the Victims' Right to Review reform', *British Journal of Criminology*, 58/3, 550–68.
- Kirchengast, K., Iliadis, M. & O'Connell, M. (2019), 'Development of the Office of Commissioner of Victims' Rights as an appropriate response to improving the experiences of victims in the criminal justice system: integrity, access and justice for victims of crime', *Monash University Law Review*, 45/1, 1–28.

In preparing for the submission of this book, I engaged the professional copy-editing services of Julia Farrell. Thank you for your patience, suggestions and meticulous attention to detail, Julia.

To my incredible family and friends, this book would not have been possible without you – thank you for your continual love and support, and for encouraging me to pursue my passion for making a difference to the social, legal and political contexts underpinning responses to victims of sexual violence. I hope that the analysis presented in this book promotes discussion on how the rights, role and status of sexual assault victims can be improved in a system that is based on adversarial exchange between the state and the accused.

Abbreviations

ABS	Australian Bureau of Statistics
ACT	Australian Capital Territory
AIFS	Australian Institute of Family Studies
AIHW	Australian Institute of Health and Welfare
ALRC	Australian Law Reform Commission
CEO	Chief Executive Officer
CPI	Consumer Price Index
CPS	Crown Prosecution Service
DPP	Director of Public Prosecutions
ICC	International Criminal Court
ILR	Independent Legal Representation
ILRC	Irish Law Reform Commission
IRE	Ireland
ISVA	Independent Sexual Violence Advisor
LASPO	*Legal Aid, Sentencing and Punishment of Offenders Act 2012*
OPP	Office of Public Prosecutions
QLD	Queensland
RAJI	Rape and Justice in Ireland
RCFV	Royal Commission into Family Violence
RCIRCSA	Royal Commission into Institutional Responses to Child Sexual Abuse (Cth)
RCNI	Rape Crisis Network Ireland
SACVR	South Australian Commissioner for Victims' Rights
UK	United Kingdom
UN	United Nations
VIC	Victoria
VIS	Victim Impact Statement
VoCC	Victims of Crime Commissioner
VPS	Victim Personal Statement
VLRC	Victorian Law Reform Commission
VRR	Victims' Right to Review
VSAC	Victorian Sentencing Advisory Council

VOCAT	Victims of Crime Assistance Tribunal
VoCC	Victims of Crime Commissioner (Victorian)
WA	Western Australia
WAS	Witness Assistance Service

1 Introduction

> The status of the victim is simply that of evidentiary cannon fodder, of witness or claimant, not of citizen with participation rights and obligations.
>
> (Braithwaite 1993: 36)

> The criminal justice system's treatment of women who allege rape has not significantly improved, and in some respects may be worse than before [victim-focused] … reforms were enacted.
>
> (Bronitt 1998: 42)

> [Victims] are denied any form of proactive participation in the trial since their interests are deemed to fall outside the remit of the criminal trial as a forum for the resolution of the dispute between the state and the accused.
>
> (Doak 2005: 299)

> Originally the adversarial system position[ed] victims … outside of a house, looking through a window and watching a black knight [the defence] and a white knight [the prosecutor] clash with one another and fight in a conflict.… [With] victims' rights initially, we open a window so that the victim – and this is where we get the information rights – could hear what was going on and gather some information. Now we have given victims some procedural rights, such as the right to participate in charge bargaining to the extent that they must be consulted. There is no obligation, though, to do anything other than to consult, and there are differences about people's understanding of what consultation is. We have given victims the right to make impact statements [and] … the right to make submissions at a parole board. So we have effectively opened the window and allowed them to step inside and where [there] are key points we think they should be heard, we invite them to be heard.
>
> (James, leading victims' rights advocate)

The rights, status and plight of crime victims have emerged as a significant 21st-century concern, occupying the forefront of legal commentary on international policy agendas. Consensus has emerged around the need to further consolidate the rights of victims to advance their standing and access to justice, although questions prevail as to how victims' rights can be secured in a system based on adversarial exchange between the state and the accused. Conceptions of fairness within adversarial justice systems are premised on the protection of an accused person's due process rights, against the might of the state, which prosecutes in the public interest. Criminal procedure thus sets out the rights of the accused and, until recently, the procedure has said very little about the rights of victims. Even so, procedural rights protections afforded to accused people are largely focused on eliciting aspects of probative evidence from vulnerable victims, including victims of sexual violence. This has led to an appetite for reform that better promotes the protection, interests and rights of victims alongside those of the state and the accused – a perspective Lord Steyn describes as '*a triangulation of interests*' (emphasis added, *Attorney-General's Reference (No 3 of 1999)* [2001] 2 AC 91, 118).

Over the past three decades, victim-focused reforms have commonly centred on the particular needs of vulnerable and at-risk victims, including victims of sexual offences, and the imperative to better support and protect their interests against adversative court processes. Recognition of the unique needs of sexual assault victims espouses the broader aims of adversarial systems, 'where attaining justice is traditionally associated with equality, fairness and respect for individual rights, encompassing those of both the victim and accused' (Iliadis & Flynn 2018: 551). The integrity of criminal prosecution processes, as noted by Kirchengast, Iliadis and O'Connell (2019: 2), more broadly relies upon 'victims' confidence that the reporting of offences will not cause further secondary harm, or exacerbate existing harm'. Indeed, research has consistently shown that consideration of victims and their interests promotes the shift in a victim's status from 'peripheral to integral' (ibid. 8), enabling victims to feel like 'important constituents in the justice system' (ibid. 2).

This book considers how three different victim-focused reforms operating across England and Wales, Ireland and South Australia can meet the participatory and procedural justice[1] needs of sexual assault victims, while maintaining the integrity and adversarial character of criminal justice. Each reform under examination offers victims enhanced information and participation rights and seeks to advance the interests and standing of victims in the criminal justice system. This book explores the extent to which each reform meets victims' procedural justice needs from the criminal prosecution process, specifically in relation to the elements of information, validation, voice and control, which are discussed later in this chapter.

The three reforms under focus include the Victims' Right to Review (VRR) scheme in England and Wales; independent legal representation (ILR) for sexual assault victims in Ireland under section 34 of the *Sex Offenders Act 2001* (Irl); and the powers of the South Australian Commissioner for Victims' Rights (SACVR) to provide ILR to victims in circumstances where their rights, interests or privacy are compromised or not adequately represented in legal proceedings. While the reforms analysed in England and Wales and South Australia are theoretically available to all crime victims, each reform is analysed in relation to sexual assault victims and the extent to which it may enable victims to feel they have attained procedural justice, and perhaps even enhanced substantive outcomes.

By focusing on reforms that advance victims' information and participation rights, the book also considers more contentious proposals for reform pertaining to whether there is scope for and merit in introducing ILR for sexual assault victims throughout Victoria's[2] criminal prosecution process to enhance victims' standing in proceedings. In doing so, the book explores whether ILR can help to address some of the key problems identified by the critiques of the prosecution process for sexual assault victims in Victoria (which are discussed in more detail later in this chapter and in Chapter 2), and, indeed, in other adversarial jurisdictions that employ similar legislative frameworks. At the same time, this book considers whether a stronger case for enhancing sexual assault victims' rights in Victoria may be made based on clearly defined information or participation rights that do not grant victims 'party' status to proceedings, such as those rights available to victims in England and Wales, Ireland and South Australia.

It is well documented in the literature that victims of crime experience difficulties negotiating access to justice within adversarial systems as their voices in proceedings are constrained due to their role as a witness (Braun 2019; Doak 2005; Holder 2018). As explored later in this chapter, however, such difficulties are often heightened for victims of sexual offences due to the nature of the offending and its protracted harms. Prospects for reform have consequently sought to address the unique needs of sexual offence victims through offering appropriate protections and supports that strengthen their evidence and confidence in the criminal justice system. The imperative to further support and protect victims, and to advance their standing and access to justice, is reflected in transnational directives. For example, the Council of Europe's *Istanbul Convention on Preventing and Combating Violence Against Women and Domestic Violence* requires that 'measures … be adopted to protect the privacy' of complainants (Article 56(1)(f)), including 'protection … from intimidation, retaliation and repeat victimisation' (Article 56(1)(a)). It also requires Member States to enact legislative changes to enable victims 'to be heard, to supply evidence and have their views, needs and concerns presented, directly or through an intermediary, and considered' (Article 56(1)(d), Council of Europe 2011). These provisions are encouraged alongside the need to 'provide victims with appropriate support services so that their rights and interests are duly presented and taken into account' (Article 56(10)(e), Council of Europe 2011). Within the current adversarial framework, however, there are increasing concerns around the contempt for sexual assault victims' rights and interests, especially insofar as their 'witness' status does not sufficiently safeguard them from unduly hostile criminal proceedings.

Disregard for victims in adversarial justice systems was not always present within the criminal justice process. Historically, victims of crime maintained an active role in determining and administering justice (Braun 2019; Holder 2018). This practice was commonplace in England and Wales, and replicated in other jurisdictions bound by similar legislative frameworks, such as Australia (Holder 2018: 5). By the 20th century, however, victims of crime were perceived as 'instruments for institutional ends' and criminal justice became situated within a public realm controlled by agents of the state (ibid.). The rationale underpinning this shift – which espoused public and open justice ideals and protection of an accused person's rights to a fair and impartial trial – limited a victim's role to that of a mere witness to proceedings (Booth & Carrington 2018; Doak 2005). Victim interests have therefore been positioned as secondary to those of the state and the accused, and their views are not legally represented unless within 'a passive context, [either] as [a] police informant or as [a] witness for the prosecution' (Kirchengast 2013: 569).

Since the late 20th century, however, crime victims have questioned how 'justice' is 'constituted and considered' (Holder 2018: 5). Knowing that the system relies on victims to report crime and cooperate as a witness for the prosecution, victims and victim advocates have critiqued their general exclusion (Holder 2018). Feminist advocates and victims' rights groups have also challenged the social, legal and political contexts that shape responses to victims, particularly victims of sexual offences, which has led to significant shifts in how victims are perceived and included in the criminal justice system as a result (Doak 2005; Iliadis 2019; Kirchengast, Iliadis & O'Connell 2019). These changes have manifested in improvements to the social and service rights of victims through enhanced access to information, compensation schemes, Victim Impact Statements (VISs)[3] and protective measures, such as the use of video testimony and restrictions on the sorts of questions that can be asked of sexual assault victims when testifying in trials (Doak 2005: 294; Iliadis & Flynn 2018: 553; Kirchengast, Iliadis & O'Connell 2019: 9).[4]

Such changes are considered to contribute positively towards the victim's sense of achieving procedural justice, providing them with the opportunity to feel like 'integral players ... rather than mere bystanders' in the prosecution process (O'Connell 2012: 1). For sexual assault victims in particular, these reforms provide a mechanism to potentially reduce the likelihood of experiencing secondary victimisation, also referred to as the 'second injury' – whereby 'the psychological impact of victimisation can be considerably exacerbated by ... the criminal justice system' (Doak 2008: 51; see also Ellison 2007; Jordan 2001). As noted by Doak (2008: 54), affording credence to victims' rights and needs is 'not only within the victim's interest, but also in the public interest' to ensure 'that victims feel able to enter into the criminal justice system' without fear of the legal process. Significantly, the movement towards acknowledging victims' rights and interests has required a reconceptualisation of the 'traditional' legal process, in that consideration must be given 'to preserving all trial participants' rights ... not just [those of] the defendant' (Gans et al. 2011: 381).[5] The emergence of victim-oriented reforms has thus been regarded as a way to better acknowledge and include victim interests, alongside those of the accused and the state. At the same time, however, victims' rights and interests continue to be reflected in conservative adversarial reform that has focused on enhancing the provision of information to victims, and, to a more limited extent, victim participation, and this has raised questions over the extent of the positive impacts the reforms have had on victims to date as they continue to occupy the status of a witness to proceedings.

Adversarial justice

The adversarial criminal justice system is a key feature of common law jurisdictions (Brienen & Hoegen 2001).[6] This system, as Flynn and Hodgson (2017: 6) contend, seeks to uphold the notions of fairness, equality and respect for individual rights. A core feature of the adversarial criminal justice system is that crime is contested between the state prosecutor and the accused – both of whom present their cases and define the issues for the jury to consider (Gleeson 2001 cited in *Doggett v The Queen* 2001: 1). The burden of proof[7] is placed on the state prosecutor, who pursues the investigation and prosecution in the public interest, and witnesses, including those who allege crime, give oral evidence in court[8] and are subject to cross-examination (Booth, Kaye & Wangmann 2019; Victorian Law Reform Commission [VLRC] 2016). Within this context, the judge assumes a relatively passive role and is not involved in investigating the alleged offence(s), deciding what charge(s) are to be brought before the accused or determining how cases ought to be conducted during the trial. They do, however, ensure that procedures and rules are followed (Gleeson cited in *Crampton v The Queen* 2000: 5). The judge also assumes responsibility for instructing the jury on how to apply the law to the evidence, which assists in their deliberations on a verdict (see, for example, *Jury Directions Act 2015* (Vic) s 5(2)).[9] After considering the evidence, the jury ultimately determines whether the prosecution has proven that the accused has committed the offence(s) charged beyond reasonable doubt (*Jury Directions Act 2015* (Vic) s 61; *Criminal Procedure Act 2009* (Vic) s 238).[10]

In the Australian High Court decision of *R v Carroll* (2002),[11] Gleeson CJ and Hayne J described the adversarial criminal trial in the following way:

> A criminal trial is an accusatorial process in which the power of the State is deployed against an individual accused of crime. Many of the rules that have been developed for the conduct of criminal trials therefore reflect two obvious propositions: that the power and resources of the State as prosecutor are much greater than those of the individual accused and that the consequences of conviction are very serious.

The adversarial approach to attaining justice thereby revolves around a 'defendant-centric conception of fairness … [that] ensur[es] a suitable legal environment for the defendant meeting the might of the state in the context of facing prosecution for a criminal charge' (Gans et al. 2011: 380). For this reason, 'fairness' is measured against how well the accused person's rights are affirmed in relation to the power of the state.[12] This reflects the principle of an 'equality of arms'

(Gans et al. 2011: 486; Kirchengast 2016c: 46), which requires that the accused person be granted a set of due process rights, including: a presumption of innocence until proven guilty; being tried without undue delay; the ability to examine witnesses and test the prosecution's evidence; legal representation, either privately administered or government-funded; and being able to appeal a conviction or sentence in a higher court (Gans et al. 2011: 379). These fair trial principles safeguard the rule of law and are considered fundamental for upholding democratic institutions and public confidence in the criminal justice system (Gans et al. 2011: 47).

The emergence of interest in victims

Within the adversarial constraints of justice processes, the focus on protecting the accused person's due process rights to ensure that there is equality of arms has 'eclipsed' the recognition of the victim's inherent interests, meaning that victims have no legitimate status and are denied active participation in the criminal justice system (VLRC 2016: 26; see also McAsey 2011). In the late 20th century, however, fuelled by feminist activism and the growth of victims' rights movements, the traditional 'state versus defendant based formulation of the fair trial began to be legislatively remodelled to spread fairness rights to witnesses' due to increasing concerns over the impacts of the legal process on vulnerable victims, particularly victims of sexual offences (Gans et al. 2011: 381). These movements sought to challenge the patriarchal systems and structures governing responses to victims of gendered crime (Iliadis, Fitz-Gibbon & Walklate 2019), especially those that 'privileged an idealised version of a victim – vulnerable, elderly victim of vicious assaults or attacks by strangers' (Booth & Carrington 2018: 294). They also aimed to address the bevy of procedural challenges impacting sexual assault victims' engagement with the criminal justice system, including their experiences of insensitive treatment by authorities, particularly the police, prosecution and defence counsel, as well as distressing cross-examination, and a lack of understanding of victims' needs more generally (Doak 2008: 51).

Within the context of adversarial trials specifically, victims are prone to aggressive cross-examination spurred by outdated myths of rape and sexuality by, or on behalf of, the very person from whom they are seeking protection. Such questioning aims to test 'the credibility and the veracity of the witness', and to elicit probative evidence that will assist in determining the accused's guilt (Booth, Kaye & Wangmann 2019: 1110). Although cross-examination is a distinctive feature of adversarial systems, questions have been raised as to whether this fair trial principle 'is the best way to establish the *truth*' (Booth, Kaye & Wangmann 2019: 1111; emphasis added). Blackstone's ([1769] 1966) centuries-old precept 'that it is better that ten guilty persons escape, than that one innocent suffer[s]' may have its roots in these considerations (Gleeson & Hayne 2002 cited in *R v Carroll 2002*: 6).[13] Blackstone's aphorism is gendered in nature and has often been cited to refer to criminal trials where alleged victims of sexual violence are called upon to testify as witnesses in support of the prosecution's case.

Indeed, research has long documented the ways in which victims of sexual violence perceive testifying in court, and cross-examination in particular, to be equally, if not more, traumatic than the crime itself (Ellison 2001; Jordan 2008; Stubbs 2003). This reality, coupled with a victim's limited role as 'witness' to proceedings, has increased the likelihood of sexual assault victims experiencing secondary victimisation. In this regard, it has been noted that victims are 'subjected to innumerable indignities ... in a system that espouses principles of respect, rights and equal treatment' (Holder 2018: 5). And although the victim's role has continued to evolve, 'the cumulative effect' of victim-oriented reform has 'not been driven by a vision of what the [victim's] role should be' and this has 'fostered inconsistencies in how victims are perceived, how they see themselves, their expectations and how they are treated' (VLRC 2016: xiv).

The Victorian context

In Victoria, Australia, the movement towards being more attentive to, and inclusive of, victims' needs and interests is evident in the 2016 appointment of a Victims of Crime Commissioner,[14] whose role is to advocate for the 'recognition, inclusion, participation and respect' of victims and to highlight the key issues victims face within the criminal justice system (*Victims of Crime Commissioner Act 2015* [Vic] s 13). Increased consideration of victims' rights within the adversarial system is also evident in the most recent report of the Victorian Law Reform Commission (VLRC), *The Role of Victims of Crime in the Criminal Trial Process* (2016). The report's main recommendation included the need to reconceptualise crime victims as participants (but not as a party) to proceedings, and to have this reflected in the *Victims' Charter Act 2006* (Vic) and the *Charter of Human Rights and Responsibilities Act 2006* (Vic). This essentially requires that more prominence be given to the victim's inherent interests by government agencies, and that victims' existing rights be respected and upheld. While this acknowledgement 'departs from the idea that a[n] ... equality of arms between the accused and the community is sufficient to ensure fairness in criminal proceedings' (VLRC 2016: 27), it does not alter the structural position of victims in the criminal justice system, as their input into the process remains the same. Therefore, any positive changes to victims' procedural justice experiences may still be limited at an operational level. In 2015, the establishment of Victoria's first Royal Commission into Family Violence (RCFV) symbolised a remarkable opportunity to transform justice system responses to victims of intimate partner violence. Amid its 227 recommendations, the Royal Commission's final report (2016) considered the need to introduce ILR for victims within specialist family violence courts in recognition of the needs of and challenges experienced by victims in civil and criminal justice processes (see Iliadis, Fitz-Gibbon & Walklate 2019). While ILR for victims of intimate partner violence has precedence within civil processes associated with applications for family violence intervention orders, the provision of ILR for victims in an applied or specialised criminal court model is a new suggestion (ibid.).

Reconceptualising sexual assault victims' rights and standing

While numerous inquiries into victims' rights have emerged within Victoria and Australia, and indeed internationally, concerns surrounding the ill-treatment of sexual assault victims by the criminal justice system continue to resonate and debate abounds as to whether and how victims' rights can be made justiciable in order to enhance victims' standing and access to justice. This site of contest is well captured by Holder (2018: 5), who notes that 'legal and conceptual recognition of victims is mired in endless controversy', with academic and policy debates characterising victims as either 'a favoured constituency' (Garland 2001: 121) redefining modern criminal justice or a 'pariah' to that same system (Rock 2007: 39). Others, such as Kirchengast, Iliadis and O'Connell (2019), and Braun (2019), similarly observe that the notion of integrating victims into justice processes remains a highly contested issue. On the one hand, proponents seek to accommodate the unique needs of vulnerable victims in criminal trials, while on the other, critics fear that increased recognition of victims and victims' rights will jeopardise the 'orthodox' nature of adversarial justice (Kirchengast 2010: 2).

These perspectives have led to different trajectories in the debates around victims' rights and have put into renewed focus the question of what form the modern criminal justice system ought to take so that sexual assault victims can be enabled to feel more like *insiders* (active participants) rather than *outsiders* (mere witnesses) within the adversarial process. At the same time, however, increased consideration and involvement of victims in the criminal justice system necessitates that a balance be struck between upholding the 'core functions of adversarialism' and acknowledging the interests of victims within this context (Kirchengast 2010: 2). Notwithstanding this consideration, general consensus has emerged around the need to further integrate victims in justice processes to enhance their standing and access to justice (Braun 2019; Holder 2018; Kirchengast, Iliadis & O'Connell 2019). As Doak explains, victims' voices remain largely constrained by their role as a witness to proceedings:

> Although many victims may feel as though they are 'owed' a right to exercise a voice in decision-making processes, such as prosecution, reparation and sentencing, the criminal justice system places such rights or interests in a firmly subservient position to the collective interests of society [and the accused] in prosecuting the crime and imposing a denunciatory punishment.
>
> (2005: 299–300; see also Cavadino & Dignan 1997)

While these issues are likely to impact a broader category of victims, there are particular concerns about the protracted effects of a lack of voice and participation in the legal process for victims of sexual violence (see, inter alia, Kelly, Temkin & Griffiths 2006; Lees 1996; McGlynn, Downes & Westmarland 2017; Smith 2018; Smith & Skinner 2017). This is especially so in light of the difficulties associated with prosecuting sexual offences and the fact that conviction rates are notoriously low (see, for example, Kelly, Temkin & Griffiths 2006). Rape prosecutions typically rely on strong forensic evidence, a victim who reports immediately and is willing to testify, and a narrative that judges and jurors will find convincing. However, obtaining physical evidence immediately following victimisation can be traumatising and victims are generally sceptical about reporting victimisation to authorities, largely due to fears of the perpetrator, the legal process and its consequences, including the distressing effects of cross-examination (Australian Bureau of Statistics 2004; Braun 2014; Daly & Bouhours 2010). Through 'intense and probing interrogation' (Henderson 2015: 90), defence techniques are used to test the veracity of the victim's claims through offensive questioning that draws upon sexual history evidence or private communications, such as medical or counselling records. And despite legislative safeguards prohibiting or limiting the use of such questioning in most adversarial jurisdictions, exceptions are made that problematically justify the admission of such evidence in court, including on the basis of concerns over the imperative for the accused person to be able to fairly test the complainant's accusations (see, inter alia, Booth, Kaye & Wangmann 2019; Iliadis 2019; Iliadis, Fitz-Gibbon & Walklate 2019; McGlynn 2017).

Rape and sexual assault investigations and prosecutions have also notoriously upheld explicit standards and expectations of how a victim should act immediately following victimisation and how they should behave during the course of proceedings (see, inter alia, Henderson 2015; McGlynn 2017; Powell et al. 2013). Social constructions of 'real' rape have historically been associated with victims who defend themselves, are assaulted by strangers, are virginal and actively resist the assault, either via force or verbal attack (Christie 1986; Estrich 1987; Hasday 2000; Lievore 2005a, 2005b; Powell et al. 2013; Walklate 2008). These stereotypes, as Powell et al. (2013: 460) explain, 'are often embedded in persistent attitudes or beliefs about rape, victim-complainants and perpetrators that serve to trivialise, deny or justify the perpetration of sexual violence'. Myths surrounding sexual violence have problematically infiltrated social and legal discourse to the extent that they often form the basis for distinguishing 'honest witnesses' from 'deceitful witnesses' (Henderson 2015: 90), particularly within the cross-examination process – which, as Conley and O'Barr (1998: 32) maintain, has a 'poignancy in the rape context that is unmatched elsewhere'.

This reliance on such stereotypes at trial constructs highly problematic ideas of sexual violence and may further discourage victims from reporting crime if their case deviates from these stereotypical understandings of what constitutes 'real' rape and a 'real' rape victim' (Powell et al. 2013: 476). Compounded by the absence of victim participation rights to challenge these preconceived ideas, and by the victim's lack of legal standing in proceedings, it is perhaps unsurprising that victims of sexual violence remain reluctant to approach the law for protection and acknowledgement of harm. These issues have resulted in victims feeling that they are denied access to both procedural justice (associated with processes) and substantive justice (associated with outcomes), and have led to a much-needed heightened focus on the rights of sexual assault victims to enhance their protection, standing and access to justice.

Procedural justice

According to leading procedural justice theorist Tom Tyler (1992: 437), 'people are most strongly affected by their evaluations of the procedure by which the outcomes are reached … irrespective of what those decisions are'. Procedural justice recognises that:

> People's evaluations of the fairness of judicial hearings are affected by the opportunities which those procedures provide for people to participate, by the degree to which people judge that they are treated with dignity and respect, and by judgments about the trustworthiness of authorities. Each of these three factors has more influence on judgments of procedural justice than do … the favorableness of the outcome of the hearing.

Essentially, Tyler (1992) argues that the extent to which people judge the legal process as fair will impact on their overall satisfaction levels with the criminal justice system and, in some cases, may have a greater influence on their satisfaction than the substantive outcome of the case. This model of justice has increasingly been used to measure sexual assault victims' satisfaction with the criminal justice system. Extending upon Tyler's initial conceptualisation, authors such as Feldthusen, Hankivsky and Greaves (2000: 83) identified the importance of 'participation, dignity and trust' in relation to sexual assault victims' procedural justice needs, including fair treatment by legal authorities such as prosecutors, lawyers and judges. More recently, Clark (2010) cited factors such as information, validation, voice and control as crucial elements in shaping sexual assault victims' procedural justice experiences. In this sense, it is believed that victims are 'less likely' to report a 'marginalizing and stigmatizing experience' with the legal system if they feel that key elements of procedural justice have been upheld (Paternoster et al. 1997: 169). Similarly, Iliadis and Flynn (2018) and Iliadis (2019) have identified a correlation between the elements of information, validation, voice and control and sexual assault victims' procedural justice needs. Drawing from Clark's (2010) conceptualisation of procedural fairness in relation to sexual assault victims, and the recent works of Iliadis and Flynn (2018) and Iliadis (2019), this book posits that the elements of information, validation, voice and control are key to shaping sexual assault victims' perceptions of procedural justice.

Much of the victimology literature supports the need to grant sexual assault victims a voice in proceedings to enhance therapeutic outcomes for them (Booth 2012; McGlynn, Downes & Westmarland 2017; Wemmers 2009). Likewise, it has been found that the prospects for victim participation that enable victims to exercise voice and control may increase the likelihood that victims' procedural justice needs will be met or, at the very least, considered, and may further promote the healing of victims (see, inter alia, Clark 2010; Iliadis 2019; Iliadis & Flynn 2018). Affording credence to victims' rights and interests also advances shifts towards increased consideration and involvement of victims in the criminal justice system, beyond that of their mere witness status. Efforts towards sexual assault law reform have therefore centred on the offering of relevant protections and supports to enhance victims' standing and perceptions of procedural justice. They also aim to ensure that sexual assault victims do not withdraw their complaint out of fear of secondary victimisation. At the same time, however, fairness to the accused remains a key concern and the advent and proliferation of 'victims' rights' should not come at the cost of adversarial due processes or the rights of the accused.

Purpose and scope

Determining appropriate 'rights' mechanisms for sexual assault victims to enhance their participation and agency as stakeholders of justice has proven to be a difficult task in light of the imperative to uphold the integrity of adversarial processes (see, for example, Kirchengast, Iliadis & O'Connell 2019). This book does not advocate exclusively for the rights and interests of sexual assault victims to the detriment of the rights of the accused, nor does it propose an overhaul to the conventional functioning of adversarial systems. Instead, this book challenges normative orientations of a victim's 'witness' status and promotes the need to reconceptualise victims as participants in (but not as a party to) proceedings with inherent rights and interests. While the book's contention challenges traditional conceptions of fairness between the accused and the community in adversarial justice systems, it does not explicitly advocate for a restructure of adversarial proceedings, but rather acknowledges the need to preserve all trial participants' rights, thereby upholding a 'triangulation of interests' (Lord Steyn cited in *R v H [2004] 2 AC 134*, 145–6; see also Kirchengast, Iliadis & O'Connell 2019).

In recognition of the unique needs of victims of sexual violence, and in light of their experiences of procedural injustice, there is an argument to be made that this category of victim would benefit from additional supports and protection against adversative court processes, including having the opportunity to participate in proceedings within certain limited contexts. This book considers how sexual assault victims' rights and interests can be secured in a system based on adversarial exchange between the state and the accused. In doing so, the book analyses three different victim-focused reforms that provide victims with increased information and participation rights in three adversarial jurisdictions: England and Wales, Ireland and South Australia (hereafter referred to as 'the focus jurisdictions'). These reforms include granting victims the right to challenge prosecutorial decisions and providing them with participation rights through ILR during certain stages of the process. The reforms in the focus jurisdictions provide a catalyst to consider whether there exists a legitimate basis (or need) for introducing ILR for sexual assault victims in Victoria in order to improve their experiences of procedural justice.

This book focuses specifically on sexual assault victims' procedural justice experiences. This focus builds upon knowledge gained from the prior literature, which has measured victims' satisfaction with law reforms and the prosecution process more generally in relation to outcomes of substantive success, namely, guilty pleas or guilty verdicts (Braun 2014; Daly 2011; Koss 2006). While retribution in the form of a guilty verdict may, to some degree, determine a victim's satisfaction with the criminal justice system, contemporary research has pointed to fair treatment throughout the process as being of equal (if not greater) significance in shaping victims' perceptions and experiences of justice (Clark 2010; Iliadis & Flynn 2018; Wemmers 2014). By analysing three victim-focused reforms through the lens of procedural justice theory, this book generates new knowledge on the extent to which sexual assault victims' expectations of justice can be met by victim-focused reforms that offer increased information and participation rights in the adversarial process. In doing so, the book also considers whether there is a need for additional (and arguably contentious) models of reform, such as the provision of ILR for sexual assault victims, throughout Victoria's criminal trial process, in order to improve victim perceptions of, and experiences with, the legal process. What follows is an overview of each victim-focused reform under focus.

The Victims' Right to Review reform (England and Wales)

The Victims' Right to Review (VRR) reform enables victims to request a review of a prosecutor's decision not to proceed with charges, the outcome of which can include a reversal of that decision when a secondary in-depth analysis of the case determines the original decision to be in error. If the original decision is upheld, a letter is provided to the victim, which details the reasons why the decision was not overturned. The VRR is accessible for all crime victims and is run by the Appeals and Review Unit within the Crown Prosecution Service (CPS).[15] It was established as a way to increase victims' confidence in the justice system by providing greater transparency and accountability in relation to the CPS's charging decisions (CPS 2016). It therefore enhances consideration and involvement of victims in the criminal justice process. While technically constituting a provision for information, the VRR reflects elements of victim participation as it provides victims with a greater voice and input into the process, which stands contrary to their traditional positioning as 'witnesses' within adversarial legal systems. In this way, the VRR reform creates an opportunity for victims' procedural justice needs to be met.

Separate legal representation: section 34 of the *Sex Offenders Act 2001* (Irl)

Section 34 of the *Sex Offenders Act 2001* (Irl) represents a distinct and significant response to sexual assault victims in the justice process. It allows victims to access government-funded ILR to oppose a defendant's application to introduce a victim's sexual history evidence in court. The provision of this limited form of ILR during pre-trial processes demonstrates that Ireland has sought to respond to the trauma associated with sexual assault victims giving evidence in court, and being cross-examined in particular. This participation right is aimed at reducing secondary victimisation and addressing victims' key procedural justice needs by offering victims a voice, a degree of control and information during the process.

Legal representation by the South Australian Commissioner for Victims' Rights: section 16 of the *Victims of Crime Act 2001* (South Australia)

The powers of the South Australian Commissioner for Victims' Rights (SACVR) are unique insofar as section 16(3)(b) of the *Victims of Crime Act 2001* (SA) allows the Commissioner to 'assist victims in their dealings with prosecution authorities and other government agencies'. This clause gives the Commissioner scope to utilise this function as a basis for justifying intervention in cases where it is deemed in the victim's best interests. This can include, for example, providing ILR to victims in circumstances where their rights, interests or privacy are compromised or not adequately represented. This reform allows victims to feel like active participants in decision-making processes – a concept traditionally alien to adversarial systems. It also represents an avenue for victims' procedural justice needs to be met by providing them with information, validation, a voice and a degree of control during their involvement in the adversarial system.

Legal representation for victims

Increasing attention has been afforded to examining the ways in which victims can assume a more active role in adversarial systems to reduce the harmful impacts of the criminal prosecution process for them (Braun 2014, 2019; Doak 2005; Kirchengast 2013; Kirchengast, Iliadis & O'Connell 2019; O'Connell 2012). This has included considering the means by which to grant the victim the right to be legally represented at trial (Braun 2014: 820). While contrasting quite significantly with the traditional adversarial approach to attaining justice – which sees the crime as contested between the state and the accused, meaning that victim interests are not legally represented – the use of ILR for victims is not unprecedented, although its use is generally confined to pre-trial processes in order to avoid disrupting the adversarial nature of proceedings.

The limited form of ILR available to sexual assault victims in Ireland that affords protection of victims' sexual history evidence is one such example (see Chapter 5 for an analysis of this reform). Recently, Ireland extended this provision of ILR to sexual assault victims where applications for the release of their counselling records are subpoenaed; however, further research evaluating the impacts of ILR within this context is needed (see *Criminal Evidence Act 1992* (Irl) as amended by the *Criminal Justice (Sexual Offences) Act 2017* (Irl)). In Northern Ireland, similar calls for victim ILR were made to protect victims' sexual history and confidential communications following the Gillen Review into *The Law and Procedures in Serious Sexual Offences in Northern Ireland* (Sir John Gillen 2019).

ILR of this kind exists for victims in rape shield proceedings in British Columbia and Manitoba, Canada. Victims of sexual violence can invoke section 3 of the *Victims of Crime Act 1996* (RSBC) to defend their right to privacy by opposing defence applications to admit their personal sexual history. Similarly, section 25 of *The Victims' Bill of Rights 2001* (Manitoba) provides victims with a right to free ILR when requests for personal information are sought under section 278.3 of the *Criminal Code* (Canada). And within Australia, ILR has been available to sexual assault victims in New South Wales (NSW) since 2011 to prevent or restrict the disclosure of their sexual assault communications (s299A *Criminal Procedure Act 1986* (NSW)). Although additional research is required to evaluate the impact of this provision for ILR in NSW, it is believed that this may make the process less harmful for victims (Braun 2014). While the provision of ILR to victims within adversarial pre-trial contexts is not an alien concept, the idea is still developing and remains contested.

Inquisitorial legal systems

The adversarial paradigm strongly contrasts with the victim's role in inquisitorial legal systems, where victims' needs and interests are identified as equal to those of the state (the prosecutor) and the accused (Kirchengast 2016c: 46). In inquisitorial systems, greater emphasis is placed on safeguarding victims' civil and human rights (Holder 2018) and victims are generally empowered to participate in proceedings as an auxiliary prosecutor and have access to legal representation in court (Kirchengast 2016c: 138). Kirchengast (2016c: 138) argues that such a framework 'provide[s] important substantive rights that support the role of the victim as a stakeholder and participant of justice'. In these systems, it is reasonable to assert that 'victims are at the heart of human rights thinking' (Klug 2004: 111).

In inquisitorial systems, because trials are 'directed and controlled by trial judges and are not structured as adversarial contests, it is easier to accommodate the interests of victims at trial without disturbing the adversarial balance' that is central to common law systems (Pizzi & Perron 1996: 41). The more prominent role of the judge in establishing the 'truth' also means that the prosecution and defence have a more subsidiary role (Braun 2014: 828); therefore, the contest between the state and the accused is less combative, and arguably more focused on truth seeking. An example of ILR for victims in this context exists in Germany, where the *nebenkläger* status of victims gives the victim's legal representative the role of a secondary prosecutor (Raitt 2010: 24), also known as a Private Accessory Prosecutor (Braun 2014: 826). This essentially provides the victim's lawyer with the same participation rights as the prosecutor and defence lawyer at trial (Bacik, Maunsell & Gogan 1998: 237). For sexual assault victims, a government-funded legal service exists that is mandated by the courts (*German Code* s 397a(1), 395(1)). Similarly, in Belgium and France, the *partie civile* procedure gives victims strong participation rights following the reporting stage (Raitt 2010: 24). The victim's legal representative has the right to:

- access the dossier of evidence at the end of the pre-trial investigation;
- be present in court throughout the trial;
- speak on the [rape] victim's behalf in court;
- call witnesses on behalf of the victim (subject to the judge's discretion);
- object to questions put to the victim by the defence or prosecutor;
- cross-examine the defendant;
- make submissions to the court on the law; and
- address the court as to compensation.

(Bacik, Maunsell & Gogan 1998: 182, 218)

Many other European jurisdictions, such as Spain, the Netherlands, Luxembourg and Finland, also have provisions for victim ILR, although in each country the legal representative's role varies in implementation and scope (Raitt 2010: 23). Likewise, the International Criminal Court (ICC) provides an avenue for ILR, whereby victims select a legal representative who acts on their behalf during the hearing to present their interests and concerns (ICC 2017). Unlike most inquisitorial jurisdictions, however, the right to victim ILR is generally resisted within adversarial systems, largely due to concerns associated with the structure of the common law, which does not accommodate victim participation (Braun 2014; Kirchengast, Iliadis & O'Connell 2019; Pizzi & Perron 1996). Victims are therefore regarded as the 'forgotten party' whose views and interests remain largely alienated and excluded from the criminal justice system (Rock 1993; VLRC 2016). While a stronger case for victim ILR may be made for vulnerable victims, including victims of sexual offences, the notion of ILR is still evolving and contested. And despite ILR for victims having some precedence in adversarial pre-trial processes, victims are not presently afforded representation and party standing in criminal trials. Indeed, resistance to the notion of granting victims 'party' status stems from a concern that the imposition of a third party (a victim's legal representative) may interfere with the two-sided contest between the prosecutor and the accused, thus potentially violating the accused's procedural rights (Braun 2014: 820; Kirchengast 2013: 569; Pizzi & Perron 1996: 41). Notwithstanding these concerns, Kirchengast (2011 cited in Braun 2014: 820) argues that 'legal representation for victims within clearly defined and limited parameters would not necessarily infringe upon the rights of the accused'. Doak (2008: 147) holds a similar view of the potential for ILR for victims in an adversarial context, noting that:

> While there can be little doubt that a victim's 'right to counsel' would sit very uncomfortably within the adversarial framework, it may, conceivably, not be so incompatible that it may not function at all.

This is because, as Doak (2008: 146) suggests, victim ILR would not necessarily 'interject' at certain stages of the process (that is, the charge stage or plea hearing). Instead, it could provide a forum for 'effective' victim participation and 'may help to alleviate some of the stress associated with [the victim] testifying in court – especially if the victim is a vulnerable witness' (Doak 2008: 147). O'Connell (2012: 10) similarly argues that ILR for victims could facilitate 'increased attention to victims' rights by police officers, prosecutors, magistrates and judges – and defence counsel'. In this regard, research conducted by the Canadian Crown counsel (cited in Mohr 2002: 16–17) also maintains that 'everyone takes it more seriously' when victim ILR is involved.

Some adversarial systems are progressively moving towards a system that better facilitates the role of the victim, such as through increased information rights, the right to review prosecutorial discretion, and participation rights. As mentioned above, the establishment of various Australian inquiries at the Commonwealth and state level has recently considered matters affecting victims of sexual violence and their recourse to justice through the introduction of reforms that enhance prospects for information and participation. In a similar vein to the three reform processes operating in the focus jurisdictions (see Chapters 4, 5 and 6), the inquiries found that enhanced information and participation rights potentially provide a mechanism to ensure that any decisions made, such as the decision not to prosecute, can balance the triangulation of interests among the victim, the accused and the state. While the VLRC (2016) has considered the notion of introducing ILR for sexual assault victims, it did not endorse submissions recommending its introduction.

Despite the potential benefits of ILR for victims, there is limited research in Australia or internationally that examines how victim-focused reforms operating in adversarial jurisdictions can respond to sexual assault victims' needs, and enhance their access to information or level of participation within a procedural justice framework. The studies that have explored this or related topics have mainly analysed the victim's role within inquisitorial legal systems and compared this to adversarial systems (Braun 2014, 2019; Doak 2008; Kirchengast 2013). While such research has provided a pivotal point of comparison between victims' rights across the two systems, there exists scope to consider the possibility of transferring knowledge and practice between adversarial systems, and how similar models of reform might operate in different international adversarial contexts. It is often difficult to imagine how victims' rights in inquisitorial systems would translate to adversarial systems, largely due to the vast structural differences that exist between the two legal frameworks, which impact the victim's level of participation within both systems such that victim ILR is not considered to readily fit within an adversarial system in the same way that it does within an inquisitorial justice system. Some studies have examined how victim ILR may be implemented in a way that 'transcends inquisitorial and adversarial systems for systems of international law and justice, providing a possible model that better allows for the hearing of the … victim within the criminal prosecution process of common law' (Kirchengast 2013: 573). In this vein,

Doak (2005) has explored the role of victims in adversarial and inquisitorial systems and considered the 'normative barriers' that obstruct victim participation rights in adversarial systems. These studies have provided an important and comprehensive overview of what enhanced victim participation rights might look like within adversarial systems, taking into account the potential benefits and limitations. They also provide insight into how victim participation reforms operate within inquisitorial systems. However, they have not directly analysed the potential for enhanced victim participation rights in adversarial systems in terms of how the reforms might positively or negatively impact victims' procedural justice experiences.

This book sets itself apart from prior studies by examining victim-focused reforms that offer victims increased information and participation in adversarial justice systems and considering whether such reforms can meet sexual assault victims' expectations of procedural justice, taking into account both the benefits and potential limitations of the reforms. Significantly, this book also explores whether there is scope for ILR for sexual assault victims within Victoria's legal system, and whether one of the reforms operating in the focus jurisdictions – arguably representing an incremental step to legal representation – would be a more viable option to introduce in Victoria at the present time.

Research design

This book is based on a cross-jurisdictional study of three victim-focused law reforms across three adversarial jurisdictions: England and Wales, Ireland and South Australia. Ireland and South Australia offer victims participation rights through ILR, while England and Wales have introduced the VRR reform that enhances the provision of information to victims. Although these three reforms are fundamentally different in nature, they each offer victims greater input into the process, in contrast to the traditional role of victims in adversarial justice systems. An analysis of the reforms in regard to the ways they operate and how they may positively and negatively attend to sexual assault victims' procedural justice needs also allows for consideration of whether similar reforms could be implemented in adversarial systems more broadly, including within Victoria. While two of the three reforms are theoretically available to all victims of crime, this book focuses primarily on the ways in which the reforms impact sexual assault victims' experiences and perceptions of procedural justice. As noted above, this focus was chosen because of the complexities associated with sexual assault investigations and prosecutions, and the difficulties sexual assault victims experience in the legal process.

This book is informed by interviews[16] conducted with 26 high-level criminal justice professionals (judges, prosecutors and lawyers – $n=10$), victim support workers ($n=9$) and key policy and government stakeholders responsible for creating, implementing and working with the three reforms under study ($n=7$). The participants were representative of a variety of experience and seniority across the four interview locations, and included practising solicitors/barristers, victims'

Table 1.1 Participant groups

Category	*Number of participants*
Criminal justice professionals	10
Victim support workers	8
Key policy and government stakeholders	8

commissioners, members of the judiciary, victim counsellors, victims' rights advocates, policy advisors, and researchers. They were selected because of their roles, experience with the reforms and understanding of the victim's role within adversarial systems more generally.

The participants were asked to draw from their expertise and experiences when discussing the victim-focused reforms in their jurisdiction and the differences between the theoretical and practical application of the reforms. They were also asked to comment on their understandings of procedural justice and the ways in which the outcomes of the reforms impact victim satisfaction with the criminal justice process.

All participants possess the authority to describe and reflect upon the reforms operating in their respective jurisdictions and the extent to which the reforms address, or neglect, victims' procedural justice needs. Additionally, the participants were invited to provide insight into their criminal justice experiences more broadly, and in turn to reflect on the viability of ILR for sexual assault victims generally. In order to situate the authority of the voices in this research, the participants were assigned to one of three categories, which broadly reflected their role and/or status (see Table 1.1).

Table 1.2 also shows the distribution of participants' professions across each jurisdiction.

As illustrated in Table 1.3 below, all participants were assigned pseudonyms to ensure their anonymity. Given the small number of interviews, confidentiality was a key issue. It was also particularly important that the data was substantiated by the level of authority and roles of the interview participants, without divulging the identity of the participants or which organisation they worked for. The participants were assigned a pseudonym that included a brief, but deliberately

Table 1.2 Distribution of participant groups across the focus jurisdictions

	Criminal justice professionals	*Victim support workers*	*Key policy and government stakeholders*
England	1	4	5
Ireland	1		2
South Australia	3	1	1
Victoria	5	3	

Table 1.3 Participants' pseudonym, role and jurisdiction

Participant pseudonym	*Description of their role*	*Jurisdiction*
Kate	Managing Lawyer, CPS	England and Wales
Adelle	Policy researcher, victim support organisation	England and Wales
Georgia	Policy researcher, victim support organisation	England and Wales
Sophie	Victims' rights advocate and campaigner	England and Wales
Olivia	Policy advisor, victim support organisation	England and Wales
Emily	Sexual assault clinical lead counsellor	England and Wales
Chloe	Leading victims' rights authority	England and Wales
Eva	Rape crisis support worker	England and Wales
Anna	Sexual abuse and violence researcher	England and Wales
Mark	Criminal justice support officer	England and Wales
David	Principal officer working within a national gender-based violence organisation	Ireland
Joanna	CEO, sexual violence support centre	Ireland
Abby	Leading policy researcher, DPP	Ireland
Xavier	Criminal justice professional	South Australia
James	Leading victims' rights advocate	South Australia
Robert	Manager, WAS	South Australia
Zoe	Sexual assault crisis response and counselling coordinator	South Australia
Victoria	Criminal justice professional	South Australia
Hannah	Criminal justice professional	Victoria
Oscar	Leading victims' rights advocate	Victoria
Bianca	Manager, victim support agency	Victoria
Wendy	Manager, victim support agency	Victoria
Simone	Member of the Victorian judiciary	Victoria
Natasha	Judge of the Victorian County Court	Victoria
Ashley	Judge of the Victorian County Court	Victoria
Sean	Member of the Victorian judiciary	Victoria

vague description of their role, thereby providing authority to the voices represented in the book's analysis while still respecting participant confidentiality.

While recognising the significant contribution that victims' views would add to this research, a decision was made to utilise the voices of victim support advocates, criminal justice authorities and key policy and government stakeholders to represent victims, in order to reduce the potential distress that involvement in such research could cause, particularly given the focus on sexual assault. This may be considered a limitation of the research; however, it avoids the possibility of victims experiencing distress or discomfort when asked to reflect on their criminal justice experiences. Given the authority and expertise of the participants interviewed, and their experience working directly with victims and/or the reforms, the data obtained can be assumed to provide a reliable indication of the experiences of sexual assault victims.

It is also acknowledged that the uneven spread of interviews across jurisdictions and the fact that only 26 interviews were conducted in total may be considered a limitation of the study. However, given the authority of the participants interviewed, the spread and size of the sample do not detract from the richness of the data and analysis presented. More qualitative data does not necessarily translate into more or better information. As qualitative research is concerned 'with meaning', samples may vary in their recruitment and size without diminishing the veracity of the findings (Crouch & McKenzie 2006). In this regard, Mason (2010) affirms that 'frequencies [in analyses] are rarely important in qualitative research, as one occurrence of the data is potentially as useful as many in understanding the process behind a topic'. This research monograph adopts a similar view that qualitative samples must be large enough to ensure that participants' perceptions are revealed, 'but at the same time if the sample is too large, data becomes repetitive and, eventually, superfluous' (Mason 2010: 2). Moreover, due to the authority of the participants involved, most had expertise relevant to the three reforms under study and were therefore able to provide rich insights and perceptions in relation to the operation of these reforms and whether they positively or negatively impact upon victims' procedural justice experiences. In these instances, the participants' perspectives and perceptions of the reforms outside their own jurisdictions were even deemed to be valuable.

In addition to the interviews that inform the analysis presented in this book, the research is supplemented by a quantitative analysis of a statistical dataset unique to this study on the VRR reform operating in England and Wales. The dataset contains information on the number of review requests and reviews undertaken, the outcomes of reviews, and the types of cases referred for review. This dataset represents the first time such data has been made available. The research also draws upon four case studies from South Australia demonstrating the role of the SACVR, and an analysis of primary source documents in relation to South Australia and Ireland.

Analysis

Interviews

Four main interview schedules were developed for the four locations in which the interviews were conducted (see Appendices A, B, C and D). The different schedules allowed me to elicit the most accurate responses from the participants depending on their experience with the reform(s) being discussed. The underlying themes of the four schedules were the same, as the questions were focused on gathering information related to how the reforms operate and in what ways they address victims' procedural justice needs. Most participants were able to speak with some degree of knowledge about the reforms in all three jurisdictions. However, in circumstances where the participants did not have extensive knowledge of a particular jurisdiction, the questions were reframed to elicit reflection on adversarial systems more broadly to allow for comparative analysis of responses. For example, questions that related to the possible benefits and limitations of implementing ILR for sexual assault victims in Victoria were reframed to instead ask participants to consider the potential benefits and limitations of the introduction of ILR for sexual assault victims in an adversarial system generally.

Data captured from the interviews was analysed using a thematic and comparative approach. The interview schedule in each jurisdiction focused primarily on the reform relevant to that jurisdiction (see Appendices A, B, C and D). However, each schedule also included questions on the reforms operating in the other focus jurisdictions, which meant that most interviewees spoke about every reform and jurisdiction examined in this study. This allowed me to extract themes from the data and draw comparisons to identify any trends that arose in the interviewees' responses, both between jurisdictions and within the same jurisdiction.

Quantitative dataset

The interview data in this research is supplemented by statistical data on the VRR reform that was provided by a participant in England (Kate, managing lawyer, CPS). Quantitative data utilises 'numerical representation[s] … for the purposes of describing and explaining the phenomena that those observations reflect' (Babbie 2010: 414). In line with Babbie's (2010: 407) observation that quantitative analyses 'can strengthen qualitative studies', the use of a quantitative dataset in this study provides a more comprehensive picture of how the VRR is operating, in particular as it sheds light on some of the gaps between the theoretical objectives and practical application of the reform.

The quantitative dataset complemented the qualitative analysis in this research as it contributed insight into some of the key issues the participants identified. The dataset included information on the numbers of review requests and reviews undertaken in England and Wales, the outcomes of the reviews, and the types of cases referred for review. This data shed light on the trends in the CPS's decision-making within the context of the VRR reform. It represents the first time that such data has been made available, therefore providing a unique opportunity to contribute new knowledge on the VRR's operation and outcomes.

The quantitative dataset was analysed by comparing the number of review requests made and reviews undertaken with the outcomes of reviews and the types of cases referred for review. By examining the case types referred for review and comparing them with the review outcomes, I was able to identify how many sexual assault cases were overturned through the VRR and how many decisions were upheld in sexual offence cases. A limitation of this statistical data is that the CPS is only required to record data on offence types that are dropped post charge; that is, once the case has proceeded beyond the police investigation. This means that there is no data on what sorts of cases are not being proceeded with in the first instance. This was significant because this limited my capacity to fully understand or critique prosecutorial pre-charge decision-making and whether offence types, situational factors or victim characteristics influence prosecutorial decision-making when a case is not proceeded with in the context of the VRR reform.

Primary source documents

The examination of primary source documents, including legislation, reports, case law and formal guidelines, informed understanding of how various victim-focused reforms were operating and their intended objectives. These documents were sourced from England and Wales, Ireland, South Australia and Victoria. The documents supplemented the qualitative analysis as comparisons were made between the theoretical objectives of the reforms (as stipulated in the legislation) and their practical application (as reported by the participant responses). As such, the analysis of these documents provided a basis from which to identify and interpret where sexual assault victims' experiences of procedural justice fell short of their needs and expectations. Some of the reports analysed, such as *The Legal Process and Victims of Rape* (1998) and *The Role of Victims of Crime in the Criminal Trial Process* by the VLRC (2016), also supported some of the key criticisms of the system raised by the interview participants.

Case study analysis

In addition to interviews and primary source documents, the discussion of the SACVR presented in Chapter 6 was supported by an analysis of four case studies (Case A, Case B, Case C and Case D), which were provided by an interviewee in South Australia (James, leading victims' rights authority). The four cases represent real examples of how the SACVR can intervene to provide ILR to sexual assault victims. According to section 16(3)(b) of the *Victims of Crime Act 2001* (SA), the Commissioner can 'assist victims in their dealings with prosecution authorities and other government agencies'. However, this clause does not clearly explain how or when the Commissioner may assist victims. The four case studies provided clear examples of how the Commissioner may utilise this function. This is an important contribution considering the vague description of the SACVR's powers offered in the legislation.

Key terms and definitions

As defined in section 3(1)(a)(b) of the *Victims' Charter Act 2006* (Vic), a victim is considered a person 'who has suffered injury … or has died … as a direct result of a criminal offence, whether or not that injury [or fatality] was reasonably foreseeable by the offender'. This means that, by legal definition, a person is considered a 'complainant' or 'witness' until a guilty verdict is reached. An individual's victim status and capacity to claim a victim title in law is thus dependent upon a guilty finding. Ellison (2007) puts forward the view that the term 'complainant' diminishes the lived experiences of victims of sexual violence and overlooks the possibility of revictimisation within the legal process. This book extends the definition of victim to also include 'a person alleged by the prosecution to be a victim prior to a determination of guilt' (VLRC 2016: xxi); individuals who have experienced victimisation, but have not reported it to the police; and individuals who have reported their victimisation to the police, but charges were not proceeded with, were dismissed or were withdrawn, or a not guilty verdict was reached.

A decision was made to extend the definition of victim used in this book to reflect the difficulties associated with sexual assault investigations and prosecutions, including, but not limited to, the preconceived biases about sexual assault and sexual assault victims that affect decision-making throughout the legal process (Taylor 2007) and the low reporting rate of sexual offences to authorities. This book thereby recognises that there are a range of factors impacting the substantive outcome in sexual assault cases and that people who allege sexual violence still experience feelings of victimisation regardless of the legal outcome. The term 'survivor' is also used by feminist researchers to describe people who have experienced sexual violence because it is believed that the term 'victim' implies notions of 'disempowerment and passivity that belie the resilience and strength demonstrated after rape' (Smith 2018: 4; see also Papendick & Bohner 2017). At the same time, however, the term 'survivor' has been critiqued because it may imply that survivors 'no longer struggle' with the impacts of victimisation (Smith 2018: 4). Pursuant to the 'victims' rights' orientation of this book, the term victim will be used to refer to people who have experienced sexual victimisation. In recognition of the particular needs of victims of sexual violence, whose agency, autonomy and control have been violated, the term 'victim' can be seen to validate an individual's experiences within the criminal justice system where 'the high standard of proof required for conviction' cannot often do so (Smith 2018: 4). Additionally, this book focuses on female sexual assault victims. This is not to overlook the sexual victimisation experiences of individuals who fall outside this gender; rather, the decision was made to acknowledge that sexual offences reflect gendered issues of dominance and power, with the majority of sexual assaults being perpetrated by men that are known to female victims (Jordan 2008; Radford 2006; Walklate 2005; Wilcox 2010).

The terms rape, sexual assault and sexual violence will be used interchangeably, and are defined as 'a range of violent behaviours … [including] unwanted touching, sexual harassment and intimidation, coerced sexual activity, sexual assault and rape and … other physical violence and threat to life' (Dean, Hardiman & Draper 1998: iii). For the purposes of the analysis presented in this book, sexual violence is understood as:

> both a consequence … and reinforcement of power disparities between individuals and in society. Attitudes, beliefs, laws and other social structures which allow or support the power of one group over another, or which allow or support violence, contribute to the problem of sexual violence in society.
>
> (Dean, Hardiman & Draper 1998: iii)

Book structure and chapter overview

Drawing from interviews conducted with 26 high-level criminal justice professionals, legal stakeholders and victim support workers, and a quantitative dataset unique to the research, this book's mix-method empirical study critically examines whether (and indeed how) victim-focused reforms that offer victims increased information and participation rights in England and Wales, Ireland and South Australia can meet sexual assault victims' procedural justice needs when operating in an adversarial framework. In doing so, the book considers whether there is the potential to transfer knowledge and practice across adversarial systems by way of introducing a VRR-style reform or ILR for sexual assault victims in Victoria or other adversarial systems more broadly.

The central aim of the book is to present the findings obtained from a doctoral research project that was the first of its kind to examine victim-focused reforms across three adversarial jurisdictions. It considers whether and how ILR could be introduced for sexual assault victims in Victoria's criminal prosecution process, or whether a limited form of ILR, such as the ILR available to victims in Ireland or South Australia, or perhaps a VRR-style reform, would be a more viable option for Victoria at the present time. The book provides an evidence base to inform policy and practice directions across adversarial systems contemplating enhancing the rights of sexual assault victims. This introductory chapter provides the contextual basis for the research and identifies the motivation for, and purpose and scope of, the project, considering the nature of the adversarial system and the victim's limited involvement within that system.

Following this introductory chapter, which outlines the research design and approach, ethical considerations, and definitions of key terms, Chapter 2, entitled 'Tracing the interest in victims, victims' rights and sexual assault law reform', addresses issues relating to victims' limited involvement and role in criminal justice systems, along with others pertaining to the ill-treatment of sexual assault victims in adversarial justice processes. It also provides an overview of the literature and debates that foreground the book's main objectives. It focuses on three key areas: (i) identifying and situating victims' rights and interests as synonymous to those of the accused and society; (ii) the competing 'triangulation of interests'; and (iii) the key challenges sexual assault victims experience in the criminal prosecution process. The discussion focuses on illuminating the rationale for enhancing victims' rights, and explores the most significant victim-focused reforms that have emerged across adversarial systems, including within Victoria. In doing so, Chapter 2 outlines the key benefits and limitations of victim-focused reforms with regard to the ways they address and represent victims' rights and interests in the prosecution process. It also highlights the contribution of this study to criminological and socio-legal scholarship.

Chapter 3, entitled 'Procedural justice', presents the theoretical framework supporting this research. It explores the concept of the vengeful victim and defines procedural justice theory as the view that fair *processes* leading to decisions generally have greater significance for victims than do substantive case *outcomes*. Chapter 3 explains how the following four key elements are crucial to meeting sexual assault victims' procedural justice needs: information, validation, voice and control.

Chapter 4, 'Providing a check on prosecutorial decision-making: an analysis of the VRR reform', is the first of four analysis chapters. This chapter examines the implementation and operation of the VRR reform with reference to its key benefits and limitations. This reform provides a unique mechanism for victims to challenge prosecutorial discretion. While technically constituting a provision of information, the VRR has the ability to rectify inappropriate prosecutorial discretion, and may result in a reversal of the original decision and ultimate conviction. Chapter 4 considers the ways in which the reform addresses or neglects victims' procedural justice needs throughout the prosecution process.

Chapter 5, 'Separate legal representation for victims under section 34 of the *Sex Offenders Act 2001* (Irl)', analyses the limited form of ILR to which sexual assault victims are entitled in Ireland in circumstances where the defence seeks to adduce the victim's sexual history evidence in court. The victim representative's role within this context is to challenge the defence's application to admit such sexual history evidence. Constituting a form of victim participation, this reform is distinct within adversarial systems in allowing a unique level of victim involvement. Chapter 5 analyses the reform with reference to its perceived benefits and limitations, and considers the extent to which it meets victims' procedural justice needs.

Chapter 6, 'Victim participation through the SACVR', details the unique and substantive powers of the SACVR, which extend to providing legal representation to victims in certain criminal proceedings where victims' rights and interests have not been sufficiently met. This chapter analyses the benefits and limitations of the SACVR's powers with reference to how they impact on victims' procedural justice experiences.

Chapter 7, 'The prospect of ILR for sexual assault victims within Victoria's criminal prosecution process', is the final analysis chapter. It considers whether there is scope for ILR for sexual assault victims within Victoria's prosecution process. This chapter explores the notion of ILR for sexual assault victims within an adversarial system, and the key criticisms and potential benefits of such a reform within Victoria's adversarial system and in what sort of contexts it could operate. Chapter 7 also considers whether sexual assault victims' rights could be enhanced within Victoria by the adoption of reforms similar to the victim-focused reforms operating in the three focus jurisdictions, in order to offer victims a greater role and input into the process, and to address their procedural justice needs.

Chapter 8, 'Concluding comments', highlights the study's significance and contribution to criminological and socio-legal scholarship, and summarises its four main findings: (i) the gaps between the theoretical aims and practical application of victim-focused reforms, (ii) that such reforms act as a 'sticking plaster' for the broader issues inherent to adversarial systems, (iii) the need for incremental change in adversarial systems, and (iv) the need to reconceive adversarial systems using a triangulation of interests framework. The conclusion reiterates the arguments of the book, including that the role and status of sexual assault victims need to be enhanced through legal reform, and identifies that a meticulous approach is required to ensure that any victim-focused reform meets its intended objectives and addresses victims' procedural justice needs. Future research directions and the potential limitations of the study are also outlined.

Notes

1 As Flynn and Hodgson (2017: 6) contend, adversarial systems seek to 'encompass procedural justice ideals (measured by perceptions of fairness within the legal *processes* used) and substantive justice ideals (measured by perceptions of fairness in the *outcomes* of those legal processes)'.
2 This book considers whether there is scope for and merit in introducing ILR for sexual assault victims within the state of Victoria in Australia.
3 A VIS is referred to as a Victim Personal Statement (VPS) in other common law jurisdictions, such as England and Wales (*Criminal Practice Directions* [2013] EWCA Crim 1631).
4 See Ellison (2007) for a discussion of the restrictions placed on the defence questioning a victim on their prior sexual history.
5 See also section 13 *Charter of Human Rights and Responsibilities Act 2006* (Vic).
6 The common law is a system of jurisprudence that is premised on the notion of doctrinal precedent. It refers to a system in which judges create laws and former court rulings form the basis for determining decisions in subsequent cases of a similar nature (Dainow 1966–67). The terms 'common law system' and 'adversarial system' are used interchangeably throughout this book and imply the same meaning. Australian common law systems also incorporate criminal code systems; see, for example, *Criminal Code Act 1899* (QLD) and *Criminal Code Act Compilation Act 1913* (WA).
7 As stated in Australia's *Criminal Code Act 1995* (Cth) Division 13.1, 'the prosecution bears a legal burden of proving every element of an offence relevant to the guilt of the person charged'.
8 Vulnerable witnesses can now give evidence via video link in some adversarial jurisdictions (Daly 2011; Flynn 2012).
9 That is, unless a plea negotiation is made and the case does not proceed to a contested trial.
10 In criminal trials, 'beyond reasonable doubt' refers to the standard of proof in which the judge or jury must be certain that the accused is guilty of the crime(s) (*Evidence Act 2008* (Vic) s 141(1)).
11 *R v Carroll [2002] HCA 55; 213 CLR 635 at 643 [21].*
12 A fair trial in an adversarial system is commonly focused on upholding the due process rights of the accused. This includes safeguarding the rights of the accused in order to ensure equality before the law (Packer 1968).
13 *R v Carroll [2002] HCA 55; 213 CLR 635 at 643 [21] citing Blackstone, W, Commentaries ([1769] 1966 reprint) Bk 4, c 27, 352.*
14 Greg Davis APM was formally appointed as Victoria's first Victims of Crime Commissioner on 8 March 2016 (see *Victims of Crime Commissioner Act 2015* [Vic]). Fiona McCormack, former CEO of Domestic Violence Victoria, was appointed as Victoria's second Victims of Crime Commissioner and commenced her role on 8 July 2019.
15 The CPS is equivalent to the Office of Public Prosecutions (OPP) in Victoria, which prosecutes indictable offences in Victoria's County and Supreme Courts and conducts criminal appeals in the County Court, the Court of Appeal and the High Court of Australia (OPP 2017).
16 Ethics approval was obtained from the Monash University Human Research Ethics Committee (MUHREC) prior to commencing the fieldwork (Approval Number: CF15/106-2015000050).

2 Tracing the interest in victims, victims' rights and sexual assault law reform

Introduction

> In the onward march to the unattainable end of perfect justice, the court must not forget those who, though not represented, have a legitimate interest in the court's exercise of its jurisdiction.
>
> (Justice Brennan cited in Jago v District Court of New South Wales (1989) 168 CLR 23)

> Bourgeoning social movements generally critical of the dominance of the state, combined with the exclusion of victims historically, saw victims mobilise to react to the crisis of their lack of agency in criminal justice, both institutionally, and at common law.
>
> (Kirchengast 2006: 159)

A significant number of studies have examined victims' rights and level of involvement in the criminal justice system (Booth 2016; Braun 2014, 2019; Daly 2011; Doak 2008; Erez 2000; Kirchengast, Iliadis & O'Connell 2019; Wemmers 2013). Although these studies have varied in nature and scope, there has been a strong focus on rape and sexual assault victims in the literature, given the harmful nature of such offences, which is often exacerbated by secondary victimisation resulting from the adversarial process (see, inter alia, Braun 2014; McGlynn 2017; Smith 2018). Much of the existing literature examining sexual assault victims' rights and experiences of the criminal justice system has focused on the difficulties associated with reporting (Jordan 1998, 2001, 2004a, 2004b), the selectivity of cases that are prosecuted (Bows & Westmarland 2016; Christie 1986; Dowds 2015; Estrich 1987), as well as the challenges arising at trial, including those related to establishing consent (Burgin 2019; Dowds 2018; Flynn & Henry 2012; Larcombe et al. 2016; Powell et al. 2013; Smith 2018) and cross-examination (Australian Law Reform Commission [ALRC] 2010; Bacik, Maunsell & Gogan 1998; Booth, Kaye & Wangmann 2019; Lees 1993, 1996; McGlynn 2017). Alternatives to trial, such as restorative justice mechanisms (Daly 2017, 2011, 2002; McGlynn, Westmarland & Godden 2012) and, to a more limited extent, specialist courts (see Bond et al. 2017; Iliadis,

Fitz-Gibbon & Walklate 2019), have also been a key focus in the literature on victims' rights and experiences within the criminal justice system. Other research has focused on contrasting a victim's role in the inquisitorial legal system with their role in the adversarial system (Braun 2019; Kirchengast 2013, 2016c). Most of these studies have typically emphasised the absence of the involvement of victims in adversarial justice systems, including their general lack of voice and input into legal processes, and how these issues are exacerbated for victims of sexual violence (see, generally, Clark 2010; Sir John Gillen 2019; VLRC 2016).

Given the structure of the adversarial system, which has not traditionally accommodated victim involvement and input into the prosecution process, law reforms focused on improving victims' rights have been slow to emerge, with the most prominent changes first taking place in the 1990s (Daly 2011; Erez 2000). Symbolically, victim-focused reforms represent a significant shift towards enhancing the rights and status of victims, who have struggled to attain some form of recognition within the criminal justice system. While such reforms have been advocated as providing victims with a greater opportunity to feel included in the process, some commentators have argued that current reforms are inadequate in effectively responding to victims' procedural justice needs (Braun 2019; Clark 2010; Holder 2018). As such, general consensus has emerged around the need to enhance sexual assault victims' rights in adversarial proceedings, albeit that such 'rights' propositions vary in their recommendations and scope (see, inter alia, Braun 2014, 2019; Kirchengast, Iliadis & O'Connell 2019; O'Connell 2015b).

In Victoria, specifically, there has been increased attention afforded to victims' rights over the past three decades (VLRC 2001, 2003, 2004, 2016). In particular, emphasis has been placed on considering the ways in which the prosecution process could be made less traumatic for sexual assault victims, and various studies and reports have recommended ways to enhance victims' rights within Victoria's criminal justice system (see, inter alia, Kirchengast, Iliadis & O'Connell 2019; RCFV 2016; VLRC 2016, 2015b, 2004). Recent commissions of inquiry in Victoria, including the VLRC's (2016) report on *The Role of Victims of Crime in the Criminal Trial Process* and the RCFV (2016), have shed light on the ongoing procedural challenges experienced by crime victims, particularly victims of domestic, family and sexual violence – many of which have long been documented in decades of academic literature. These inquiries also considered victim-focused reforms operating within other adversarial legal systems, including the potential role of ILR for victims in the criminal trial process (see Iliadis, Fitz-Gibbon & Walklate 2019 for an analysis of the RCFV (2016) recommendation for ILR for intimate partner violence victims). The VLRC (2016) similarly raised the potential role of legal counsel for victims, but ultimately did not endorse its recommendation. It did, however, consider the need for an associated reform, including the possibility of introducing a VRR-style reform, such as has been operating in England and Wales since 2013 (CPS 2016),[1] as well as the need to strengthen the powers of the Victorian Victims of Crime Commissioner to a degree akin to those held by commissioners in other

Australian states, such as South Australia. At a Commonwealth level, the Royal Commission into Institutional Responses to Child Sexual Abuse (RCIRCSA 2017) also recommended the introduction of a scheme that gives victims the right to review prosecutorial decisions. This would provide victims with substantive rights to justice where they perceive miscarriages of justice, including, for example, where the prosecutor's decision not to proceed with a case is deemed wrong by the victim or if the victim believes that the prosecutor made an error in making the decision. These recommendations are reflective of the reforms under focus in this book. However, in the absence of empirical evidence detailing how these reforms can be brought to life, this book draws on international experiences and perspectives to explore the possibilities for such reforms within the Victorian context.

This chapter presents an overview of the scholarly literature that identifies the motivations underpinning victim-focused reforms, the types of reforms that have been implemented, and the critiques levelled at such reforms. The chapter begins by considering the emergence of scholarly interest in victims, drawing upon some of the key theoretical perspectives that have traditionally shaped understandings of victims and their experiences, and have become the catalyst for debates around the 'rights' victims should be afforded. This discussion will then form the basis for identifying how sexual assault victims are perceived and treated within the criminal justice system, and how greater recognition of victims and their rights arose from the collective efforts of women's rights movements and victims' rights activists. The chapter then explores the key challenges experienced by sexual assault victims within legal processes as identified within the existing literature and considers the conflict among the interests of victims, prosecutors (the state) and the accused, pointing to the significance of conceptualising victims within a 'triangulation of interests' framework. Following this, the chapter provides an overview of the most significant victim-focused reforms introduced in Victoria, which offer victims information and participation rights. Where applicable, the chapter also indicates whether similar reforms exist in the three focus jurisdictions. It presents a review of the literature and the key findings of the relevant research, including studies that have critiqued these reforms based on their harmful impact on victims' experiences of the legal process.

To remain consistent with the focus of this book, this chapter primarily focuses on sexual assault victims' experiences, even where the reforms discussed are available to all crime victims. The chapter concludes by demonstrating that there has been a significant shift in Victoria towards greater inclusion of victims and victims' rights in the legal process; however, there are a range of issues that continue to impact on victims' ability to experience procedural justice. As such, the chapter provides a framework through which to examine how victim-focused reforms operate in adversarial jurisdictions outside Victoria, particularly those that offer enhanced information and participation rights to victims, and to what extent such reforms are meeting victims' procedural justice expectations. This provides a basis for the book to explore whether ILR could operate for sexual assault victims in Victoria, or whether any of the three reforms examined in the analysis chapters would be more viable options for the Victorian context.

The emergence of interest in victims

The initial interest in victims and their plight, both within and beyond the criminal justice system, arose from a belief that greater understanding of crime and its occurrence could only be obtained through a systematic study of victims (Erez 1989: 236; O'Connell 2008: 91). The study of victims and victimisation was believed to be both an expansion of criminology's primary focus on crime and criminals, and an additional means to gain a more profound and comprehensive understanding of the production of crime (Erez 1989: 236). This view suggests that, prior to the emergence of victimology, academic investigations of victims were not only rare, but also underdeveloped. Early criminological research 'concentrated most squarely on the analysis of crime, criminals and criminal justice', and the criminal justice process 'tended somehow to obliterate the victim' (Rock 1994: 11). While victimology is a relatively young and developing discipline, in the context of criminology and socio-legal inquiry the study of crime victims and victimisation has been labelled an 'essential complement to criminology's well-established research on offenders' (Fattah 2000: 18). Victimology has thus confirmed itself as an emerging and significant area of study (Karmen 2013: 2).

Victimology is concerned with the study of victims and their victimisation experience, from the behaviour of the victim and offender prior to the offence; and the aftermath of the crime, including the impact of the injuries and losses on the victim (such as physical, financial or emotional damage); to the social and legal responses to the victim and their experiences, including the actions taken by criminal justice agencies to respond to and manage victimisation (Dussich 2006: 116; Karmen 2013: 2; O'Connell 2008: 92).

Despite the recognition victimology has received as a field of study, its standing, nature and significance continue to generate widespread debate. Concepts such as 'victim', 'victim status', 'victims' rights' and 'victimisation' are contested and remain 'malleable and far from universal' (Dignan 2005: 35). Differing understandings of victims and their experiences have also influenced the role and treatment of victims in different jurisdictions and at various stages of the criminal justice process. The chorus of diverse interpretations of victims has also impacted victims' rights and level of involvement in the criminal justice system, and the notion of victims having 'rights' within the structural constraints of adversarial systems remains highly disputed. The following section unpacks the evolving social constructions of victims and their experiences, and considers the influence of Christie's (1986) 'ideal' victim construct on how victims of sexual violence have come to be perceived and treated within adversarial justice systems.

The 'ideal' victim and sexual assault: victim-blaming and victim-defending

Initial scholarly discussions of victims were concerned almost exclusively with the victim's role in contributing to, provoking or causing their own victimisation (Fattah 2000; Mendelsohn 1940, 1963; Von Hentig 1940; Wolfgang 1957).

Early victimology scholars such as Mendelsohn (1940, 1963 cited in O'Connell 2008: 93) drew attention to the notion of the 'victimal', as opposed to the 'criminal', focusing on the victim's culpability in the genesis of a crime. Von Hentig (1948) and Mendelsohn (1956) created typologies that categorised victims according to their degree of accountability, with the guiltiest victims distinguished from the guiltless victims. In *The Criminal and His Victim* (1948: 436), Von Hentig states that 'a victim who consents tacitly, co-operates, conspires, or provokes ... is one of the causative elements' of crime. Expressions such as 'victim-blaming' and 'the duet frame of crime' affirm the victim's involvement in crime according to precipitation theory, which perceives the victim as an essential accessory to the crime committed against them (Von Hentig 1948; Mendelsohn 1963 cited in O'Connell 2008). The crimes most commonly examined in victim precipitation theory include sexual assault and rape, aggravated assault, domestic violence and homicide (Mieth 1985: 209; Miers 1989). This theory appears to be based on some gender bias, given that women are more likely to be sexually and violently offended against by men (Jordan 2008; Radford 2006; Walklate 2005; Wilcox 2010).

Within victim precipitation theory, a victim is attributed a status that deviates from Christie's (1986) construction of the 'ideal' victim. Christie (1986) identified five criteria that one must fit in order to be considered an 'ideal' and 'blameless' victim, including that the victim must be: (i) weak – either sick, old or very young; (ii) doing something respectable at the time of the offence; (iii) in a public place during the daytime; (iv) vulnerable in relation to the 'big bad' offender; and (v) unknown to the offender (Christie 1986: 19). Christie's (1986) classification of the 'ideal' victim supports Estrich's (1987) construction of the 'real' rape scenario, which characterises rape as an act of violent, forceful penetration committed by a stranger in a public place. However, the reality is that most sexual assaults are perpetrated by someone who is known to the victim and often occur within a private place, such as the victim's home (Daly & Bouhours 2010: 566; see also Kelly, Lovett & Regan 2005; Mahoney, Williams & West 2001). Likewise, the 'ideal' victim is generally portrayed as someone who sustains physical injuries while trying to resist an attack (Christie 1986; Estrich 1987), but rape does not always result in sustained visible injury, and resistance and physical injury are not required to prove 'nonconsent' (Daly & Bouhours 2010: 566; see also Burgin 2019). Indeed, it is common for victims to 'freeze' and 'cooperate' out of shock and fear (Jordan 2008; Powell et al. 2013; Tuohy 2017). Stereotypes around 'real' rape also require that victims report the offence(s) immediately, yet much research indicates that victims are hesitant to report due to the shame associated with their victimisation and the fear of not being taken seriously or believed (Jordan 2004a; Hanly, Healy & Scriver 2009). This is demonstrated in the reflections of a Rape and Justice in Ireland (RAJI) survivor in Hanly, Healy and Scriver's (2009 cited in RCNI 2010: 6) study:

> I didn't want anyone to know what happened. I did not report the rape because I was too ashamed at what happened to me at my age. I didn't think anyone would believe me and I did not want my children to find out what happened to me.

While Christie's (1986) notion of the 'ideal' victim and Estrich's (1987) 'real' rape stereotype reflect highly problematic and empirically false constructions of rape (Bows & Westmarland 2016; Ehrlich 2001), Stevenson (2000) observes that in order to secure criminal convictions, it is necessary for rape victims to be 'unequivocal victims'. Indeed, studies have found that allegations that do not readily align with the 'ideal' victim or 'real' rape categories are more likely to be viewed and treated with scepticism by criminal justice authorities (Jordan 2008; Lievore 2005a, 2005b; Powell et al. 2013), and are less likely to result in prosecution (Brown, Hamilton & O'Neill 2007; Ellison & Munro 2009). As Hanly, Healy and Scriver (2009) argue, 'real' rape scenarios disadvantage the majority of cases that do not fit within these stereotypes. While a plethora of research and commentary has sought to counteract these harmful and misconceived stereotypes, media, legal and social discourse continues to perpetuate the 'real' rape and 'ideal' victim stereotypes. In recent commentary on the issue, Victorian Police Assistant Commissioner at Family Violence Command, Dean McWhirter, (cited in Tuohy 2017) stated:

> Myths and misconceptions [of sexual violence] are so strong and embedded in mainstream understanding [that they] impact every decision right through to the criminal process … they have a key impact on how a victim is treated and on attrition rates.

This view is shared by Bows (2019: 10) in the United Kingdom (UK), who notes that 'criminal justice campaigns often reflect (and possibly reinforce) the stereotype' and that this prevents victims who do not fit within 'real' rape stereotypes from reporting to the police.

Additionally, while there appears to have been a general increase in the number of reported rapes and sexual assaults to the police over the past two decades, prosecution and conviction rates remain notoriously low globally. For example, in 2017, the Australian Bureau of Statistics documented 25,837 reports of sexual violence by victims to the police. This is a gross under-estimate of the probable number of people who experienced sexual violence in Australia in that year (Precel, Dexter & Marsh 2019). Of the 25,837 victims who reported to the police, 4797 resulted in charges being brought against their perpetrator within a month. For the remaining victims – just over 80 per cent – the investigation was either discontinued or remained ongoing. Statistics from England and Wales reveal that the CPS prosecutes 58.3 per cent of reported sexual offences and convicts at a rate of just under 5 per cent of recorded cases (Office for National Statistics 2018). The operation of the criminal law in response to sexual violence has also contributed to the high rates of attrition in these cases (Kelly, Lovett & Regan 2005; Lees & Gregory 1993).[2]

Additionally, as noted by Fitz-Gibbon (2014: 74), 'the barriers that women encounter in having their stories heard within the confines of a law traditionally made by men for men' have prevented victims from reporting sexual violence due to the fear of being disbelieved or discredited. The (in)capacity of victims of sexual violence to seek and obtain justice within the male-centric confines of adversarial justice systems is raised throughout this book. The 'ideal' victim and 'real' rape stereotypes are also considered as factors that impact a victim's capacity to experience procedural justice from as early as the stage of reporting to the police.

Public versus private interests: the state versus the victim

Police

Situations that continue to give rise to victim dissatisfaction with police discretion include those where the validity of victims' claims are challenged upon reporting (Gans et al. 2011; Jordan 2004a, 2004b; RCNI 2012). In the context of sexual offence cases, Jordan (2004b: 49) explains that:

> The responses of criminal justice system agencies to women rape complainants have reflected patriarchal legacies of thinking and representation. Legal discourse has reinforced views of women as inherently deceitful, their word as typically flawed.

This is evident in the victims' testimonies presented in Jordan's (1998) study. For example, one victim observed, 'I went seeking help but then it turned and I was accused of false allegations' (Jordan 1998: 23). Another victim explained how her claims were challenged upon reporting because she did not fit the stereotypical construct of an 'emotional' victim:

> I think that was something that they really couldn't understand, that I was so calm. There were no tears, there was no hysteria, there was nothing, and I think they couldn't accept that I wasn't dissolving.
>
> (Jordan 1998: 23)

Another study conducted by Jordan (2004b) similarly highlights the police's tendency to draw upon 'real' rape stereotypes when responding to sexual assault victims. Jordan (2004b: 84) refers to one participant, Lydia, who, upon reporting her victimisation to the police, was blamed for not having left a 'terrible' husband and was advised not to pursue charges due to her 'apparent lack of [physical] injuries and because … marital rape was very hard to prove'. A study conducted by Hanly, Healy and Scriver (2009) also reflects the 'real' rape standpoint – a RAJI survivor in that study expressed:

> I was made to feel it wasn't a serious sexual assault. I was phoned a few days later. Garda stated 'you were seen on CCTV footage kissing this man'. I was devastated. A kiss did not encourage a sexual assault.
>
> (2009 cited in RCNI 2010: 9)

It is unsurprising then that Hanly, Healy and Scriver (2009 cited in RCNI 2010: 6) found that 42 per cent of victims who made a report 'seriously considered' withdrawing their complaint as the legitimacy of their allegations was measured against 'ideal' victim and 'real' rape stereotypes, thereby downplaying the victims' credibility. This impedes opportunities for sexual assault victims to experience and gain some form of validation through the legal process, even where cases cannot proceed due to the evidential difficulties associated with attaining a conviction. These examples also act as a reminder that victim precipitation views continue to exist in a contemporary context, whereby the victim is frequently considered to be at least partly responsible for the crime.

More recently, research conducted by Segrave, Wilson and Fitz-Gibbon (2018) found that, even since the inception of the RCFV in 2015 and the delivery of its final report in 2016, police attitudes towards intimate partner violence victims remain negative and inconsistent. In their study, they found that new recruits and experienced police alike associated 'genuine' victims of intimate partner violence with Christie's (1986) 'ideal' victim construct, resembling 'those who cooperated with police, took responsibility for the situation and followed through with the criminal justice process, and ultimately, had limited contact with police, as their response to their abuse was immediate and definitive' (Segrave, Wilson & Fitz-Gibbon 2018: 99).

Policing scholarship that examines gendered violence has long documented the prejudices and adverse attitudes held by the police in response to victims. These responses, as Segrave, Wilson and Fitz-Gibbon (2018: 102) contend, are 'rooted in a masculine policing ethos', which has traditionally seen family, domestic and sexual violence as a 'low-status task within policing – one which distracted from "real" police work and … enabled the exercise of police discretion in ways which often involved decisions not to invoke the criminal law' (see, inter alia, Douglas 2012; Loftus 2009). It is within this context that Segrave, Wilson and Fitz-Gibbon (2018: 103) observe that police attitudes and responses to victims are 'inextricably intertwined with wider debates surrounding the salience and power of "power culture"' in which high levels of discretionary power have resulted in unfettered decision-making processes (see also Chan 1997, 2003; Reiner 2010). Noting that the justice system relies on victims' confidence that the reporting of crime will not exacerbate existing harm, cynical police responses to victims of sexual violence have deterred them from reporting and impacted their perceptions of procedural justice. However, even when victims do report and the case proceeds to prosecution, research has consistently pointed to the bevy of procedural challenges impacting victims' engagement with the criminal justice system, including (but not limited to) their anticipation that prosecutors will protect their rights and interests against adversative court processes.

Prosecutors

In its latest report, the VLRC (2016: 13) states that, 'legally and operationally', the state is considered the wronged party – not the victim (VLRC 2016: 13; see also McDonald 2011: 67). Zehr (2005 cited in Doak, Henham & Mitchell 2009:

654) similarly observes that 'the state is conceived as the notional "victim", while those who have actually suffered the primary consequences of the offending behaviour are viewed as awkward outsiders to the process'. In this context, Crown prosecutors do not have to routinely prioritise the interests of victims, but instead are required to 'exercise a broad discretion, strongly rooted in the public interest' (Doak 2005: 303).

Scholars have put forward the view that a prosecutor's role should be reformed to reflect the emergence of the interest in victims and their rights. For example, in 2001, Nichols wrote that a prosecutor should act as a 'pure advocate and representative of the crime victim'. Others have similarly maintained that prosecutors should act as 'avengers' and 'seek justice' on behalf of victims (Pirro 2004). On the other hand, some authors, including Plater and Line (2012), have argued that prosecutors, as impartial ministers of justice, must not lose sight of the fact that they act on behalf of the public at large. They state that prosecutors should not become 'crusaders' for justice, nor should they be expected to perform as crime victims' lawyers (Plater & Line 2012; see also *Dix v Attorney-General [2002] AJ No 784*). To this end, Plater and Line (2012) caution that the prosecuting lawyer must be astute to avoid being cast as 'the creature of a private interest' when exercising their discretionary powers (*R v Milton Keynes Magistrates' Court; ex parte Roberts [1995] Crim LR 225*).

In Doak's (2005: 306) examination of the relationship between victims and state prosecutors, he refers to empirical studies that suggest 'that prosecutors are fundamentally unable to take into account the private interests of the victim while pursuing the public interest in the prosecution'. Ellison (1997 cited in Doak 2005: 306) shares this view, maintaining that there is an:

> inherent tension in the idea of an objective 'minister of justice' presenting evidence to the court dispassionately as part of the overall public interest in pursuing a conviction, whilst at the same time performing any sort of support or protective function in relation to the victim.

This conflict is notable in research conducted by Temkin (2000) and Shapland, Willmore and Duff (1985), who highlight the inconsistencies in the treatment of victims by prosecutors, with many victims feeling as though prosecutors are 'uninterested in their cases' and that their views are 'poorly represented' (Doak 2005: 306). Reflecting on sexual assault cases specifically, McDonald (2011: 69) notes that many victims are unaware that they are classified only as complainants or witnesses to proceedings. It is therefore not surprising that victims often believe prosecutors are *their* lawyers, who should prioritise *their* needs, rights and interests. This undoubtedly leads to feelings of disappointment when victims discover that the prosecution must prioritise the state's interests over theirs (McDonald 2011: 69). In this regard, Ellison (1997 cited in Doak 2005: 306) highlights that prosecutors are less likely to conduct cases with the 'same degree of zeal' as the defence. However, Doak (2005: 306) suggests that this may be partly due to the statutory limitations placed on the prosecution, which prohibit them from cross-examining the accused unless it is deemed relevant in very specific circumstances (see, for example, *Criminal Justice Act 2003* (UK) s 101).

In the sexual assault cases that proceed to trial, the harm associated with victims testifying and being cross-examined is well documented, as discussed in more detail later in this chapter (Lees 1996; Bacik, Maunsell & Gogan 1998). The harm may become exacerbated by prosecutors taking no action to safeguard victims' interests. For example, a survey conducted by Brown, Burman and Jamieson (1992) examining Scottish sexual offence trials found that prosecutors frequently failed to protect victims from character attacks. This is because 'too many objections to the questions of the defence counsel can make the jury suspicious because it implies that the prosecution is hiding something' (Braun 2014: 824). An English study conducted by Sweeting et al. (2008), which evaluated the Victims' Advocate Scheme, similarly found that the potential for conflict between prosecutors and victims was concerning given the prosecution's duty to disclose information about the victim, which may work against the victim's interests. In some instances, the information disclosed can even assist the defence (Gans et al. 2011), which increases the likelihood that victims will experience procedural injustice in their dealings with prosecuting authorities.

Another issue that contributes to the fraught relationship between victims and prosecuting authorities revolves around the inadequate provision of timely information relating to a case's progression, and decisions being made without sufficient victim consultation, for example, in relation to plea negotiations (Flynn 2012).[3] This issue is highlighted in Flynn's (2012: 80) study, in which she draws attention to the non-transparent nature of plea negotiations in Victoria, which rely upon 'the discretionary powers of the prosecution'. The outcome of a plea negotiation can involve the prosecution reducing the seriousness of the charge(s), thereby downplaying the severity of the offence(s) committed, or withdrawing one or more charges in order to secure a guilty plea (Flynn 2012: 79). Early guilty pleas have been identified as having a range of potential benefits for victims – for example, sparing victims from having to endure lengthy trials, which in some cases can take up to two years to resolve. They also eliminate the burden of having to testify in court and the resultant likelihood of being revictimised through the trial, especially during cross-examination (see Doak 2005: 306; Flynn 2012: 82, 88). However, Flynn (2012: 80) argues that the absence of formal acknowledgement of the practice of plea negotiations within Victoria means that the public must 'rely solely upon trusting those who engage in discussions to ensure the process, and resulting agreements, uphold … judicial principles, such as consistency, accessibility, equality and fairness'. And this process should include the timely provision of information to and adequate consultation with victims, in accordance with victims' entitlements to information under section 9(c) of the *Victims' Charter Act 2006* (Vic).

Flynn (2012: 89) also highlights a potential limitation for victims under section 22(1)(a) of the *Victims' Charter Act 2006* (Vic), which prohibits victims from pursuing civil action against the prosecution if there is a belief that the prosecution failed to uphold their rights to information. As Flynn (2012: 89) explains, section 22(1)(a) essentially safeguards the prosecution from being held accountable for not adhering to their statutory requirements. This means that victims' rights can be disregarded – for example, if the prosecution fails to inform the victim of a decision to engage in plea negotiations, the victim is precluded from taking civil action against the state. Consequently, the Act poses a barrier to victims' justice needs being met.

Another issue related to the *Victims' Charter Act 2006* (Vic) identified by Flynn (2012) involves the degree to which the prosecution will act in accordance with the victim's interests. Flynn (2012) claims that, to a significant extent, the key principles governing responses to crime victims in Victoria, as outlined in the *Victims' Charter Act 2006* (Vic), are upheld by prosecutors. As a prosecutorial participant in her study explained, 'we are very conscious of the role and place of the victim in the criminal justice system' (Flynn 2012: 91). This suggests that prosecutors are, to some extent, able to find a balance between upholding the public interest and having regard to victims' interests. However, Flynn's (2012: 91) analysis also revealed various limitations associated with the practical application of the *Victims' Charter Act 2006* (Vic) and the extent to which prosecutors uphold their obligations to victims. In particular, 'workload pressures' and 'victim perceptions' stood out as two key issues for the prosecutorial participants (Flynn 2012: 91). The increased workload of prosecutors in recent years, as driven by the requirements outlined in section 9 of the Charter, was described by Participant I in Flynn's (2012: 91) study as 'labour intensive'. In discussing such comments, Flynn (2012: 91) observes that, 'although [prosecutors did] not directly stat[e] that victim consultation does not occur, the potential negative implications of Prosecutor I's comments are quite high'. This lack of consultation may deny victims the opportunity to experience procedural justice by way of receiving information and feeling included in the process.

The second limitation Flynn (2012) identifies relates to victims' understandings of the prosecution's role. Statements by prosecutorial participants such as 'the victim is not our client. I think that could be a misperception, they may think we are now acting for them' and 'this is the Office of Public Prosecutions, not the Office of Private Prosecutions, so we have regard to what victims have to say, but it is not determinative' (Flynn 2012: 91–2) exemplify that, while regard is given to victims, the prosecution's role cannot be misconstrued for one that is primarily representative of victims' interests. This acts as another reminder that the victim's interests are peripheral to those of the state in adversarial systems, despite the victim being the individual most impacted by the crime.

Police and prosecutors cannot adequately protect victims' interests because they ultimately represent the state. This, coupled with the victim's limited role in the process, has prompted the need to reconsider the ways in which victims' rights and interests can be better upheld in order for victims to experience a greater sense of procedural justice. Doak's (2005) examination of the parameters of the prosecution's role in relation to victims in the UK has led him to conclude that 'it is not clear whether the adversarial structures of the criminal hearing, or indeed the public interest which underpins criminal prosecutions, could accommodate any expansion in the role of the [CPS]' (Doak 2005: 207). Although the CPS has taken on additional responsibilities to enhance the rights and interests of victims (see Chapter 4), Doak (2005) argues that this is unlikely to have a positive impact on victims' experiences in the criminal justice system. Instead, he questions whether the introduction of ILR for victims would relieve prosecutors from 'certain responsibilities towards victims, and as such [prosecutors] would be less likely to encounter conflicts of interest in their role as "ministers of justice"' (Doak 2008: 147). Indeed, Doak (2005: 307) suggests that this could 'save the prosecutor from having to juggle two roles which are ultimately incompatible'. This question is equally applicable within Victoria given the issues raised in Flynn's (2012) study. The potential for providing legal counsel to victims, and the possibility of introducing a scheme that advances victims' rights to information, has also gained traction in key Australian commissions of inquiry into crime victims' rights and role. At a state level, Victoria's RCFV (2016) recommended that ILR be introduced for complainants' within specialist family violence courts. The VLRC (2016) also considered the potential role of legal counsel for victims and documented the possibilities and implications of introducing ILR for victims in Victoria. At a Commonwealth level, the RCIRCSA (2017) did not consider the role of private counsel for victims specifically, but it did recommend the introduction of a VRR-style reform that would give victims the right to request a review of prosecutorial decisions. These inquiries, and the potential value of these reforms in Victoria, will be discussed at more length in Chapter 7. The following section extends the discussion of critiques of the prosecution process for victims of sexual violence, as outlined in the introductory chapter.

Is the adversarial criminal trial a 'degradation ceremony' for victims?

The adversarial criminal trial has been criticised for creating a hostile climate in which the victim feels used as a mere witness to provide testimony that assists the court to reach a verdict. This quest for a verdict can be pursued at the expense of the victim's interests, through the use of selective questioning during cross-examination, a partial presentation of facts, aggressive argument, and psychological attacks on the victim (Herman 2005: 571–2). The nature of this fact-finding process, where defence counsel conduct an 'intense and probing interrogation' (Henderson 2015: 90) of the victim to test the veracity of their claims, is widely recognised as problematic (Booth, Kaye & Wangmann 2019; Iliadis, Fitz-Gibbon & Walklate 2019). Herman (2005: 574) argues that 'if one set out intentionally to design a system for provoking symptoms of traumatic stress, it might look very much like a court of law'. This is especially so for victims of violent crimes, such as rape and sexual assault. Indeed, research conducted by Booth, Kaye and Wangmann (2019: 1108) suggests that the courtroom is 'an extension of the violence' endured by victims (see also Ellison 2001; Stubbs 2003). These criticisms highlight the conflict arising from the triangulation of interests, whereby victims can become revictimised through the trial.

In analysing the adversarial criminal trial, Bankowski and Mugham (2001) draw upon the work of Garfinkel (1956), who coined the notion of a 'degradation ceremony'. They contend that criminal justice proceedings have less to do with delivering justice and more to do with publicly labelling and stigmatising deviance (the offence) and deviants (the offender). Their analysis focuses on the dynamics of court proceedings and how they produce adverse effects for offenders, causing them to be 'stripped' of their 'expectations' of justice (Bankowski & Mugham 2001: 331). Bankowski and Mugham (2001: 333) draw attention to the implications of this, noting that:

> To degrade someone, is, in part, to destroy all capacity for self-determination, all ability … 'to predict the future and thus to prepare for it'. In court, the future, for the defendant, is determined by others.

While acknowledging that the criminal trial can produce similar effects for victims, Bankowski and Mugham (2001) centre their analysis on offenders. However, their findings relating to the adversarial trial as a degradation ceremony for offenders are also relevant to victims, especially in light of a significant volume of research that suggests that victims feel revictimised by court processes (Booth, Kaye & Wangmann 2019; Clark 2010; Iliadis 2019; Iliadis, Fitz-Gibbon & Walklate 2019; O'Connell 2006). The adversarial trial thus may also 'degrade' victims and 'destroy all [of their] capacity for self-determination' (Bankowski & Mugham 2001: 333).

Lees (1993: 14; 1996) describes the cross-examination of victims as degrading and humiliating, as it often leaves them feeling denied of any sort of validation and control, exacerbating their sense of vulnerability throughout the process (see also ALRC 2010: 1116; Bacik, Maunsell & Gogan 1998). Yet cross-examination is a key feature of the adversarial criminal trial. It is designed to allow the defence to 'confront and undermine the prosecution's case by exposing deficiencies in a witness' testimony' (ALRC 2010: 1334). In doing so, the defence is able to produce a story in court that could potentially work in favour of the accused and thus discredit the prosecution's case and the victim's testimony (Rock 1993: 29). Morison and Leith (1992: 144) suggest that the defence often performs the cross-examination in a fierce way, intended to make victims feel 'fragile'. Rock (1993: 29) likewise contends that, towards the final stages of the cross-examination, counsel may 'work themselves up [in]to a climax', using repetitive questioning tactics that accuse victims of false victimhood. The fierce and assertive nature of such questioning has been referred to as the 'slamming' phase (Mazengarb 1964: 190), 'damag[ing] the witness beyond repair, or destroying' her (Hilbery 1946: 35). The trauma associated with cross-examination generally is highlighted in Resick's (1987) study examining the experience of 200 victims of rape and robbery in the criminal justice system in the United States. In her study, rape victims reported that the prospect of having to testify in court was one of the most fear-inducing factors (Resick 1987: 475). Van de Zandt, who conducted research into 150 rape cases prosecuted through the Australian courts, similarly found the cross-examination process to be experienced negatively by victims, arguing that it amounts to 'state-sanctioned victimisation' (Van de Zandt 1998: 125).

Within the trial context, little (if any) regard is given to the impact of the crime on the victim. This is reflected in the comments of a participant in Clark's (2010: 33) study, who explains:

> The focus in the legal system is on events that happened: he did this on this day to me. Whereas there wasn't much focus on the actual impact … the impact that it's had on the victim and everyone else is enormous. I think there needs to be more consideration taken about that.

Yet many scholars believe that this common experience of the criminal justice system, as described in the quote above, is far removed from the needs and expectations of victims. As Herman (2005: 574) argues:

> Victims need social acknowledgment and support; the court requires them to endure a public challenge to their credibility. Victims need to establish a sense of power and control over their lives; the court requires them to submit to a complex set of rules and bureaucratic procedures that they may not understand and over which they have no control. Victims need an opportunity to tell their stories in their own way, in a setting of their choice; the court requires them to respond to a set of yes-or-no questions that break down any personal attempt to construct a coherent and meaningful narrative. Victims often fear direct confrontation with their perpetrators; the court requires a face-to-face confrontation between a complaining witness and the accused.

Sexual assault victims are confronted with unique issues in the cross-examination stage, during which the defence counsel seek to elicit probative evidence that will counteract the victim's claims. For example, the defence may argue for the admissibility of a victim's sexual history evidence or private communications in court (see, for example, Iliadis 2019; Iliadis, Fitz-Gibbon & Walklate 2019). While there are now legislative safeguards that prohibit the use of a victim's sexual history evidence and private communications (such as medical or counselling records) in many adversarial jurisdiction,[4] the legislation still allows for examination of such in 'exceptional circumstances'.[5] The impacts of this clause are discussed more extensively in Chapter 5, but include drawing upon pre-existing beliefs about the 'ideal' rape victim and 'real' rape stereotypes to inform such questioning. As Jordan (2008: 75) argues:

> Rape trials are particularly notorious for the way in which the credibility of the victim is attacked in court, with the emphasis typically placed on showing how she may have 'asked' to be raped or in some way brought the attack upon herself.

Bankowski and Mugham's (2001) degradation ceremony is therefore especially relevant to sexual assault victims, as their prior sexual history or private communications could be revealed and criticised if they deviate from the socially constructed idea of an 'ideal' rape victim. This can impact a victim's justice outcome, including whether a case results in a guilty verdict, the severity or type of sentence imposed, and whether victims experience a sense of procedural justice in court.

In this regard, research conducted by Hanly, Healy and Scriver (2009) found that the prospect of being cross-examined on one's prior sexual history or related private matters was a leading factor contributing to high attrition rates in sexual assault cases in Ireland (RCNI 2012). In their report, Hanly, Healy and Scriver (2009: 366) describe this type of attrition as falling within the 'improper attrition' category, referring to:

> [a]ttrition that arises from non-evidential, illegitimate grounds ... [which] includes all cases that are pushed out of the criminal justice system for any of the following reasons: fear, prejudice, poor investigation or procedures, weariness/frustration or unjustifiable legal rules.

These authors distinguish this from the notion of 'proper attrition', which they refer to as 'attrition that reflects the evidential requirements of the criminal justice system' (Hanly, Healy & Scriver 2009: 366). In sexual assault cases generally, most attrition falls within the 'improper' category (Hanly, Healy & Scriver 2009). For this reason, Hanly, Healy and Scriver (2009) argue that protecting victims from intrusive questioning and adversative court processes is not only crucial to keeping them engaged with the process, but also benefits the criminal justice system, as it can potentially protect the public from dangerous sex offenders.

The adversarial nature of the criminal trial thus engenders a hostile environment for sexual assault victims, and does not support them to relay their victimisation experiences. This often leads to victim dissatisfaction with the process, procedurally unjust outcomes and high attrition rates – all of which increase the likelihood of secondary victimisation. As Herman (2005: 574) argues, 'the wishes and needs of victims are often diametrically opposed to the requirements of legal proceedings', which means that victims will likely continue to experience procedural injustice throughout the prosecution process, and the conflict arising from the triangulation of interests will prevail.

A triangulation of interests

Common law systems have moved towards greater consideration and involvement of victims in criminal justice proceedings. This has necessitated a shift from the 'individualization of the offender to individualization of the victim' (Wolfgang 1982 cited in Erez 2000: 165). Some scholars have suggested that the need to be more inclusive of victims could be perceived as paralleling the notion of 'just deserts' (Erez 2000: 166).[6] Others have argued that it is less about vengeance and more about increasing victim status and involvement in the criminal justice system by addressing the traditional lack of input by victims in legal processes (Erez 2000; O'Connell 2012). In 1989, Justice Brennan of the Australian High Court claimed that justice is better served when victims' interests are taken into account in court proceedings:

> In the onward march to the unattainable end of perfect justice, the court must not forget those who, though not represented, have a legitimate interest in the court's exercise of its jurisdiction.
>
> (*Jago v District Court of New South Wales (1989) 168 CLR 23*)

Similarly, within the UK, Hoyano supports the protection of a fair trial, but notes that a 'quadrangulation [of interests] between the defendant, the alleged victim, other witnesses, and the public' can still be taken into account. Hoyano (2014: 12) asserts that:

> It is not only the defendant who can lay claim to the right to a fair trial, but all participants, and so the court has an obligation to ensure that judicial processes are conducive to a trial that is fair to all.
>
> (Hoyano 2014: 12)

In this regard, a fair trial arguably seeks to ensure the integrity of the verdict by protecting the rights and interests of the accused, the public *and* the victim. In light of this, the past three decades have witnessed a shift towards victim interests being considered as a crucial component of the legal process (Doak 2005; Iliadis 2019). While the adversarial system has a duty to uphold the due process rights of the accused, the VLRC (2016: xiv) recently suggested that 'fairness to the accused does not preclude recognition of the victim's interests'. In maintaining this view, the VLRC (2016: xiv) claims that:

> Fairness is a dynamic concept, changing over time alongside changes in community values and expectations. Increasingly, it is recognised that the public interest can be served not only by safeguarding the rights of the accused and the independence of the prosecution but also by taking into account the victim's interest. Procedures and rights that regulate the contest between the prosecution and defence have been supplemented by reforms that allow for the victim's interest to be taken into account, although only to the extent that fairness permits in an adversarial system.

On this basis, the VLRC (2016: xiv) emphasises that the 'interrelationship of the three – victim, accused and community – is mutual and complementary, not exclusory', and that there is scope to consider all three perspectives without compromising the principles upon which the adversarial system is based. It is within this *triangulation of interests* framework that this book is based.

The rise of women's and victims' rights groups

Over the past four decades, feminist activists and women's movements have challenged the patriarchal systems and structures that contribute to violence against women and sustain the law's response to sexual assault victims as a form of oppression, impacting women's equality, freedom and access to justice. These movements have critiqued the 'social, legal and political contexts governing responses to victims of gendered violence' (Iliadis, Fitz-Gibbon & Walklate 2019), especially those that privilege 'an idealised version of a victim' (Booth & Carrington 2018: 294). Htun and Weldon (2012: 549) argue that such movements are 'critical to understanding the origins of progressive social policies that explicitly challenge the established social order ... [and] develop oppositional consciousness, imagine new forms of social organisation, and mobilise broad social action to generate understanding and support'. By cultivating a *progressive social policy* response, feminist activists and women's rights movements advocated for extensive changes to be made with regard to how society perceives and responds to victims of gendered violence, both within and beyond the law.

In the early 1970s, crime victims similarly initiated a rights' movement that sought to highlight the 'injustices and imbalances' impacting victims within adversarial justice systems (Karmen 1992: 158). The establishment of victims' rights groups marked a significant milestone for victims because they brought to life common law jurist William Blackstone's precept that when crime occurs there are two victims – 'the actual person who is harmed or suffers a loss, and the state, whose law is violated' (cited in O'Connell 2012: 1). The establishment of victims' rights groups also became a catalyst for the developing awareness of victims, including of their marginalised place in the criminal justice system; the creation of support services and education initiatives; research on victims; and the push for law reforms that would improve victims' experiences in the legal process (Karmen 1992: 158). Significantly, this movement prompted a shift in the status of the victim from 'outsider *par excellence*' (Ryan 2003: 68) to the 'centre of contemporary discourse' (Garland 2001: 11).

While both movements led to different trajectories in the debates around victims' rights and the development of rape law reform, some feminist scholars argue that the language of 'victims' rights' erases feminist history and struggle (see, for example, Htun & Weldon 2012). Karmen (1992: 159), on the other hand, states that, despite several differences in 'priorities and world views', both movements mobilised to transform justice system responses to victims of gendered crime and reinforced the following five key critiques of the criminal justice system:

> 1) That criminal justice personnel – the police, prosecutors, defence attorneys, judges, probation officers, parole boards, corrections administrators – were systematically overlooking or neglecting the legitimate needs of crime victims until they began their campaign; 2) that there was a prevailing tendency on the part of the public as well as agency officials to unfairly blame victims for facilitating or even provoking crimes; 3) that explicit standards

> of fair treatment were required to protect the interests of complainants and prosecution witnesses … 4) that people who suffered [physical] injuries … ought to receive reimbursement … and 5) that the best way to make sure that victims could pursue their personal goals and protect their own interests was by granting them formal rights within the criminal justice system.
>
> (Karmen 1992: 159)

Women's and victims' rights groups were thus critical of the ways in which victims of sexual violence were treated in the criminal justice system, particularly in light of their historically marginalised status as women in the first instance, and as witnesses to proceedings in the second (Iliadis 2019). Informed in large part by these critiques, these groups applied ongoing pressure to challenge the traditional 'state versus defendant based formulation of the fair trial', advocating for legislative changes intended to 'spread fairness rights' to victims (Gans et al. 2011: 381). In advancing this argument in relation to victims of gendered crime, Fitz-Gibbon (2014: 74) writes that 'women have historically been assigned the role of the gendered "other"' within the criminal justice system. In a similar vein, Susan Currie (1995: 14) describes how:

> The realities of women's lives have been invisible in the law because women have not been able to tell their stories, because they have not been listened to and because they have not been believed.

Feminist activists and victims' rights groups accordingly promoted increased consideration of the interests of victims of sexual violence (who are generally women) alongside those of the accused and the community in the pursuit of justice, thus reaffirming Lord Steyn's conception of a 'triangulation of interests' (cited in *R v H [2004] 2 AC 134, 145–6*).[7]

The emergence and development of victim-focused reforms

The development of victims' rights reforms is complex, multilayered and varied, and any changes may be limited in their ability to meet victims' expectations (Skelton & Frank 2004; Strang 2002; Wright 2004; Zehr 2003), largely due to the wide range of differences in victims' needs and the nature of the adversarial system (Skelton & Frank 2004; Strang 2002; Wright 2004; Zehr 2003). As Zehr (2003: 69) maintains:

> Victims have many needs. They need chances to speak their feelings. They need to receive restitution. They need to experience justice: victims need some kind of moral statement of their blamelessness, of who is at fault, that this thing should not have happened to them. They need answers to the questions that plague them. They need a restoration of power because the offender has taken power away from them.

Yet, even in light of such differences in victims' needs and expectations, common law systems are moving towards greater recognition of victims' rights and involvement of victims within the prosecution process.

At an international level, greater recognition and involvement of victims have led to the development of the *Declaration of Basic Principles of Justice for Victims of Crime and Abuse of Power* by the United Nations (UN) in 1985, which outlines victims' entitlements and states that victims should:

- Be treated with compassion and respect for their dignity, irrespective of characteristics like age, gender, race, religion and so on;
- Have access to justice, including being allowed to present their views at the appropriate stages of the proceedings;
- Be informed of the progress of investigation and criminal proceedings, as well as court outcomes; and
- Be afforded measures to protect their privacy, ensure their safety and minimise inconvenience.

(s 6(a))

As noted in the introductory chapter, the Council of Europe's *Convention on Preventing and Combating Violence Against Women and Domestic Violence* (or the Istanbul Convention) also advocates for improved policies, support services and discourses around the violence women and girls experience.

In various countries globally, victim-focused reforms have been introduced in conjunction with administrative changes to procedures and services for victims. This has included the establishment of victim support services that assist victims to negotiate the criminal justice process, as well as training the police in how to respond to sexual assault incidents and provide assistance to victims throughout proceedings.

In Australia, specifically, victim recognition and related reform became a prominent focus in the 1980s. In the context of sexual assault law reform, the development of victim recognition has differed across Australian jurisdictions, taking place at various stages. However, Daly (2011: 3) explains that there has been a widespread emphasis on expanding the definition of rape and sexual intercourse and shifting the focus of consent away from the victim's behaviour to the offender's behaviour. Further reforms have focused on restricting the admissibility of evidence on a victim's sexual reputation or past behaviour, and allowing victims to give evidence via video technology or while accompanied by a support person (ALRC 2010: 1121–2; Braun 2014: 820). Other changes have included increased information rights, such as those outlined in the *Victims' Charter Act 2006* (Vic), and participation rights, such as through the provision of a Victim Impact Statement (VIS).[8] These changes have been aimed at redressing problems such as low reporting rates, the insensitive treatment of victims by the police, police perceptions of high rates of false reporting, the trauma of the courtroom experience, low prosecution and conviction rates, myths and misconceptions around the 'ideal' victim and 'real' rape experiences, and victim dissatisfaction with the criminal justice process more generally (Daly 2011: 3; Mason 1995: 53).

Flynn (2012: 74) argues that these changes have included the development of positive social responses, such as the introduction of rape crisis centres, and legal reforms, including the 'recognition of previously unacknowledged offences as "real" crimes, for example, domestic and family violence, and rape in marriage'. The victim, at least to some extent, is now recognised and has some involvement in criminal justice proceedings, although, as Flynn (2012: 75) argues, 'this position continues to operate within an adversarial framework, which restricts the victim from having a determinative say in the prosecution of their case'.

Key victim-focused reforms

Changes to the definition of consent

When rape laws were initially codified in adversarial legal systems, two central elements of the statute required that non-consent had to be proved and that the perpetrator exerted force – both reflecting 'real' rape myths (Easteal 1994: 202). To date, extensive changes to rape law have been introduced across many adversarial jurisdictions with regard to expanding the definition of consent (Daly 2011). These changes have been considered pivotal in providing legal clarity during trials and reinforcing the notion that resistance and injury are not required to prove non-consent (ALRC 2010; Burgin 2019). Larcombe (2011: 698) highlights that 'particular attention has been addressed to instituting what has been called a "communicative model" of sexuality'[9] in order to improve the procedural justice experiences of sexual assault victims and to redress the issues associated with their fear of reporting. As such, Larcombe (2011: 697–8) argues that these reform efforts not only reflect evolving 'standards and expectations regarding both sexual conduct and the appropriate treatment of sexual assault victims in criminal trials', but also function to 'address the significant "justice" gap between rape reports and trial outcomes'.

In Australia, every jurisdiction with the exception of the Australian Capital Territory (ACT) has a statutory definition of consent based on free agreement, free and voluntary agreement, or consent freely and voluntarily given (ALRC 2010). These definitions are reflective of the recommendation put forward by the UN Division for the Advancement of Women that states that legislation should approach consent as 'unequivocal and voluntary agreement' and that the accused should be obligated to prove the actions they took to 'ascertain whether the complainant/survivor was consenting' (cited in ALRC 2010).

In Victoria, the *Crimes Act 1958* (Vic) defines consent as 'free agreement' and outlines consent-negating circumstances in which a person does not freely agree to sexual activity. These include, but are not limited to, a person: (i) submitting to the act due to fear or force; (ii) submitting to the act due to fear of harm; (iii) submitting to the act due to being unlawfully detained; (iv) being asleep or unconscious; and (v) being so affected by drugs or alcohol that they are incapable of freely consenting (*Crimes Act 1958* (Vic) s36). South Australia defines consent as when 'the person freely and voluntarily agrees to the sexual activity' (*Criminal Law Consolidation Act 1935* (SA) s46(2)) and lists consent-negating circumstances similar to those outlined in the *Crimes Act 1958* (Vic) (see *Criminal Law Consolidation Act 1935* (SA) s46(3)). England and Wales have also broadened the definition of consent, placing emphasis on an individual's free capacity to make a choice to participate in the act without fear or force (*Sexual Offences Act 2003* (UK) s74 & s3(2)). In Ireland, section 2(1)(a) of the *Criminal Law (Rape) Act 1981* (Irl) defines rape as an act where 'he [sic] has unlawful sexual intercourse with a woman [sic] who at the time of the intercourse does not consent to it'.

Although the expanded definition of consent can be regarded as a significant step towards acknowledging the true nature of sexual violence and its impacts on victims, authors such as Larcombe (2011), Armstrong (2004) and Gotell (2007) have criticised the effectiveness of its implementation, suggesting that it does not meet 'its intended effects' in practice (Larcombe 2011: 698). In particular, Larcombe (2011: 698) states that the decision of the Victorian Court of Appeal in *Worsnop v The Queen ('Worsnop')* in 2010 provides an example of rape law reform 'not achieving' its aims. Larcombe (2011: 698–9) argues that in the case of *Worsnop*:

> The Court held that a jury direction on the 'mental' or 'fault' element for rape, introduced by the *Crimes Amendment (Rape) Act 2007* (Vic), … had not altered the law in the ways imagined by the 2007 Act's drafters and supporters. *Worsnop* determined that a jury cannot convict for rape if they find there is a reasonable possibility that the accused held an honest belief in consent (however unreasonable or mistaken). On this point, the Court found that both the Explanatory Memorandum accompanying the *Crimes Amendment (Rape) Bill 2007* (Vic) and the *Victorian Criminal Charge Book* … were incorrect. Consequently, when the trial judge in *Worsnop* directed the jury in accordance with the *Criminal Charge Book*, an error in law was made.

Larcombe (2011: 699) contends that 'the regrettable irony' in this case was that the *Crimes Amendment (Rape) Act 2007* (Vic) 'was designed to make jury directions in rape cases clearer … [to] reduce the likelihood of any error or appeal'. However, as a result of the court's ruling in *Worsnop*, this identified 'error' resulted in substantial 'miscarriage[s] of justice … in a number of subsequent [case] decisions' (Larcombe 2011: 699). Larcombe (2011: 699) concludes that there is a pressing need for further reforms to 'give effect to the objectives of the [*Crimes Amendment (Rape) Act 2007* (Vic)]' – namely, revolving around reasonable belief in consent – because 'immunity should no longer be provided for an accused whose belief in consent is the result only of distorted views of female sexuality' (Larcombe 2011: 711).

Victim Impact Statements

One of the most significant victim-focused law reforms is the VIS. VISs vary in their implementation and scope across common law jurisdictions; however, their main purpose is to provide victims with the opportunity to express the impact of the crime upon them to the court, including any physical, emotional or psychological damage, as well as loss or damage to their property (Erez 1991; Erez, Roeger & O'Connell 1996; Victims Support Agency 2009). VISs are one of the earliest and most significant legislative responses that encourage victim participation during the sentencing stage of the criminal justice process (Daly 2011: 16; Erez 2000: 166).

Prior to a sentence being imposed, a VIS is read to or by the judge, which outlines the impact(s) of the offence(s) on the victim. The main purpose of the VIS is to explain the harm that the crime has caused the victim so that the judge can consider these factors when determining what sentence to impose. The VIS therefore has the capacity to influence sentencing outcomes. Legal scholars such as Goldstein (1984) and Erez (1990) believe that the provision of this information can lead to enhanced proportionality and accuracy in sentencing, thus bolstering the aims of punishment (Erez 2000; Talbert 1988).

Overwhelmingly, VISs are considered to have had a positive impact on victims, providing them with the opportunity to feel recognised as participants in the process (Erez 2000; O'Connell 2012). They also reinforce the notion of a triangulation of interests, as they act as a reminder that 'behind the "state" is a real person with an interest in how the case is resolved' (Kelly 1987 cited in Erez 2000: 167). Victim participation rights, such as through the use of VISs, can also have therapeutic benefits for offenders. For example, the adoption of therapeutic jurisprudence for offenders enhances their understanding of the impact of their actions on victims, particularly when there is victim input into the process (Booth 2014b; Erez 2000; Wexler & Winick 1996; Wiebe 1996). Increasing victim participation rights in the criminal justice system is therefore often advocated on the basis of improved therapeutic outcomes.

Each Australian jurisdiction has provision for VISs in criminal proceedings (O'Connell 2012), as do other common law systems including England and Wales, and Ireland. In Australia specifically, VISs were first introduced in South Australia in 1989 (*Criminal Law (Sentencing) Act 1988* (SA)). This occurred as a result of the South Australian Government establishing a committee of inquiry into victims of crime to review the needs of victims (Erez, Roeger & O'Connell 1996). Victoria introduced the VIS into legislation in 1994 (*Sentencing Act 1991* (Vic)), with the intention of facilitating 'increased satisfaction by victims with the criminal justice system' (Victims Support Agency 2009). Additionally, Booth (2012) states that granting victims a voice in decision-making can assist with 'cooling out'[10] victims (see also Goffman 1952). The provision for victim participation through a VIS is therefore often supported on the basis that, even where the court does not consider the content of the statement, allowing victims to articulate the impact of the crime upon them can assist with their healing.

Notwithstanding the perceived benefits of VISs, contention over their effectiveness has made them one of the most examined victim-focused reforms (Booth 2014a, 2014b; Daly 2011; Erez 1991; Erez, Roeger & O'Connell 1996; Victims Support Agency 2009). A key reason for this is that VISs are not consistently implemented. For example, section 13(1) of the *Victims' Charter Act 2006* (Vic) states that victims are entitled to make a VIS 'unless the court orders otherwise'. This means that in some circumstances this right may be taken away. An example of this occurred in a Victorian Magistrates' Court in 2010 when the magistrate refused to hear the VIS of a sexual assault victim due to his view that the plea hearing was running overtime (Johnston 2010). The victim in this case described this experience as feeling like she 'didn't get justice at all. I feel let down. It's just shattered me' (cited in Johnston 2010). Similar victim experiences have been identified in England and Wales. Roberts and Manikis (2012) examined data from the Witness and Victim Experience Survey and found that, for the 2007–10 period, fewer than half (42 per cent) of victims recalled being informed about their right to make a Victim Personal Statement (VPS) and almost half (45 per cent) stated that they had not been given the opportunity to make a VPS.

The impact of victims not knowing about their right to make a VIS or not being given the opportunity to provide one has been highlighted by Henderson (1985 cited in Erez 2000: 168), who claims that 'victims who feel that their input has been ignored by judges may become embittered and resentful' towards the criminal justice process. Similarly, O'Connell (2006: 2) argues that a lack of support for VISs by judicial officers increases a victim's dissatisfaction with sentencing outcomes and loss of confidence in the criminal justice system generally. As reported by the Canadian Department of Justice (2001: 10), VISs 'are powerful but only if the system enforces what they have created … Sometimes it is as if no one cares [if you complete one] but Victim Services'. The impact of granting victims a 'right' to make a VIS but no legal right to enforce it is captured by Professor Caroline Taylor, who states that this 'completely undermines and subverts the intention of the legislation, which was introduced to finally give victims of crime a voice in the criminal justice system' (cited in Houlihan & Campbell 2010).

An additional concern associated with VISs has been identified in relation to plea negotiations (Flynn 2012). When plea negotiations take place, charges are likely to be altered and therefore the facts that are presented to the court must also be changed to reflect those amended offences, thereby limiting how much information the court can legally take into account from a VIS prior to a sentence being imposed (Flynn 2012: 83–4). Flynn (2012: 83) argues that this limits the opportunity for victims to express their views and have input into proceedings, as their version of events is substantially curtailed, and therefore the court does not hear the 'entire story'.

Accordingly, while reforms like the VIS can assist victims to some degree – that is, if their VIS is heard in its entirety – O'Connell (2006: 1) claims that they have not 'altered the structural position of the victim in the criminal justice system'. In Victoria, this can be attributed to the fact that a VIS is a victim's only opportunity to formally participate in proceedings. Thus, victims continue to remain 'recipients of information rather than … participant[s] in the [prosecution] process' (Refshauge 2013).

Victims' Charter Act 2006 (Vic)

Another key victim-focused reform is the establishment of a declaration or charter of victims' rights, and all Australian states and territories have introduced either one or the other. In Victoria, specifically, the *Victims' Charter Act 2006* (Vic) is significant in that it provides some form of legal recognition of victims and acknowledges that they have been adversely affected by crime. It requires that victims be treated with respect, courtesy and dignity by prosecuting agencies, investigating bodies and victim support services, and be provided with adequate and timely information about the legal process and their case (*Victims' Charter Act 2006* (Vic) s6 & 7). The *Victims' Charter Act 2006* (Vic) outlines 12 principles that govern the responses of criminal justice authorities and victim support agencies when dealing with crime victims. These include that victims be:

- Given clear, timely and consistent information about [their] rights and entitlements and, if appropriate, be referred to victims' and legal support services;
- Told by police of key progress in the investigation;
- Told about the prosecution, including charges laid, court dates and times, court outcomes and any appeals lodged, as well as any substantial changes to charges;
- [Provided with explanations about] the court process;
- As far as is practical, … protected from unnecessary contact with, and intimidation by, the accused, their family, supporters and defence witnesses while … at court;
- [Informed about] a VIS which will be taken into account by the judge in sentencing the offender, and have access to help when preparing the VIS;
- [Afforded measures to have] personal information [protected] in accordance with the *Privacy and Data Protection Act 2014* (Vic);
- Included on the Victims' Register if an adult offender is sentenced to prison for a violent crime against [them], receive specific information regarding the release of the offender, and have [their] views taken into account by a parole board when any decision about parole of the offender is being considered.

(Ibid.)

Significantly, the *Victims' Charter Act 2006* (Vic) ensures the provision of information to victims, as it gives them the right to be kept informed about crucial stages in a case's progress, as well as support and protective measures to improve their criminal justice experiences (Flynn 2012: 89). In relation to section 9 of the *Victims' Charter Act 2006* (Vic) in particular, Flynn (2012: 89) argues that it represents an important milestone for victims because:

> For the first time in Victoria's history, [it] places a statutory obligation on prosecutors to inform victims of any decisions to modify the charge(s) being proceeded with, and any decision to accept a guilty plea to a lesser charge(s).

While symbolically the Act marks an important shift, there are, however, some limitations associated with its practical application, such as those discussed above in relation to section 22(1)(a), which could prevent benefits arising for victims from having this right to be kept informed. On this basis, there appears to be merit and scope in revising the *Victims' Charter Act 2006* (Vic) to ensure that victims' rights to information are upheld and that their prospects to participate in the legal process are increased in order to enhance the likelihood that victims will experience procedural justice. This may involve enhancing victims' access to formal remedies where perceived failures to uphold victims' rights have been identified. Providing victims with the ability to pursue complaints through administrative or cognate civil processes, such as the ability to address prosecutors to seek a review of their decisions, may help to ensure that victims' rights to information are upheld and have clout in practice.

Reconceptualising the role of sexual assault victims

While there has been a significant shift towards greater inclusion of victims and their rights in the criminal justice system, their minimal role in the process, coupled with the identified shortcomings of recent reforms, has limited the opportunity for victims to experience procedural justice. Drawing upon empirical studies conducted in the Australian states of Victoria and New South Wales, numerous authors, including Bronitt (1998: 42), have observed that, even since the introduction of victim-focused reforms, 'the criminal justice system's treatment of women who allege rape has not significantly improved, and in some respects, may be worse than before the reforms were enacted'. Stubbs (2003: 23) similarly identifies that legislative changes to the victim's role have been 'limited in effectiveness' because of the 'resilience of cultural mythologies about women and sexuality'. This is especially evidenced by the fact that current legal reforms have not impacted on reporting or conviction rates in sexual assault cases, nor have they improved victims' experiences or perceptions of the criminal justice system (Australian Bureau of Statistics 2004: 54–7; Braun 2014: 820; Daly & Bouhours 2010: 619).

Recently, the VLRC (2016: 23) advanced this view, noting that while the victim's role has continued to evolve:

> The cumulative effect of the reforms have [sic] not been driven by a vision of what it should be; nor is there an adequate description of what it has

> become. The ambiguity this has created causes inconsistencies in how victims are perceived, how they see themselves, their expectations and how they are treated.

In a similar vein, Kirchengast (2016b: 2) argues that:

> The twenty-first century criminal trial is increasingly reconceived in form and substance, yet victims remain controversial and contested participants of justice, despite being increasingly connected to the criminal trial.

As a result, in its latest report the VLRC (2016) proposes that there is a need to reconceive the victim's role and level of contribution in the criminal justice system. In particular, the VLRC (2016: 41) recommends that the role of a victim be characterised as that of a 'participant' (rather than a witness) – 'but not a party' – to proceedings, and that this should include:

- treating victims with respect and dignity
- providing information and support
- a level of participation in court processes and decision-making
- protection from trauma, intimidation and unjustified interference with privacy during the criminal trial process
- having the ability to seek reparation.

(VLRC 2016: xv)

These rights and entitlements are already outlined in statute, such as within the UN *Declaration of Basic Principles of Justice for Victims of Crime and Abuse of Power 1985*, the *Victims' Charter Act 2006* (Vic), the *Sentencing Act 1991* (Vic), the *Criminal Procedure Act 2009* (Vic) and the *Evidence Act 2008* (Vic). In this regard, Kirchengast (cited in VLRC 2016: 29) states that 'a substantial rights framework is already in existence' so victims are already, in some capacity, 'included in, and protected during, the adversarial criminal trial process'. However, the VLRC (2016: 29) claims that the development of victims' rights has been limited in Victoria because:

> [the] language and conceptual basis of the victim's role has not evolved in line with the changes to the role itself … [Therefore, it] has contributed to the fragmented development of victim-oriented laws and policies, and a related lack of compliance [with victim-focused reform].

Thus, despite many changes to their role and level of recognition, victims, and sexual assault victims in particular, continue to experience alienation and exclusion from the prosecution process. For these reasons, O'Connell (2012) argues that victims' rights remain a secondary consideration in the legal system and that there exists scope for further reform. Daly (2011) points to the need for new and more 'innovative' ways of addressing these issues, for example, through restorative justice mechanisms that offer victims an 'informal' environment in which to discuss the impact of the crime upon them and redress the harm (Daly 2011: 10). Other authors, such as Braun (2014), have explored the prospect of ILR for sexual assault victims by considering how different forms of ILR operate in inquisitorial systems, such as Germany. Doak (2005: 294) similarly investigates the position of victims within adversarial systems amid legislative changes to the victim's role and considers 'arguments for a more radical course of reform that would allow victims to participate actively in criminal hearings as they are able to do in many European jurisdictions'. Meanwhile, Kirchengast (2013: 568) analyses 'the rise of victim lawyers in common law jurisdictions' and argues that 'access to private counsel is an important development in criminal justice that allows for the expression of the agency of the victim as a significant stakeholder in adversarial systems of justice'.

Recent inquiries, including the RCFV (2016) and the RCIRCSA (Cth), have considered how the rights of victims could be enhanced to advance their standing, protection and access to justice. As mentioned earlier in this chapter, this has included examining the means by which victims can be empowered to review prosecutorial discretion through a VRR-style reform (such as is available to victims in England and Wales) or through the introduction of ILR for victims in emerging Victorian specialist family violence courts.[11] In the absence of evidence-based research detailing how these reforms could be achieved in Victoria in practice, there is a need to explore the possibilities these reforms lend themselves to.

This book advances these debates by examining victim-focused reforms in adversarial jurisdictions that have enhanced victims' information and/or participation rights in the legal process, including through ILR, and considers the extent to which such reforms meet (or neglect to meet) victims' procedural justice needs. This will provide a basis from which to consider whether there is scope for ILR for sexual assault victims in Victoria, or whether any of the victim-focused reforms operating in the focus jurisdictions may be more viable alternatives for Victoria's adversarial system.

Concluding remarks

By way of concluding, it is clear that the emergence of interest in victims, victims' rights and sexual assault law reform has impacted the level of recognition afforded to victims of sexual violence. This chapter has provided an overview of the emergence of interest in victims by referring to the early literature and activism that shaped initial understandings of victimology, victims and their victimisation experiences. In particular, it considered the problematic construction of an 'ideal' victim as one who readily meets the criteria associated with 'real' rape scenarios (Christie 1986; see also Bows 2019; Bows & Westmarland 2016; Ehrlich 2001; Estrich 1987). It then explored the motivations underpinning feminist and victims' rights movements and in what ways these movements encouraged extensive changes with regard to how victims are perceived, responded to and treated within criminal justice systems.

In light of the traditional parameters of the adversarial system, which has positioned victims as witnesses to proceedings, the chapter considered the notion of a 'triangulation of interests' between the accused, the community and the victim. It drew upon the literature suggesting that justice can be better served when victims' interests are taken into account in proceedings (Justice Brennan 1989 cited in *Jago v District Court of New South Wales (1989) 168 CLR 23*; O'Connell 2012; VLRC 2016), despite this conflicting with the traditional adversarial mode of justice. The chapter explored how victims continue to be marginalised and excluded in a range of ways – for example, by feeling as though their rights and interests are not adequately upheld by the police and prosecutors, who primarily represent the public interest. It further demonstrated the conflict arising from the triangulation of interests by exploring how the trial can create a 'degradation ceremony' for victims, thereby exacerbating the harm associated with their victimisation.

The chapter also discussed the emergence, development and types of victim-focused reforms, with a particular focus on Victoria. It examined key victim reforms that have been implemented to provide victims with rights to information, such as the *Victims' Charter Act 2006* (Vic), and participation, including through the VIS. While acknowledging the significance of these reforms, the chapter highlighted the criticisms emerging in the literature, which reveals various gaps between the theoretical and practical application of the reforms. This leaves scope to consider how sexual assault victims' procedural justice experiences can be improved through other reforms that offer victims increased rights to information and/or participation that are upheld in practice.

Notes

1 The VLRC (2016: xxii) recommended that a similar scheme be introduced in Victoria (Australia), which would give victims a statutory right to request an independent review of prosecutorial decisions. However, the Victorian Government has yet to respond to this recommendation (Flynn and Freiberg 2017). Submissions cited throughout the VLRC (2016) report also pointed to the need to establish a system of review for victims in Victoria, such as the VRR operating in England and Wales (Iliadis 2015 cited in VLRC 2016: 71).

2 Attrition refers to the loss of cases within the criminal justice system, from as early as police investigations through to the trial stage (Jehle 2012; Kelly, Lovett & Regan 2005; Lees & Gregory 1993).

3 Flynn (2012: 79) defines plea negotiations as involving:

> [A] police prosecutor, or a Crown prosecutor or solicitor from the OPP engaging in an informal discussion with a defence counsel on an accused person's likely plea, and the possibility of negotiating the charge(s), case facts and/or the prosecution's likely sentencing submission.

4 Legislative safeguards prohibiting the use of a victim's sexual history evidence in court exist across all the focus jurisdictions – see *Sex Offenders Act 2001* (Irl) s34; *Criminal Procedure Act 2009* (Vic) s352(b); *Youth Justice and Criminal Evidence Act 1999* (UK) s41; and *Evidence Act 1929* (SA) s34(L)(1)&(2).

5 See, for example, *Criminal Procedure Act 2009* (Vic) s352(b).

6 The concept of 'just deserts' maintains that 'the level of punishment must be proportional to the seriousness of the crime' (Starkweather 1992: 857).

7 See also *R v A (No 2) [2002] 1 AC 45.*

8 Also referred to as a Victim Personal Statement (VPS) in England and Wales (see *Criminal Practice Directions* [2013] EWCA Crim 1631).

9 The 'communicative model' of consent is based on 'an ideal of mutuality in emotional and physical gratification' (McSherry 1998: 35). Under this model, Flynn and Henry (2012: 172) maintain that 'if one person is seeking to have sex with another person, they must take steps to find out if that person is willing to have sex with them'. Thus, they argue that 'if a person does not say or do anything, they are not consenting to the sexual act' (Flynn & Henry 2012: 172).

10 Booth (2012: 215) draws upon Goffman's (1952) 'cooling out' conceptual framework to demonstrate how:

> various legal structures and processes … [can assist with] manag[ing] and contain[ing] the emotional tension in the courtroom, as well as assist victims to adjust to the legal constraints and the compromise inherent in their position [as a witness] in the process.

11 See Iliadis, Fitz-Gibbon and Walklate (2019), for an analysis of Recommendation 60 of the RCFV (2016), which included the need to provide all Magistrates' Court of Victoria headquarter courts and specialist family violence division courts with 'facilities for access to specialist family violence service providers and legal representation for applicants and respondents'.

3 Procedural justice

Introduction

> The common law, and even some statutes, recognise that confidence in the criminal justice system and the part it has to play in creating and maintaining a liberal democratic and civilised society depends on it being, and being seen to be, fair and treating those involved in it with humanity and respect.
>
> (The Honourable Richard Refshauge cited in Gans et al. 2011: v)

> Procedural reform might, in the victim's perception, be more important than substantive legal change. Victims seemed more distressed by prevailing procedures, including the lack of information conveyed to them by the criminal justice system agencies and their lack of recognition as a party to the process, than by the dispositional outcomes. The indicators were that a greater involvement with the system may lead to a reduction in the level of discontent.
>
> (Sebba 1996: 200)

Sexual assault victims' expectations of justice are multi-layered and varied depending upon a range of factors relating to the circumstances of the offence, the individual victim and the victim's relationship (if any exists) with the accused (Clark 2010; Herman 2005). As victims' needs and expectations vary, so too do the sorts of answers and justice mechanisms they seek in order to help regain the power they have lost and redress the harm done to them. Following the crime, victims may question why the offence happened to them, how they can return to life before experiencing victimisation, whether they will be believed if they choose to report, what justice might entail, what justice remedies are available, how the truth is legally discovered, how offenders will be held accountable, what an appropriate punishment is for the crime, and how the harm(s) they have experienced might be redressed (Herman 2005: 571). Such questions (and answers) hold some complexity for sexual assault victims, considering the traumatic nature of their victimisation, which, as discussed in Chapter 2, is often exacerbated by criminal justice procedures. As Herman (2005: 573) contends, sexual violence offences are 'intractable and so impervious to the formal remedies of the law', making the attainment of justice for victims difficult.

Some victims' expectations of justice may align with more traditional understandings of just outcomes, for example, having the offender tried, found guilty and receive some form of punishment that reflects the severity of the crime committed. For other victims, however, obtaining justice through the legal process may take the form of the perceived fairness of the processes leading to the decisions made, such that the process allows them to feel like they are listened to, believed and kept informed of the case's progression. Notwithstanding the differences among victims' needs and perceptions, research consistently reveals that, when the legal process is fair, it increases victims' 'satisfaction with justice' (Erez 2000: 165) and improves victims' justice experiences (see Clark 2010; Feldthusen, Hankivsky & Greaves 2000; Herman 2005; Tyler 1992, 2007). This reflects the premise of procedural justice theory – that a focus on fair *processes*, rather than the *outcomes* of those processes, is crucial to meeting victims' justice needs.

This chapter explores the relevance of procedural justice theory for meeting sexual assault victims' needs and expectations from the criminal justice process. In doing so, the chapter begins by discussing the powerful myth of the vengeful victim. It draws upon the literature that suggests that victims' perceptions and expectations of justice do not necessarily correlate with vengeful outcomes. Instead, victims' satisfaction with the justice system often depends more on the level of information and input they have in legal processes. Information and participation can thus provide victims with a greater opportunity to experience equitable and fair legal processes, which in turn may enhance their perceptions of justice, regardless of the substantive case outcome (Lind & Tyler 1988). The chapter advances understandings of procedural justice theory, drawing upon the four key elements that have been found to address sexual assault victims' needs and expectations in relation to the legal process: information, validation, voice and control. The chapter explores the degree to which these often overlapping elements are reflected within current criminal justice processes, and how they may influence sexual assault victims' criminal justice experiences. As will be demonstrated through the discussion presented in this chapter, employing procedural justice theory as a framework for analysis is instrumental in analysing the potential benefits and limitations of the victim-focused reforms examined in the subsequent analysis chapters with regard to the ways they address or neglect victims' needs and expectations. It also provides a useful basis for considering whether there is scope for ILR for sexual assault victims in Victoria.

The myth of the vengeful victim

Historically, the victim was responsible for administering punishment upon the offender before state-based criminal justice systems emerged to 'curb the danger of vendettas and blood feuds and set limits on arbitrary, cruel, and excessive punishments' (Herman 2005: 576). Given that the state is now considered the wronged party, it also has responsibility for criminal investigations and prosecutions, and for establishing and administering punishment, which is to be applied 'fairly and rationally in proportion to the seriousness of the crime' (Herman 2005: 575). The idea that the state will be less vengeful and punitive than the victim is rarely challenged, even amid an ever-increasing tough-on-crime political agenda that tends towards harsher punishment of offenders, for example, through the introduction of mandatory minimum sentencing.

Resistance to victim input into the legal process has often been premised on the view that integrating 'victims into the process may be a way of accomplishing the goal of harsher punishment' (Erez 2000: 168; see also Henderson 1985 & Hellerstein 1989). For example, according to Erez (2000: 166), punishments based on the notion of 'just deserts' have paralleled 'the rise of a vocal victims' movement seeking to improve the plight of victims in the criminal justice system, and rectify their traditional lack of voice in legal proceedings'. This has created tension between the 'demands to provide victim input rights and attempts to increase sentence uniformity and reduce its severity' (Erez 2000: 169). This tension has thus resulted in considerable opposition to integrating victims into proceedings, as some believe that 'vengeful' victims will impose their 'punitive' views at the expense of offenders (Erez 2000: 169).

Research on victim participation in legal proceedings, however, has challenged the view that victims merely seek vengeance by way of securing a conviction and punitive punishment (Jordan 2008; Kelly 1982). Not only has research recognised that harsher sentences do not deter crime, but it has also found that harsher sentences are not always conducive to victims' needs. This was evident in a study conducted by the Centre for Innovative Justice (2014) in Victoria on sexual offences, which found that longer sentences do not reduce, prevent or redress sexual offending. Instead, they can make the accused person more likely to contest allegations and less willing to take responsibility for their offending, which would be counter to the victim's desire for validation of the offence and offender accountability (Centre for Innovative Justice 2014; Clark 2010). Jordan (2008: 29) similarly highlights how proceeding through the legal process does not always align with sexual assault victims' expectations of justice. This is because, upon reporting, victims do not always expect that the offender will be caught and convicted; rather, they may be seeking 'to regain a sense of personal safety, and to have their experience validated' (Jordan 2008: 29). Such views are reflected in the following comments provided by sexual assault victims in Clark's (2010) study:

> I really wanted … the criminal justice system to acknowledge that the crime had been committed and the enormous impact that it had on my life. I didn't want the perpetrator to go to jail or anything like that, I just wanted an acknowledgement or something – but I didn't get it, so I felt pretty ripped off.
>
> (Brenda cited in Clark 2010: 30)

> I wanted to make sure he didn't do it to anyone else. I kept quiet for 20 years, so I wasn't so much after [substantive] justice. I just wanted to protect others from him and that was my primary goal in going there [to the police].
>
> (Justin cited in Clark 2010: 30)

These statements suggest that victims may approach the criminal justice system for validation of their victimisation experiences, and/or for altruistic reasons – to keep others safe from potential harm (Clark 2010: 20). An American study conducted by Kelly (1982), in which 100 rape victims in the Washington, DC area were interviewed, supports these findings. Kelly (1982) found that victims welcomed the idea of conviction, but that ultimately a conviction contributed little towards their overall satisfaction with the justice process. Another American study of rape victims in Boston conducted by Holmstrom and Burgess (1978) identified that many victims felt ambivalent about the offender's conviction, either because they felt 'sorry or bad about what happened' or they perceived the offender as requiring 'help, not the prison sentence that he received' (Holmstrom & Burgess 1978: 256).

Furthermore, an Australian study conducted by the Australian Institute of Family Studies (AIFS) (2014: 4.1) examined the effects of victim-focused reforms in relation to victims' criminal justice experiences at a multi-jurisdictional level and found that victims' perceptions of justice 'are formed with reference to the totality of the victim/survivors' experiences within the process'. The AIFS (2014: 4.1) went on to state that:

> Justice is not defined by the *outcome* of the process, but rather the *experience* of the process … for the majority of [victim/survivor] participants, … [justice] was a matter of providing validation, information and respect.

This view is supported by the responses of two stakeholder participants in the AIFS (2014) study, who noted that:

> With law, they see [conviction] as 'that's the end'.... That is what justice is. A conviction is justice and that is the only way you can have any sense of justice, but I think what we're hearing is that's not necessarily the case. Justice is different.
>
> (Counsellor/Advocate Group 1, Jurisdiction 1 cited in AIFS 2014: 4.1)

> It's important in terms of that whole sort of procedural justice type area – that people are seen to be treated respectfully and seen as important. And I think sometimes, when you talk to people down the track, the outcome obviously is important at the time, but some people are managing really well after a not guilty verdict, other people aren't … So it's not all about the verdict, and hopefully there is something about being treated as a person properly, because a lot of people feel they haven't been respected

> [or] believed ... By treating them in the right way and showing that you've put some time and effort into their matter, ... they might get a different view on it [the legal process].
>
> (Victim Support Group 2, Jurisdiction 2 cited in AIFS 2014: 4.1)

These findings suggest that 'retribution is not the sole concern for victims' (Kelly 1982: 19), but rather that experiencing fair treatment, such as receiving validation, may indeed hold a higher level of importance. This supports the key principles of procedural justice theory insofar as it relates to perceptions of fair *processes*. Procedural justice theory also maintains that a key factor determining whether processes are perceived as fair is that victims have a degree of 'process control' (Tyler 1988). When an opportunity for victim input is provided, it is believed that victims will experience enhanced levels of satisfaction with the legal process regardless of the outcome (Lind & Tyler 1988). While convictions and the severity of punishment imposed upon the offender can determine, to some degree, victims' perceptions of a just outcome, their expectations of justice can extend well beyond punitive outcomes. This means that justice in the form of retribution is not the only driver, nor is it the most significant factor impacting a victim's level of satisfaction with the criminal justice system (Clark 2010; Herman 2005; Holder 2018; Holmstrom & Burgess 1978; Jordan 2008; Kelly 1982; Tyler 2007). Therefore, a greater understanding of victims' justice needs is necessary – one that allows for more nuanced and comprehensive insight into the factors that impact and shape sexual assault victims' perceptions of justice.

Theorising justice from the victim's perspective

In conceptualising justice from the victim's perspective, various scholars have attempted to understand 'when and how victims feel justice has been restored' (Wemmers 2014: 40). Despite differences in the underlying rationale, most models incorporate the ideals of *fairness* and *equality*, and there is usually a focus on the *outcome*. This can be seen in the distributive justice model. Social psychologists define distributive justice as referring to 'the fair distribution of outcomes or resources' (ibid.). It upholds equality ideals as it 'posits that fairness is achieved in social relationships when people feel that they are getting back what they are putting into a relationship' (Walster, Berscheid & Walster 1973 cited in ibid.). Applying this theory to crime victims, one may consider the proportionality between the harm suffered by the victim and the offender's punishment (see Jones, Parmentier & Weitekamp in this volume of Wemmers 2014). This closely links to the notion of 'just deserts' because it upholds the ideal of formally recognising victims as affected participants in the criminal justice system (Starkweather 1992: 854). Other elements considered within this model of justice are the notion of needs-based distribution, which fosters personal development and healing of the victim; and distribution that is based on equality, which supports fair and equitable distribution of resources (Deutsch 1975; Wemmers 2014). Needs-based distribution would include prioritising victims with the greatest need, for example, in relation to them obtaining support from victim services (Wemmers 2014: 226).

More recently, some scholars have proposed more critical and multifaceted conceptualisations of justice in order to further advance understandings of what justice might mean from a victim's perspective (see, for example, Holder 2018; O'Connell 2015a). The development of new justice theories has largely been due to ongoing victim dissatisfaction with the criminal justice process. In this regard, a more comprehensive understanding of the factors that impact and shape victims' justice experiences may lead to improved criminal justice procedures and ultimately enhance victims' perceptions of justice.

Procedural justice theory

Instrumental for understanding outcomes?

The theoretical framework underpinning this book is procedural justice theory. Procedural justice treats the significance of fair processes (the *how*) as equal to, if not more important than, the outcome (the *what*) (Barsoux & Manzoni 1998: 2). In the criminal justice system, procedural justice refers to the perceived fairness of procedures underlying decision-making processes (Burke & Leben 2007; Feldthusen, Hankivsky & Greaves 2000; Lind & Tyler 1988; Tyler 1992, 2007). In this context, fairness includes ensuring that the role and treatment of both parties (victim and offender) be fair and consistent, and that their rights are simultaneously upheld (Tyler 2007).

Thibaut and Walker (1975 cited in Wemmers 2014: 40) were the first theorists to identify procedural justice as 'a key determinant of people's justice judgments'. They proposed that procedures are crucial to ensuring fair outcomes as they provide 'a means to an end' (Thibaut & Walker 1975; see also Wemmers 2014). Later theorists, such as Lind and Tyler (1988), considered procedural justice as signifying one's value or worth to a group. In other words, if people feel a sense of acceptance and belonging, they are more likely to feel like valued group members. Hence, a key determinant of procedural justice is being treated with dignity, worth and respect (Feldthusen, Hankivsky & Greaves 2000; Tyler 1992). By applying this understanding to crime victims, it can be assumed that victims are more likely to experience a sense of belonging and worth if they are included in the legal process and have their voice heard in a fair and equitable manner. This is supported by the findings of Feldthusen, Hankivsky and Greaves's (2000) study on sexual assault victims' experiences with the legal system when making claims for compensation. They found 'participation, dignity and trust, [as well as] the role of legal actors', to be key elements informing victims' perceptions of procedural justice (Feldthusen, Hankivsky & Greaves 2000: 83). Other studies have also identified that victims value being treated fairly, even in cases where a conviction is not forthcoming (Burke & Leben 2007: 6). Respectful treatment is therefore a crucial component of fair legal processes and, according to Lind and Tyler (1988), is perceived as independent of the case outcome.

Despite the emphasis on fair processes, a common misconception about procedural justice theory is that people will be satisfied with *any* outcome, even where that outcome significantly contrasts with their initial desire (Tyler 2007: 26). Within the context of prosecution processes, this may create a false perception that victims are satisfied with no conviction or charges not being brought against the offender. This is not always the case. However, victims may be *more* willing to accept non-conviction if the procedures followed are perceived to be fair and consistent (Tyler 2007: 27). In other words, fair processes can make unfavourable outcomes more palatable (Tyler 1992, 2007). This can be seen in Feldthusen, Hankivsky and Greaves's (2000) study, for example, where sexual assault victims mostly prioritised therapeutic goals, including obtaining recognition of their victimisation and accountability of the offender. And this was identified as facilitating a victim's 'reconnection with ordinary life' (Feldthusen, Hankivsky & Greaves 2000: 69). The significance of reconnecting 'with ordinary life' (Feldthusen, Hankivsky & Greaves 2000) is also discussed by Herman (1997), who argues that, for sexual assault victims, this can lead to regaining the power, control and autonomy that they lost as a result of the crime.

Significance and relevance

Within criminology and socio-legal scholarship, procedural justice theory has often been utilised to analyse public perceptions of police legitimacy (Hinds & Murphy 2007; Tankebe 2013), as well as victims' and accused persons' levels of satisfaction with court proceedings (Burke & Leben 2007; Tyler 2007). For example, a study conducted by Tankebe (2013) evaluated public perceptions of police legitimacy in relation to procedural justice and found that a perception of legitimacy in the police was a key factor in determining people's willingness to cooperate with the police and legal authorities more generally (see also Engel 2005). Tankebe (2013) considered whether the police:

- use rules and procedures that are fair to everyone;
- provide opportunities for unfair decisions to be corrected;
- make decisions based on facts, rather than their own personal opinions;
- treat you with respect if you had contact with them for any reason; and
- clearly explain the reasons for their actions to people they deal with.

In relation to court proceedings, Burke and Leben (2007: 7) evaluated accused persons' compliance with court orders and found that, where there was a perception of fairness in the procedure, the accused was more likely to comply with the order. They explained, 'procedural fairness reduces recidivism because fair procedures cultivate the impression that authorities are both legitimate and moral' (Burke & Leben 2007: 7). Paternoster et al. (1997: 169) similarly contend that, '[o]nce the perception that legal authorities are legitimate has been shaped, compliance with the law is enhanced, even when it conflicts with one's immediate self-interest'. That is to say, even if an accused person 'fail[s] to obtain the outcomes they desire … they are more willing to accept and abide by the decisions of judges when those decisions seem to have been made fairly' (Burke & Leben 2007: 7). This ideology underpinning procedural justice has led Paternoster et al. (1997: 166) to claim that an accused's 'compliance [with court processes] may depend as much or more on the procedural fairness of sanction delivery as it does on the characteristics of the sanction imposed (i.e., its certainty and severity)'.

Other researchers have focused on the significance of procedural justice in exploring victims' needs within the criminal justice process (Clark 2010; Feldthusen, Hankivsky & Greaves 2000; Holder 2018), and the degree to which various victim-focused reforms meet these needs (Erez 2000; Iliadis 2019; Iliadis & Flynn 2018). While numerous studies have measured victim satisfaction with the legal process according to elements situated within a procedural justice model (Doak 2005, 2008; Herman 2005; Shapland, Willmore & Duff 1985; Strang 2002; Wright 2004; VLRC 2016; Zehr 2003), fewer studies have *explicitly* focused on examining victims' experiences of the legal process using a procedural justice framework (AIFS 2014; Clark 2010; Erez 2000; Iliadis 2019; Iliadis & Flynn 2018; Miller & Hefner 2013).

Clark (2010) is one scholar who has conducted research looking *explicitly* at sexual assault victims' needs from the criminal justice system based on procedural justice theory. Specifically, Clark (2010: 29) examined how victims 'personally understand justice and how this applies to various aspects of criminal justice processes'. Clark's findings reveal four key elements that are crucial to meeting sexual assault victims' procedural justice needs: information, validation, voice and control (Clark 2010: 29). Drawing from Clark's (2010) conceptualisation of sexual assault victims' procedural justice needs, more recent research by Iliadis and Flynn (2018) has used this theory to determine victims' satisfaction with the VRR reform in England and Wales (see Chapter 4). Likewise, Iliadis (2019) also used this model to determine whether sexual assault victims were experiencing procedural justice when exercising their right to ILR to oppose defence applications for the introduction of their sexual history evidence in court (see Chapter 5).

Erez (2000) has explored the significance of procedural justice for victims in relation to VISs and found that a VIS can promote victims' 'psychological healing' as it enables them to present 'their side to decision-makers' (Erez 2000: 176). In turn, this allows victims to feel a degree of 'process control' (Tyler 1988) and can increase their satisfaction with the justice system, 'regardless of the outcome' (Lind & Tyler 1988). Scholars such as Miller and Hefner (2013) have also examined how procedural justice can be successfully achieved for victims (and offenders) through restorative justice processes. In particular, they found that restorative justice provides a mechanism to ameliorate the harms caused by the criminal justice system and, significantly, enhances perceptions of procedural justice (Miller & Hefner 2013). Another study conducted by the AIFS (2014) identified that victims' needs from and perceptions of fairness within the legal process aligned more closely with being believed, receiving emotional support, having a voice and being informed about the progress of their case (AIFS 2014: 4.1).

Other studies have *implicitly* explored victims' perceptions of, and experiences with, the criminal justice system, and have typically emphasised the system's inability to address (sexual assault) victims' justice needs (Doak 2005, 2008; Herman 2005; Shapland, Willmore & Duff 1985; Strang 2002; VLRC 2016; Wright 2004; Zehr 2003), particularly in relation to information, validation, voice and control (Clark 2010: see also Doak 2005; Erez 2000; VLRC 2016).

Key elements of procedural justice theory

Tyler (2006: 23) defines procedural justice in terms of: voice, meaning one's ability to participate in the case by expressing and having one's viewpoint heard; neutrality, consistency and transparency in court processes and how decisions are made; respectful treatment of all parties; and trustworthy authorities (see also Burke & Leben 2007; Spencer 2017). King (2009: 191) identifies similar elements as making up procedural justice, including validation, respect and voice. Leventhal (1976, 1980) likewise states that the following criteria are likely to influence one's perceptions of fairness within a legal procedure: consistency in fair treatment of all victims and offenders; the ability to suppress bias to prevent favouritism; decision quality and accuracy, such that outcomes are based on objective, well-informed decision-making; correctability, which involves being able to contest and correct inaccurate or unfair decisions (such as through a VRR scheme – see Chapter 4); representation, which allows both the victim and the accused to be involved in decision-making processes (such as having ILR in certain circumstances – see Chapters 5 and 6); and ethicality, which considers 'the degree to which the decision-making process accords with general standards of fairness and morality' (Leventhal 1980 cited in Tyler 1988: 105).

Drawing from the body of literature on victims' needs (Clark 2010; Herman 2005; Skelton & Frank 2004; Strang 2002; Tyler 2007; Wright 2004; Zehr 2003), this book defines the following four elements of procedural justice as critical to meeting sexual assault victims' needs from the criminal justice system: (i) information – keeping the victim informed at all stages of the case's progression and *before* decisions are made; (ii) validation – including believing the victim's account of their victimisation experiences, and treating the victim with respect and dignity; (iii) voice – providing victims with the opportunity to narrate their story to a supportive and receptive audience, and to have this story acknowledged and; (iv) control – giving the victim some sense of control within their case, particularly in regard to the decisions made. These four elements continue to emerge in the literature as factors impacting sexual assault victims' experiences of and overall satisfaction with the criminal justice system (Clark 2010; Erez 2000; Herman 2005; Jordan 2008), and as such they will underpin the theoretical analyses of the victim-focused reforms presented in this book. Each element is discussed in turn below.

Information

A common need consistently identified by crime victims is the desire to be kept informed at all stages of the case's progression through the criminal justice process (Johns 2002; Maguire & Bennett 1982; Sebba 1996; Shapland, Willmore & Duff 1985; Strang 2002; Wright 2004). This was illustrated in a study conducted into victims' attitudes towards court processes in the UK, which identified information and support as two leading requirements of victims from the court process (Ames et al. 2003). In particular, victims expressed the need for 'emotional support and counselling, information about how the court works ... visits to the court, help and advice about compensation, and transport to the court' (ibid. 45). In relation to the pre-trial process, Ames et al. (2003) used a confidence scale from least to most confident to identify the needs of victims. Victims who were identified as being least confident with the criminal justice system were more likely to be victims of serious personal crimes, have very specific needs, have a relationship with the offender, have no prior experience with the criminal justice system, require ongoing support, and feel traumatised by their victimisation experience (ibid.). Conversely, victims who were identified as being most confident with the pre-trial process included those who had prior experiences with the criminal justice system and had been kept well informed throughout the pre-trial process (ibid.).

A Victorian survey conducted by the Victims Support Agency and Victoria Police found that support and information were lacking in the delivery of the criminal justice system (Victims Support Agency 2013: 5). Of the 605 victim and witness respondents, over 60 per cent of victims who attended court said that they did not receive support. A further 32 per cent stated that they had not received any information or details regarding the court process, or how to go about receiving information about the outcome of their case (ibid.). These findings are evident in one participant's comments: 'I was unaware of [the] victims of crime program. I found that on the net myself' (victim respondent cited in ibid. 15). Another participant explained that they were not 'informed of [the victim] impact statement before the trial' and were not provided with information to understand why the offender got 'off the charges' (victim respondent cited ibid. 15). Recent Victorian commissions of inquiry, including the VLRC (2016) and the RCFV (2016), likewise highlighted the imperative to keep victims informed throughout the criminal justice process. Noting that victims' early interaction with the justice system can be crucial to keeping them engaged with the process, the VLRC (2015: 4) identified that 'victims need to be treated with respect and provided with information and support'. The VLRC (2015: 19) maintained that the provision of information and support can also contribute to enhanced procedural justice outcomes for victims.

An Irish study conducted by Hanly, Healy and Scriver (2009 cited in RCNI 2010: 14) drew attention to the lack of information victims reported receiving in the criminal justice system:

> I was looking for a code book, a guide book for a long, long time of what to expect next so I could be prepared. And no such things exist of course, but I asked advice from the Rape Crisis Centre and I used the hotline continually which was great because you really do need people to talk to.
>
> (RAJI survivor cited in RCNI 2010: 14)

Sexual assault victims in Clark's (2010) study also identified having accessible information as a crucial component of their justice needs. This is especially important given the complex nature of the criminal justice system, which one participant described as 'a foreign land' (Clark 2010: 31). The participants in Clark's (2010: 31) study expressed the need for practical information relating to the different stages of the process, the key players involved, their own role in proceedings, the potential consequences for them of engaging with the legal process, and the potential outcomes, as highlighted in the comments below:

> I would want someone from the criminal justice system to come to me and speak very clearly – not get caught up in a whole lot of legal mumbo jumbo, but speak very clearly to me – and say what were my options [and] the procedures that would be gone through.
>
> (Rose cited in Clark 2010: 31)

> It would be better if they explained, 'well look, we've made a decision, can we make some time to see you? This is how the system works', you know, and explain to me something or even say, 'Um, look, I acknowledge that this happened to you; however, our system, blah blah blah'. I don't know how they made the decision [not to prosecute the offender].
>
> (Penny cited in Clark 2010: 32)

These statements reveal that providing victims with clear and consistent information, and relaying the information in a way that they can understand, will enable victims to consider their options and manage their expectations in accordance with the standard of proof in sexual assault cases. It can also help victims to better understand why cases may not be able to proceed or why certain decisions are made. Ultimately, Clark (2010: 31) found that when information was provided to victims it informed their decisions about whether or not to continue to engage with the criminal justice process.

Providing information to victims can also contribute to their long-term recovery and positively influence their perceptions of the justice process (Heenan 2014; Shapland, Willmore & Duff 1985; Strang & Sherman 2003). Sebba (1996: 96) contends that victims are less likely to be disappointed by substantive outcomes than they are by the failure of the police to inform them of decisions made – for example, in relation to non-arrest, release on bail or a decision to engage in plea negotiations – which reiterates the significance of information in addressing victims' procedural justice needs.

As adversarial systems are currently operating, however, it appears that victims are not consistently receiving adequate information. This failure thus brings into question the extent to which victims' rights are being upheld in accordance with charters governing their rights to information, such as the *Victims' Charter Act 2006* (Vic) (see Chapter 2), and the failure undermines the fundamental objective of such reforms of treating victims with dignity and respect. This may then further entrench a victim's feelings of exclusion and vulnerability in the process, which is particularly concerning given that most victims already suffer high levels of anxiety, stress and trauma in the aftermath of the crime (Cook, David & Grant 1999; The Honourable Judge Ian Gray 2014). These findings emphasise the need for the provision of more consistent, transparent and reliable information to victims to allow them to feel that their procedural justice needs are being met, or, at the very least, considered (The Honourable Judge Ian Gray 2014).

Validation

The second key element of procedural justice theory requires that victims receive some form of validation of their experiences (Clark 2010; Iliadis & Flynn 2018). This is particularly relevant for sexual assault victims, as very few cases proceed and few convictions are recorded. In reflecting on victims' experiences in her study, Clark (2010: 32) notes:

> Being believed is a stepping-stone to attaining acknowledgement, validation, victim status and support … Participants who felt that their allegations were met with disbelief felt that their credibility was judged and the seriousness of their claims were undermined.

Jordan's (2008: 75) account of victims' experiences in her book *Serial Survivors* offers a similar view: 'for those who sought redress in the criminal justice system, the single greatest shock was the discovery of just how little they mattered'. This links in with a victim's status in the criminal justice system, where legal recognition as a victim can only be attained when (and if) there is a guilty verdict. Until such a verdict is reached, the law only considers victims as witnesses, which may remove or limit any potential for victims to experience some form of validation from criminal justice authorities. Examples of this are evident in Clark's (2010) study, in which victims spoke of being treated with scepticism by the police:

That seemed to be the conclusion after they'd interviewed [the offender]:

> 'Oh [he says] he didn't do it, so let's not go any further. It's not worth it – your word against his. He's an upstanding member of the community, he's

> done this, that and the other. You're just a nobody who has a mental illness'. So yeah, in a way I think that I was made out to be a liar … I got the impression, from their point of view, the system doesn't work in these [sexual assault] cases.
>
> (Kane cited in Clark 2010: 32)

> I was judged on my sexuality. My sexuality impacted on their enthusiasm, if you like – their support for the case that they were prosecuting, because I'm a lesbian. And the sexual assault – they said that I was consenting. Their perception was that it was minor, that it wasn't serious.
>
> (Amanda cited in Clark 2010: 320)

Procedural justice theory recognises that validation is important not only for legal recognition of the crime, but also for victims whose matters do not proceed, for example, due to the high standard of proof required in sexual assault cases. Research indicates that the number of false complaints is very low in sexual assault cases (Heenan & Murray 2006; Kelly, Lovett & Regan 2005), which means that, even where legal recognition of the crime cannot be obtained, the validity of a victim's claims should not be challenged. Considering the sensitive and harmful nature of sexual assault, victims need justice system officials to acknowledge the seriousness of their victimisation experience and its impact on their life (Clark 2010). Communicating to sexual assault victims that they are believed also increases the likelihood that they will seek specialised support, which can contribute to their healing (Campbell 2006; Clark 2010; Flood & Pease 2006; Lievore 2003).

Within procedural justice theory, being validated includes feeling believed from as early as the initial reporting of the crime. Indeed, as discussed previously, while some victims may only feel validated if the offender is charged and convicted, it has generally been found that if victims are listened to and believed, they are more likely to report satisfaction with the criminal justice system, regardless of substantive case outcomes (Clark 2010). However, as demonstrated within the literature and by the quotes above, validation is often lacking in sexual assault victims' criminal justice experiences. This discourages victims from reporting the crime and increases improper attrition levels (Clark 2010; Hanly, Healy & Scriver 2009).

In its current form, the adversarial system often does not provide an opportunity for sexual assault victims to feel validated (Clark 2010; Iliadis 2019). This is particularly evident at the reporting stage, when victims frequently receive adverse responses from the police – their first point of contact with the legal system (Jordan 2001, 2004a, 2004b; Kelly 2002; Segrave, Wilson & Fitz-Gibbon 2018). It is also evident throughout the trial itself and during the cross-examination stage in particular, when 'misleading or confusing' questions are asked of victims to belittle or insult them (Booth, Kaye & Wangmann 2019: 1111). Thus, a limitation of the adversarial system is that it denies victims of their status unless there is a guilty verdict, thereby replicating the harm of their victimisation as victims feel disbelieved (Jordan 2013; Madigan & Gamble 1991; Temkin & Krahé 2008).

Conveying to sexual assault victims that they are believed is thus a key element to meeting their procedural justice needs and can make victims more willing to accept case outcomes, regardless of what they might be. The significance of validation will be further explored in the analysis chapters, in relation to the ability of the reforms discussed to provide an opportunity for victims to feel validated.

Voice

It has been well established in the literature that providing victims with a voice in the criminal justice system enables them to feel acknowledged, included and empowered (Burke & Leben 2007; Clark 2010; Doak 2008; Erez 2000; Iliadis 2019; Iliadis & Flynn 2018; O'Connell 2012). The importance of voice is confirmed in the procedural justice literature, which suggests that 'people consistently judge procedures as fairer when they are given an opportunity to express themselves in the decision-making process' (Van den Bos 1996 cited in Wemmers 2014: 40). Burke and Leben (2007: 12) found this to be so even in situations where people are 'told that their voice will have *no* impact on the decision' of the substantive outcome. In relation to sexual assault victims, Clark's (2010: 34) study identified that victims need to be given the opportunity to narrate their story to a supportive and receptive audience, to provide 'the full context' of the offending, and to communicate 'the impacts of the assaults' to authorities.

In contrast to inquisitorial systems, victims typically have no 'right to be heard' in adversarial systems (Spencer 1997 cited in Doak 2005: 299) and are denied participation rights, 'since their interests are deemed to fall outside the remit of the criminal trial as a forum for the resolution of the dispute between the State and the accused' (Doak 2008: 35). This means that, aside from the VIS, victims have no opportunity 'to put their own side of the story to the court in their own words, but must confine their explanation of events within the parameters of the questions posed by the advocates' (Doak 2008: 251). Yet having the ability to convey the impact of the crime has been identified as a key component of victims' procedural justice needs (Clark 2010: 34). This was demonstrated in Clark's (2010: 34) study, in which many victims expressed the need to have their 'day in court'. However, this expectation was subdued when sexual assault victims discovered what their role would entail within the adversarial system and how trial processes can impact victims' capacity for self-determination within the criminal justice process (Easteal 1998; Lees 2002; Orth 2002; Taylor 2004). In this regard, a comment from a victim in Clark's (2010: 34) study reveals how victims become 'manipulated, humiliated [and] degraded':

> In the end it was disempowering … There was no space to speak my truth whatsoever. And the words that I had spoken, the contexts were twisted and used to say the opposite to what I meant … It didn't just not enable me to speak my truth, it actually spoke lies using my words.
>
> (Hannah cited in Clark 2010: 34)

This comment is particularly concerning given that reporting sexual assault often comes with many challenges for victims (Clark 2010; Jordan 2004a, 2004b). The impacts on victims of having to tell their story to the court are already so damaging and are exacerbated when the focus is on victim 'credibility rather than truth' (Clark 2010: 34; see also Taylor 2004). The effects of victims not having adequate input also extend to them feeling sidelined by the process, with their views and interests essentially overlooked (Herman 2005: 581), leading to secondary victimisation.

Due to the structure of the adversarial justice system – being a contest between the state and the accused – victims' voices are generally not integrated into proceedings. For this reason, it has been argued that 'the wishes and needs of victims are often diametrically opposed to the requirements of legal proceedings' (Herman 2005: 574). While the VIS gives victims an opportunity to express the impacts of the crime upon them, in most adversarial jurisdictions completion of a VIS is the only formal right victims have to express their views. More recently, some adversarial jurisdictions, including Ireland and South Australia, have moved somewhat contentiously towards introducing victim-focused reforms that allow victims to have more of a voice in proceedings. The analysis chapters consider the extent to which these reforms accommodate victims' voices and enhance victims' procedural justice experiences.

Control

The formal classification of victims as 'complainants' and 'witnesses' in the criminal justice system means that they are afforded little, if any, control over the decisions made in their case (Clark 2010: 34). In referring to the marginal position victims occupy in the criminal justice system, McBarnet (1983: 300) states, 'if victims feel that nobody cares about their suffering, it is in part because *institutionally* nobody does'. Research has also shown that victims are surprised at the lack of control they have over case decisions and how their interests are peripheral to the system (Clark 2010; Herman 2005; Iliadis 2019; Koss 2006). According to the victims in Clark's (2010) study, their concerns should be considered 'central to their case' (Clark 2010: 34). As one victim reflected:

> I'm a person being violated in … one of the worst ways a person could be violated, and I get this letter to say, 'Sorry it's not really important'. For the criminal justice system to say, 'Well it's not worth pursuing', that's the bit that's been the hardest. Apart from the abuse itself, that part has been really hard. It almost felt like being abused again.
>
> (Penny cited in Clark 2010: 34)

This comment demonstrates the lack of control victims have in the legal process, particularly in terms of their ability to contest prosecutorial decisions in instances where they do not agree with those decisions. It also highlights the disjuncture between the interests of the victim and those of the state (Clark 2010: 34; see also Booth, Kaye & Wangmann 2019). As Clark (2010: 34) describes:

> The prioritisation afforded to proceeding with certain cases over others seemed to denigrate the value of their [the victim's] experience, question their [the victim's] credibility as a person and repeat the position of insignificance that the perpetrators put them in.

With the exception of England and Wales, which allow victims to contest some prosecutorial decisions (see Chapter 4), victims have very limited control within adversarial systems. This can be a significant barrier to reporting:

> In actually initiating that police statement, once it gets in the process, I felt [that] I was handing over a lot of control to them. And basically, they wanted me to follow through with it. It was sort of like, 'Well, we're going to do all this work for you. You know, if you go and pull out, this is your credibility at stake'. And I found that difficult to handle.
>
> (Rose cited in Clark 2010: 34)

Another victim in Clark's (2010) study drew attention to the lack of control she had once she reported, as the police then exerted almost total control over the case:

> We were advised that if we made a statement, then the police, if there was enough evidence as they believed in the statement, that they would charge him [sic]. And I kind of thought that that was a bit unfair, because you know, I really only just wanted them to know that there was a man out there with this problem and how they could protect other people.
>
> (Felicity cited in Clark 2010: 34)

These comments demonstrate that a victim's ability to regain control through involvement in the criminal justice system is very limited. This is problematic in light of research that emphasises 'process control' as a crucial element of victims' procedural justice needs (Tyler 1988). In this vein, Wemmers (2014: 40) has found that a victim's ability to 'maintain control over the decision and control over the process' will help to 'maximise [satisfactory] outcomes'. This includes giving victims a more active role in proceedings – one that ensures that their voice is heard and their rights consistently upheld (Clark 2010: 35). It could also involve granting victims the opportunity to have input into key decisions made, for example, in relation to plea negotiations, or being able to contest prosecutorial decisions.

The ability for victims to exert some sort of control in decision-making processes has recently been raised by the RCIRCSA (2017) in Australia. In its final report, the Commission found that 'justice had been delayed and/or denied for many of the most vulnerable victims' (Iliadis & Flynn 2019). It recommended that every prosecution office in Australia 'establish a robust and effective formalised complaints mechanism to allow victims to seek an internal merits review of key decisions' – akin to the VRR scheme operating in England and Wales (RCIRCSA 2017: 105). As discussed at more length in the next chapter, the implementation of this suggestion could enable victims to experience a greater sense of control over decision-making processes, which could contribute towards enhanced procedural justice outcomes. The analysis chapters to follow will demonstrate the importance of victims regaining a sense of control that they may feel they have lost as a result of the crime(s), and how this contributes to a victim's recovery and perceptions of justice.

Concluding remarks

Procedural justice theory holds great significance and relevance as a framework for understanding the needs and expectations of sexual assault victims in adversarial systems of justice. The common misconception underpinning the myth of the vengeful victim, which views victims as seeking punitive outcomes for offenders, is not supported by the extant literature. Instead, what is clear is that other factors play a role in facilitating 'just' outcomes for victims. A large body of literature supports the notion that fair legal processes are a key determinant of victims' perceptions of justice. When fair procedures are followed, unfavourable outcomes are made 'more palatable' (Lind & Tyler 1988: 67). While sexual assault victims' justice needs may vary in nature and scope, there is evidence to suggest that the elements of information, validation, voice and control play a significant role in shaping victims' perceptions and experiences of procedural justice.

4 Providing a check on prosecutorial decision-making

An analysis of the VRR reform[1]

Introduction

> I think it's a very useful insight by us [the CPS] as to what's going on in our own organisation, and [considering] some of the decisions that I've overturned, I don't understand why the prosecutor didn't go ahead … Our CPS board … have asked us for reports in my unit because we're quite unique and we have an overview of the work of the whole of the CPS service … they want to know how the areas are doing, how they're dealing with this, what their decisions are like, trends in decision making across the country – you know, we get one area that will produce a certain level of decision making which is quite different from another area and we want consistency. It shouldn't be a postcode thing. You shouldn't have someone prosecuted depending on where you live, and so having our unit enables us to have an overview as to what's going on in the service, otherwise the only way you would know is by complaints or by people taking us to the High Court, and of course you only go to the High Court if you've got the money to do it so that's quite unfair on people. So I think it has been good for the CPS and it's also good to see what we're doing well.
>
> (Kate, managing lawyer, CPS)

> It's important that the victims are actually considered in each stage of the process – to be heard on what their views are – because it is them that are directly impacted by [the decisions], so they need to have as much choice and control over what's happening next, as much as they possibly can.
>
> (Georgia, policy researcher, victim support organisation)

Prosecuting authorities maintain a high level of discretion in carrying out their everyday professional duties, including having the power to decide whether or not, and how, to proceed with a case. As Flynn (2016: 567) explains, such decisions 'are governed by discretionary judgments of the evidence's sufficiency (prospect of conviction) and public interests'. Traditionally, these decisions have not been subject to any external scrutiny or review. However, as Davis (1969: 81) questions, 'Why should the prosecutor's charging decision be immune to review by other officials and immune to review by the courts, even though our legal and governmental system elsewhere generally assumes the need for checking human frailty?'. This question was the focus of a High Court case in 2011 (*R v Killick [2011] EWCA Crim 1608*),[2] in which the court considered whether victims of crime have a 'right' to seek a review of the CPS's decision not to prosecute. In making its determination, the Court recognised the finality of this largely unfettered decision-making power, stating that, 'for the victim, there must be a right to seek a review of such a decision'.[3] As a result of the Court's ruling in *Killick*, victims in England and Wales now have the opportunity to challenge the prosecutor's decision not to proceed with charges through the VRR.[4]

The VRR is theoretically accessible to all crime victims and is intended to acknowledge and, where deemed appropriate, correct prosecuting decisions not to lay charges, proceed with a charge(s), proceed with certain charge(s) or present evidence, when a secondary in-depth analysis of the case determines the original decision to be in error. The VRR is managed by a special division within the CPS – the Appeals and Review Unit – and adopts the principles established in *Killick* and set in Article 11 of the *European Union Directive*,[5] which outlines minimum standards for the rights, support and protection available to victims.

In this way, the VRR reflects the CPS's broader efforts to be more transparent in its decision-making processes, to show more sensitivity to victims, and to improve victims' confidence in the criminal justice system. The VRR also advances shifts towards increased consideration and involvement of victims in the criminal justice process generally and captures the broader aims of the British legal system, in which attaining justice is traditionally associated with equality, fairness and respect for the individual rights of both the victim and the accused.

This chapter focuses on the extent to which the VRR responds to victims' procedural justice needs, with reference to the four key elements identified in Chapter 3 – information, validation, voice and control. The chapter examines the extent to which victims experience and gain validation, information, voice and control from the reform. It begins by presenting a detailed overview of the VRR process, including how victims can exercise their rights under the VRR, the specified timeframes surrounding requests, how decisions over whether to accept review requests are made (and by whom), and the procedures involved in the conduct of reviews. Although the VRR is available to all victims, this chapter focuses primarily on the VRR in relation to sexual assault victims. It then considers the benefits and limitations of the VRR, and how it may positively and negatively impact on victims' experiences and perceptions of the criminal justice system. In doing so, the chapter focuses on the extent to which the VRR responds to victims' procedural justice needs (noting the apparent focus placed on victims during its development), and comments on the extent to which victims experience satisfaction as result of this victim-focused reform.

The VRR process

The shift towards greater inclusion and consideration of victims in the criminal justice system in large part underpins the creation of the VRR. In addition to this, greater scrutiny of prosecutorial charging powers that emerged in the wake of the Glidewell Review of the CPS in 1998 has also lent itself to a system that favours review of prosecutorial decision-making. The Glidewell Report identified 'serious tension between the police and the CPS, with a tendency for each party to blame the other if the case failed' (Huxley-Binns & Martin 2014: 160). The report's main recommendation was to 'place the CPS representatives into police stations to form a single integrated unit in charge of assembling and managing case files, able to call on the police to obtain more evidence where necessary' (Huxley-Binns & Martin 2014: 160). This reform – known as the statutory charging process – has been rolled out across England and Wales, and requires that the CPS, in conjunction with the Association of Chief Police Officers, advise the police prior to charges being laid on what the appropriate offences are based on the law, and also review the police brief to determine what charges the offender should face in serious and complex cases (Flynn & Freiberg 2017). It is within the context of these victim-focused frameworks involving increased oversight that the development of the VRR must be placed.

The VRR is theoretically accessible to all victims, as defined by the *Code of Practice for Victims of Crime 2015* (UK)[6], subject to some restrictions. Eligibility is initially assessed based on whether the victim's case adheres to one of four qualifying decisions whereby the prosecutor decides to:

- Not lay any charges (pre-charge stage);
- Discontinue all charges (referred to as 'withdrawing' all charges at the Magistrates' Court level);
- Not offer (particular) evidence; and/or
- Leave all charges in the proceedings to 'lie on file' (this occurs when the CPS decides not to proceed with charges, and requests that charges not be proceeded with unless leave is granted by a court).

(CPS 2016)

In addition to these restrictions, victims are not able to access the VRR if:

- The police exercise their independent discretion not to investigate a matter, or not to investigate a case further (whether in consultation with the CPS or not), in which case, a full file of evidence is not provided to the CPS;
- A single charge or charges are discontinued, but another charge(s) relating to that victim proceeds (this includes where the matter resolves through plea negotiations);
- A single charge or charges are substantially altered but proceedings involving that victim continue (this includes where a case resolves through plea negotiations);

- The case resolves through an out-of-court disposal (this option is intended for low-level, often first time offending where a prosecution is not considered to be in the public's interest and includes alternative outcomes to prosecution, such as cautions); and/or
- The victim requests that proceedings be stopped.

(CPS 2016)

In cases that satisfy the eligibility requirements, victims are encouraged to submit a review request within five working days of the CPS decision being made; however, a request can be made up to three months after the victim is notified of the decision (CPS 2016). To lodge a request, victims must contact the CPS Appeals and Review Unit by email, phone or letter, detailing the decision and requesting that it be reviewed. There is no requirement for a reason or justification to accompany the request.

As outlined in Table 4.1 above, the first step of the review process involves the matter being transferred to the jurisdiction where the original decision was made, after which the CPS attempts to resolve it locally. This entails the relevant CPS office either providing to the victim a full explanation of the rationale underpinning the original decision or, in some cases, deciding to overturn the original decision without going through the full review process. If the former occurs and the victim is still not satisfied, the case is directed to the Appeals and Review Unit or the Area Chief Crown Prosecutor (depending on the nature of the qualifying decision),[7] who then conducts a final examination of the case.

Table 4.1 Stages of the VRR process

Decision not to charge/discontinue/offer no evidence
↓
Communication to victim informing them of decision and VRR (time limit in Victims' Code)
↓
Request for VRR (time limit for submission = normally seven calendar days but in any event within three months)
↓
Local resolution → Case resolved/further explanation given/case referred for review (time limit from receipt of enquiry = 14 days)
↓
Review: (overall time limit – six weeks)
↓
Outcomes A: Decision not to charge/discontinue overturned → initiate further investigation/ prosecution (where appropriate) B: Decision to offer no evidence overturned → provide an apology C: Decision upheld → case concludes
↓
Communication of reviewed decision to victim (CPS 2016)

This independent review involves an examination of the evidence, in particular, whether there is sufficient evidence to warrant a conviction on the original charges and whether or not proceeding with a prosecution is in the public's interest. Based on this assessment, the person tasked with reviewing the decision determines whether the original decision was correct and, as outlined below, the decision is then either reversed or an apology is provided to the victim (CPS 2016).

In every case, the victim is informed of the outcome of the review by written response. In cases where the original decision to discontinue proceedings or not to charge is found to be incorrect, the review may result in proceedings being reinstated. However, this remedy is not available in cases where the qualifying decision was to offer no evidence. This is because such decisions are considered final and therefore proceedings cannot be reinstated. In these instances, redress is limited to an explanation and apology (CPS 2016). Despite this, the VRR Interim Guidance specifies that the 'quality and thoroughness of the review undertaken will be no less than a review undertaken for any other category of case' (CPS 2016). The guidelines further emphasise that the fundamental issue being addressed in these cases is whether the original decision was incorrect, and, if it was, this should be acknowledged even where it cannot be altered (CPS 2016).

The VRR: addressing victims' procedural justice needs

On paper, the VRR appears to meet the various elements of victims' procedural justice needs. As outlined in Chapter 3, procedural justice involves the following key requirements being met: information, validation, voice and control. In this regard, it can be argued that the VRR gives victims a voice by providing them with a mechanism with which to challenge prosecutorial decisions – a right that is alien in most common law jurisdictions. Further, the reform may enable victims to feel a sense of empowerment and control over prosecutorial decisions that have a significant impact on their lives. It can also provide a mechanism for victims to receive information and clarity as to why certain decisions are made. This is important considering the complex nature of the criminal justice system, which can be difficult to understand for people lacking a detailed knowledge of the law. And this is particularly so in sexual assault cases, where issues of consent can be difficult to clarify and charges may not be laid or may be withdrawn due to insufficient evidence or the strength of the defence's legal argument. The VRR may also provide validation of the complainant's victimisation if the original decision is overturned. However, even when validation in the form of charges being brought cannot be achieved for the victim, the justification provided in the letter may give them a greater sense of closure. Thus, the VRR can be seen as meeting victims' procedural justice needs from the criminal justice process to some extent.

Witnessing change: attaining justice

The VRR provides victims with a unique opportunity to have their cases reviewed and, where an error is identified, to have the decision overturned. In this way, the process arguably responds to victims' procedural justice needs by enabling them to have their voices heard, to exercise control in deciding whether to request a review, and to receive more information regarding the decisions made in their case. It also offers validation of their victimisation experiences by acknowledging their status as a victim in reviewing the request. The process can respond to victims' substantive justice needs in cases where the outcome provides them with a sense of justice being attained, whether via an apology or a reversal of the decision.

The ability of the VRR to respond to victims' substantive and procedural justice needs is evident in a childhood sexual abuse case that resolved because of the VRR. In this case, the victim reported historic sexual offences to the police, at which stage the CPS decided that there would be no further action and did not proceed with charges. On the victim's behalf, a victim support organisation later requested that this decision be reviewed via the VRR. After the initial review, the local CPS decided to reinstate the charges and proceeded to trial. This trial resulted in a hung jury. A second trial was run in which a unanimous guilty verdict was reached and the offender was sentenced to a maximum of 14 years' imprisonment. The case took over three years to resolve from the initial reporting of the offences (March 2012) to the offender being sentenced (April 2015). In reflecting on her experience with this case, Eva, a rape crisis support worker, explained how the victim had spent 'a lifetime … looking for justice … [something] she feels she has finally got'. She further noted how the VRR process 'had a massive impact on [the victim]' in a positive way, because it ensured that the victim remained informed and engaged throughout the 'difficult and long haul process' to attain justice. The capacity for the victim in this case to challenge the decision, gain some sense of control and have the outcome of the original decision altered demonstrates how the VRR can meet victims' procedural and substantive justice needs. As the lead police detective involved explained, all the victim 'ever wanted was to be believed' (cited in the UK and Ireland Database 2015). Had the VRR not been available, the case would never have moved beyond the victim initially reporting the offence, and her needs would never have been met or had the opportunity to be met.

In addition to justice being attained through a conviction, justice may also be achieved through the offender facing other consequences. As Kate, a managing lawyer in the CPS, explains, the punishment may extend to a 'restraining order being imposed to prevent the offender from approaching the victim'. This can be particularly beneficial for a victim's protection in the context of sexual and domestic violence, where the offender may reside in the same community (or even house) as the victim. Compensation schemes and other like remedies are also available to victims when a review takes place, thereby offering further recognition of their victimisation experience and facilitating the attainment of justice. Further to these justice remedies leading to a sense of justice being attained, the capacity for the victim to challenge a decision, gain some sense of control in their case and potentially influence prosecutorial decisions demonstrates how the VRR can align with procedural justice ideals.

Challenge, control and change

As demonstrated in the childhood sexual abuse case discussed above, numerous benefits arise for victims from utilising the VRR. A key benefit is the VRR's capacity to provide a mechanism for victims to pursue and challenge what were once finite prosecutorial decisions, theoretically creating greater accountability around the decisions being made, and simultaneously offering victims a sense of control. This right is currently unique to England and Wales, and is something all the participants in this research raised as providing major benefits. Importantly, victim support workers who had assisted victims through the VRR process noted that, in their direct experience, the VRR had benefited victims by giving them a voice, a level of validation and some control, even if the review did not alter the outcome of their case. In this way, the VRR can be seen to respond to victims' procedural justice needs, as satisfaction comes more from the process being experienced as fair rather than from the outcome itself. As Olivia, a policy advisor within a victim support organisation, explained, the VRR gives victims the opportunity to 'request for a review to take place if they feel their case … hasn't been [considered] as thoroughly as it should have [been] … or they categorically disagree with the decisions made'. Emily, a sexual assault clinical lead counsellor, similarly explained that the VRR has been significant for victims because it gives them the opportunity to express their dissatisfaction with the processes surrounding their case and have that dissatisfaction acknowledged – an important element in improving victims' perceptions of the justness of the legal process, again, regardless of the outcome of the review.

Acknowledgement was also observed by Georgia, a policy researcher working within a victim support organisation, who argued:

> It's important that the victims are actually considered in each stage of the process – to be heard on what their views are – because it is them that are directly impacted by [the decisions], so they need to have as much choice and control over what's happening next, as much as they possibly can.

Perhaps more than implicit in Georgia's comments is that the VRR provides victims with a unique way to achieve this degree of control and consideration, as it gives them an opportunity to express, and have acknowledged, their concerns about the decisions made in their case. This outcome is considered particularly important for sexual offence victims, whose feelings of harm can be further exacerbated by the criminal justice process – an experience Chloe, a leading victims' rights authority, describes as being 'so brutal' that it can 'pull you apart'. Georgia expanded on this, claiming that sexual violence victims tend to lose control over their lives and 'lose ultimate control of the incident that's happened to them'. As such, in relation to the benefits of the VRR, Eva, a rape crisis support worker, noted that 'having the VRR empowers [them] … in terms of having more control and being assured that their case is being reviewed by an independent person'.

The VRR was also identified as bringing a greater level of accountability to the largely unfettered decisions made by prosecutors. This is particularly important given the individualised nature of such decisions – a factor referred to in Flynn's (2016: 570) study of plea negotiations as 'the human nature effect' of prosecutorial decision-making, and something that depends 'on the individuals involved, [who determine] how it will go and how well it will be done'. In this regard, Adelle, a policy researcher working within a victim support organisation, observed that the CPS 'are not going to get 100 per cent of the decisions right, 100 per cent of the time'. And the VRR provides a unique accountability mechanism for decisions to be reviewed and experiences of injustice to be acknowledged and, on occasion, rectified. Emily, a sexual assault clinical lead counsellor, similarly identified the greater accountability enabled from a victim's capacity to challenge, via the review process, the exclusion of relevant evidence in a case as a key benefit. She recognised that, on occasion, there may be an oversight in terms of omitting certain evidence that could be crucial to sustaining a prosecution. She explained that, in these instances, the possibility of a review brings greater accountability to decisions. Georgia, a policy researcher working within a victim support organisation, likewise highlighted the importance of such accountability for victims, as it provides a guarantee that 'another set of eyes … [will] look over that [decision] and … mak[e] sure that decision is right'.

Another benefit of the VRR relates specifically to cases involving sexual offences, the prosecution and investigation of which are consistently recognised as highly problematic and retraumatising for victims (Jordan 2004a, 2004b; McGlynn, Downes & Westmarland 2017; Powell et al. 2013). Anna, a sexual abuse and violence researcher, noted:

> Whether everything is being done to evidence cases or whether there is some level of lazy policing happening in some forces which automatically says rape is a difficult crime to investigate, it often comes down to one person's word against the other; therefore [the prosecution] write it off.

This view is supported by a breadth of research that examines victims' lived experiences during the criminal justice process (Clark 2010; McGarry & Walklate 2015). Clark's (2010) Australian study of sexual violence victims found that the lack of status, power and control they have in the criminal justice process acts as a deterrent for victims engaging with the system and hinders many from reporting. Concerns related to prosecutorial decision-making have also been raised in research examining discretion in rape cases (Jordan 2004a, 2004b; Lievore 2005a, 2005b; Powell et al. 2013). For example, in exploring prosecutorial decisions in Australian rape cases, Lievore (2005b) found that prosecutors were most likely to take a rape case to trial when the victim was injured, when they physically or verbally resisted, when the assault was severe and/or where the offender was unknown to the victim. Accordingly, having a mechanism like the VRR that can provide accountability to, and review of, prosecutorial decision-making in sexual offence cases may be an important step in recognising and potentially responding to some of the procedural justice needs of sexual violence victims. Indeed, the participants in this study pointed to the accountability provided by the VRR as potentially offering a way to challenge and limit the problematic misconceptions and stereotypes about sexual violence that inform prosecuting decisions.

In describing the significance of the VRR in sexual offence matters, several participants argued that it could also help address some of the problems historically associated with these cases, including victims not reporting due to fears of not being believed or taken seriously (Jordan 2004a, 2004b). In reflecting on these issues, Sophie, a victims' rights advocate and campaigner, explained that 'even after the offence happen[s], victims often feel that they won't be believed if they do report', and the VRR is 'another way for [victims] to challenge that … idea of not being believed or taken seriously'. Georgia, a policy researcher working within a victim support organisation, similarly maintained:

> There are some really big confidence issues in terms of [victims] reporting. We know that reporting rates for victims of sexual offences are very low. A lot of victims are very worried about the court process and anything that can increase confidence or … [a victim's] sense that they have a stake and some rights within the process [is positive].

Sophie's and Georgia's views were shared by all participants, in that there was consistent acknowledgement that the VRR potentially provides a way to increase victims' confidence in the criminal justice process. If these views are reflective of the lived experiences of victims, then the VRR may have the capacity to increase reporting rates among victims of sexual assault.

Limited voice and limited control

While the chapter thus far has identified some of the potential benefits of the VRR scheme in terms of meeting victims' procedural justice needs, the data revealed that the effectiveness of the scheme in achieving these ideals was less evident in practice. The participants noted that, despite having the ability to request a review, victims continued to feel sidelined and powerless within the VRR process, with their voices remaining silenced. This can be seen, for example, even in the application process for the VRR scheme.

In requesting a review, victims are not asked to provide a justification for the request, and the CPS is not permitted to ask victims for the reasons informing their request. In commenting on the rationale underpinning this, Kate (managing lawyer, CPS) suggested that this is to ensure that the VRR is 'accessible' to all victims, and requiring victims to provide a justification could complicate the process. However, in a somewhat contradictory way, Kate went on to state that a key reason why victims are not required to give any explanation or to contribute (potential) evidence is that their opinion 'as to why a suspect should be prosecuted is rarely helpful'. One could accept this statement on the basis that the independent review must focus only on the evidence of the indictment, including that available to the prosecution and presented by the defence, and that the reviewer is not in a position to take any additional evidence or material presented by the victim into account, as it may not fit within the evidential rules applied at trial. Yet this may also be seen as problematising the nature of the application process, since failing to consider the victim's rationale for their request effectively marginalises their voice, which largely remains unheard in this process.

One of the pressing problems arising from the CPS not considering a victim's justification for review is that it may further perpetuate a legal culture that is infiltrated by negative stereotypes – namely, rape myths and outdated notions of the 'ideal' victim (Christie 1986; Estrich 1987). As mentioned in Chapter 2, it is common for prosecutorial charging decisions to be informed by such stereotypes (Jordan 2004a, 2004b; Lievore 2005a, 2005b). This was also made evident in an example given by Xavier, a criminal justice professional, when he explained that during his time working as a prosecutor for the CPS in England, one of his colleagues (hereafter referred to as Prosecutor A) prided his prosecutorial success on ensuring that he achieved a 100 per cent conviction rate. Prosecutor A made a blanket policy of only prosecuting the 'dead certainties' and would thus eliminate cases he deemed to be the most difficult to prosecute, including many sexual assault cases. Essentially, Prosecutor A refused to take on cases that were one-on-one in nature, where there were no other available witnesses. He referred to this practice as his 'clean, clear desk policy'. On one occasion, Xavier confronted Prosecutor A about a decision he had made in a case that Xavier deemed to be 'egregious and disgraceful'. In response, Prosecutor A stated: 'the role of prosecution obviously is to act as a filter, [and to determine whether there is a] reasonable or realistic prospect of conviction'. Prosecutor A thus claimed that this eliminates most sexual assault cases given that they are 'one-on-one' in nature. Xavier challenged Prosecutor A on his view by arguing that such an approach is 'fundamentally misconceiving your role [as a prosecutor]. Your role … is to say *is there a realistic prospect of conviction?* [It is] not to undermine or usurp the role of the jury' (emphasis added). Prosecutor A responded by asking, 'Who is going to believe them [the victims] anyway?'. This example demonstrates that some prosecutors uphold adverse decision-making in order to maintain their personal prosecuting success. However, clearly the selectivity in cases pursued for prosecution can leave some victims feeling denied of a sense of procedural justice.

More recently, in September 2019, rape prosecutions in England and Wales reached their 'lowest level in a decade' (Barr & Bowcott 2019). Data released by the CPS reveals that the number of rape convictions declined by 26 per cent, from 2635 cases in 2017–18 to 1925 in 2018–19. Furthermore, the number of prosecutions dropped by 33 per cent from 4517 to 3034 in the same period, while the number of cases charged by the police also declined by 38 per cent (Barr & Bowcott 2019). This steep decline in rape charges, prosecutions and convictions comes despite the number of reported rapes to the police more than doubling over the previous six years. In commenting on this notable decrease, the Director of Public Prosecutions (DPP), Max Hill, stated that these figures are reflective of the reduced number of cases that the police have been passing on to the CPS for prosecution. Meanwhile, other commentary on the issue suggests that 'more cases … are falling out of the system because of the CPS charging decisions [rather] than police referrals' (Barr & Bowcott 2019). These findings problematically replicate the reasons underpinning the inception of the Glidewell Review in 1998, highlighting the tension between the police and the CPS, with each party blaming the other if a case failed (Huxley-Binns & Martin 2014: 160). It appears, then, that two decades on, the very same issues pertaining to police and prosecutorial charging decisions prevail. These issues highlight the imperative for a VRR scheme, but simultaneously raise concerns over the limited input victims have in the VRR process, particularly when considering that the CPS take carriage over the VRR decision-making.

In relation to the decision-making practices within the CPS, Olivia, a policy advisor within a victim support organisation, stated that, 'whilst it [the VRR] provides victims with the impression of a greater sense of control … they are actually still within a system that controls decision-making very tightly'. In this regard, victims actually have very limited control and influence over whether decisions will be overturned. Significantly, this reveals that, although the VRR appears to offer victims a greater sense of voice and control, in practice this is rarely the case, which limits victims' procedural justice needs being met.

Transparency

Perhaps one of the most significant elements of the VRR in terms of the victim's traditionally alienated role in the system is that it brings an increased level of transparency to previously hidden decision-making processes as the VRR can provide clarity around why certain decisions are made. As Flynn (2012: 79) observes:

> Notwithstanding the often immense differences between individual victims and their victimisation experiences, a common need consistently identified by victims of crime is the desire to be kept informed at all stages of the case's progression through the criminal justice process … When such information is provided, it has been recognised that victims feel an increased level of satisfaction.

In this regard, the VRR has the potential to increase victim satisfaction with the criminal justice system, as it provides a certain level of information otherwise not accessible. For example, if a decision is made to not proceed with charges, the VRR ensures that victims are given a full explanation as to how that decision was reached and why. This can be seen in the letter shown in Figure 4.1 below, which provides an example of a letter from the CPS to a victim regarding the outcome of a review.[8]

Date

Your Ref:

Our Ref:

Dear Mr X

Victims Right to Review Scheme request in the case of C

I am writing to you as the Specialist Prosecutor dealing with this matter, following your request for a formal review under the VRR scheme of the decision of the Crown Prosecution Service not to bring a prosecution in this case.

I realise that this is a difficult time for you but I have now completed my review of the case papers provided by the police and I am able to inform you of the outcome.

Following a careful and fully independent consideration of all the available evidence, I have concluded that the decision not to prosecute this case was in fact correct. In other words, I agree with the original decision and this means that the suspect will not be charged.

I will explain as clearly as I can the reasons for the decision I have reached in this matter, but before I do so, it may help if I briefly highlight some guiding principles upon which all prosecutors must rely when reviewing cases. I apologise if this has been explained before, but it is very important that you understand the basis upon which these very difficult decisions have to be made.

When considering the case papers provided by the police, a prosecutor must apply the Code for Crown Prosecutors. In order for the case to proceed I must be satisfied that there is sufficient evidence for there to be a realistic prospect of conviction. A 'realistic prospect of conviction' means that a properly directed jury or bench of magistrates will be more likely than not to convict on the charge alleged. This is a separate test to the one the courts themselves apply; a jury or bench of magistrates must only convict if they are sure of the defendant's guilt. If there is sufficient evidence, I must then go on to consider whether it is in the public interest to prosecute.

In this case, on the day of the incident you had custody of your children. Their mother F came to your house in order to collect the children accompanied by the suspect, C. F was concerned for their welfare following the suggestion that you were drunk. An incident took place at your house in which you allege that C assaulted you. You were initially arrested yourself following an allegation that you had assaulted C and F, but not charged with any offence. The present case arises because you subsequently made a counter allegation against C.

The suspect does not dispute that he struck you. However, he asserts that any force he used was in defence of himself or F.

When considering the sufficiency of the evidence in such cases, a prosecutor must be satisfied there is enough reliable and admissible evidence to rebut the suggestion of self-defence (or defence of another). The prosecution must adduce sufficient evidence to satisfy the court beyond reasonable doubt that the defendant was not acting to defend the other person, and if he was so acting, the force used was excessive.

I have therefore considered the various witness statements carefully, together with the evidence from police officers who attended and arrested you. Although you dispute that you were drunk, all the evidence suggests that you were. I am satisfied that the weight of the evidence means that a court would conclude that you were under the influence of alcohol.

The witness statements support C's assertion that he only became involved out of concern for F after you dragged her on the floor, and that he only punched you in response to you attempting to punch him.

As in all criminal cases, the prosecution would bear the burden of proving the case so that the court is sure of the suspect's guilt. Any doubt would be resolved in the suspect's favour. Having regard to all of the available evidence, I am not satisfied that the prosecution could rebut C's assertion that he was acting in defence of himself and F. Furthermore, given the circumstances of the offence and the relatively minimal force used, I am not satisfied that the prosecution could establish that any force used was excessive. There is accordingly no realistic prospect of conviction for an offence of assault.

The fact I have reached the conclusion in this letter does not mean that I disbelieve your account. My role as a prosecutor is not to decide whose version of events I prefer, but rather to decide whether there is a realistic prospect of conviction on the evidence before me.

I realise that you are likely to be very disappointed with the decision I have reached but I am grateful that you felt able to raise your concerns about this case with the CPS. It is through such direct contact that we are able to ensure that prosecutors are making the right decisions and that we identify all opportunities for improving our service to the public.

The Appeals and Review Unit will now notify your local CPS Area of the outcome of this review.

I hope you will understand that having fully and independently reconsidered this matter, this decision is now final and no further review will be conducted by the Crown Prosecution Service in accordance with the VRR.

This decision does not, of course, affect your right to take independent legal advice in relation to this matter. If you choose to do that, I would suggest that you do so as soon as possible.

Finally, it is very important to us that those affected by our decisions understand the reasoning behind them and I hope that this detailed explanation has assisted you in that respect.

Thank you for raising this important matter with us.

Yours sincerely,

Specialist Prosecutor
Appeals & Review Unit

CC to Area CPS

Figure 4.1 Letter from the CPS to a victim regarding their review.

The letter provides a detailed explanation as to why the charges were not proceeded with. In addition, it states that the decision was not a reflection of the victim and was not made because the CPS did not believe the victim, but rather that the evidence was insufficient to proceed given the stringent rules of procedure inherent to the legal process. The letter also suggests other avenues of support available to the victim and that the victim could still seek independent legal advice should they choose to do so. In this regard, the letter can be seen to address victims' procedural justice needs by offering the victim recognition, validation and a sense of control. Importantly, it provides the victim with a detailed and transparent explanation of the decisions made in their case.

The provision of a detailed explanation was identified by all the participants as a very important and somewhat unique component of the VRR, and the prosecution process more generally – and this is particularly important given the complex nature of legal proceedings, which can be inscrutable for those unfamiliar with the law. Olivia, a policy advisor within a victim support organisation, summed this up by claiming that the VRR provides victims with 'a greater sense of transparency … to a system that is very convoluted'. She further highlighted the importance of this transparency for victims insofar as it shifts the focus from belief in the victim to 'technical' evidentiary issues. Sophie, a victims' rights advocate and campaigner, explained:

> If they are told that there is … no further action at any stage, to them that is often seen as, 'Oh you don't believe me', rather than [understanding that] it's quite a technical, evidential issue … So I guess the [VRR] could be another way to reinforce [the notion] that it's not about … not being believed, there are all these very technical reasons [why] the case has not gone forward.

Joanna, Chief Executive Officer (CEO) of a sexual violence support centre, similarly argued that victims:

> need to be told something like, 'It's not that we don't believe you, but there isn't enough evidence to bring this case to court where it can be proved beyond reasonable doubt that this happened and we don't want to put you through a gruelling court process when we don't believe there is enough evidence to prove it'. It's the idea of not being believed which can really stop and block a victim's healing process.

By providing victims with a greater understanding as to why cases may not proceed, the VRR offers them a sense of closure that they would not otherwise receive in cases when a prosecution does not follow from them reporting the offence/s. Significantly, this sense of closure was identified by those participants working with victims as offering benefits even in cases where a decision is not overturned, because, as evidenced in the letter above, the provision of a detailed explanation enables a victim to better understand the decision-making process. Kate, a managing lawyer in the CPS, explained:

> We do get people [victims] thanking us, saying thank you for at least taking the time to look at it, you've given an explanation, I didn't realise that was the reason and I'm happy now.

Olivia, a policy advisor within a victim support organisation, likewise maintained that the explanation is 'the biggest benefit' of the VRR:

> Because [while] the chances of a decision completely being overturned are probably small … there is a duty placed upon the CPS … to actually look into [the case] in depth and get back to the victim within a [set] timeframe and give them a lot more information than what they probably would have had to do when they initially made the decision.

These benefits are important considerations when evaluating whether the criminal justice system meets victims' procedural justice needs, and how communication and information are consistently recognised as elements that increase victim satisfaction (Clark 2010; Flynn 2012). Thus, while the victimisation experiences of some victims remain invalidated within one legal context (a prosecution not proceeding), the VRR represents an alternate legal mechanism that allows victims to be acknowledged, informed and communicated with in a transparent way aimed at helping them comprehend why their case did not proceed. This is also important for increasing victims' confidence in the criminal justice process itself. Knowledge and understanding are vital in upholding public trust and confidence in the legal system. Accordingly, providing more information through the VRR may 'reduce the likelihood that people will perceive a gulf between their expectations of the criminal justice system and the reality' (Victorian Sentencing Advisory Council [VSAC] 2006: 23), thereby potentially increasing confidence in the legal process overall.

Accountability

In theory, and as discussed above, the VRR offers victims a degree of control, transparency and acknowledgement in a traditionally hidden process – the prosecutor's decision-making around whether or not to proceed to trial. However, in practice, the level of accountability surrounding the VRR has been questioned, especially because it is the CPS itself who conducts the 'independent' review. In commenting on the VRR, Westmarland (cited in Shaw 2014) argues that 'what we essentially have is a panel of colleagues reviewing the decision of somebody who they may be personally friends with'. This concern was echoed by several participants in this research, who challenged the independent nature of the review process. Sophie, a victims' rights advocate and campaigner, described the VRR as 'marking your own homework essentially'; and Olivia, a policy advisor within a victim support organisation, argued that:

> The kind of anecdotal evidence that I have on a day-to-day basis is that whilst the review is a benefit … often there's not full independence of that review because obviously it's being undertaken by the same organisation.

As implicit in Olivia's comments, the VRR relies upon trust in the CPS – the very organisation whose decision the victim is questioning in the first place. Anna, a sexual abuse and violence researcher, also expressed concern around how independent the review is because 'people would ultimately want to protect their institution [and] where they work'. This is not to suggest that improper decisions are being made as part of the review process; however, some participants relayed their concern that this may be the perception victims have, which reduces the VRR's effectiveness in meeting victims' procedural justice needs.

Such concerns can be seen as stemming from the hidden nature of the legal culture more generally, which some research suggests is an exclusive community that operates in a closed environment (Fitzgerald 1989; Reiner 2010; Skolnik & Fyfe 1993; Wood 1996). The existence of this closed culture may engender a view, whether reflective of reality or not, that those within the CPS would never scrutinise each other's behaviour or decisions in ways that genuinely hold them accountable – an outcome that may create the perception that adverse decision-making cannot be identified. Similar concerns have been expressed in relation to prosecutors and plea negotiations, about which it is argued that 'the absence of transparency surrounding plea deals fuels public perceptions of clandestine outcomes, inequality and a lack of accountability in plea bargaining practices more generally' (Flynn 2012: 907). In this regard, Anna, a sexual abuse and violence researcher, observed that there is a perception that prosecutors working within an organisation like the CPS will 'stick together'. A possible outcome of this is the perception that the CPS will not want to undermine or challenge the decisions made by their prosecuting 'brothers'. In such circumstances, the accountability provided by the VRR may be reduced.

One way in which the VRR process could be imbued with greater independence is to make use of the extant multi-agency panel, which is chaired by members external to the criminal justice system who work collaboratively with the CPS to monitor prosecutorial decision-making. The role of this external body is to review randomly selected cases and examine how they were handled. In its current role, the panel is not able to change case outcomes, but it does provide a level of external oversight by making recommendations for improvement. This type of independence applied to the VRR would allow for increased transparency around decision-making processes, which would likely increase its positive standing among victims. In commenting on the potential for this type of agency to be involved in the VRR, Anna, a sexual abuse and violence researcher, stated:

> I would [be] happier with some kind of panel oversight, [a] multi-agency panel that had oversight and reviewed that decision instead ... [because] ultimately that's still somebody within the same organisation who's probably been trained in a similar way [and] probably has some of the same institutional beliefs.

She explained that adopting this type of external transparency would be beneficial as it could bring a degree of independent accountability to the VRR process, such that 'it starts to unpick' some of the gaps in decision-making processes. In this way, the VRR could become more accommodating to victims' needs and expectations.

Another issue relating to the transparency and accountability of the VRR is that there is limited data available on the process.[9] The quantitative data from this research reveals that, between 1 June 2013 and 31 March 2015, the CPS made 230,506 decisions that could qualify for a VRR. Of these decisions, a request for review was made in 2863 cases – or 1.24 per cent of all qualifying decisions. An analysis of the most recent data available on the VRR further reveals that between 5 June 2013 – four days after the VRR was introduced – and 31 March 2017, the CPS made 449,560 qualifying decisions. Of these, a request for review was made in 6743 cases – or 1.5 per cent of all qualifying decisions during this four-year period. According to the former DPP (cited in Shaw 2014), there is a low number of victims using the VRR because 'so few ... feel that they need to take up the scheme', thereby reflecting the positive work of the CPS. However, this view contrasts with the findings in this research, where participants observed that the low use of the VRR is more attributable to victims not knowing about their right to review. These concerns are not exclusive to the VRR as they are commonly raised in connection to other 'victim-focused' reforms. As mentioned in Chapter 2 in relation to the VIS, for example, victims are not always informed of their right to complete a statement.

In relation to the VRR, Emily, a sexual assault clinical lead counsellor, expressed her concern around how 'terribly publicised' the process is and observed that when she informs her clients about the prospect of having a decision reviewed, the general response is 'I didn't know that [was an option]'. Anna, a sexual abuse and violence researcher, likewise explained that very limited information about the VRR is provided to victims. Instead, she maintained that victims who have their cases discontinued receive a letter directing them to arrange 'a personal meeting with the CPS to explain their decision', as opposed to notifying them of the option to seek a review of that decision. This point was further articulated by Eva, a rape crisis support worker, who explained, 'the VRR isn't really known to victims unless they are being supported by a specialist organisation ... so even though it's in the *Victims' Code* and other documentation, it isn't really a well-known process'. These observations from those directly involved in the process therefore suggest that the low rate of review requests identified is a result of a lack of knowledge of and publicity about the VRR, rather than reflecting the true level of victim satisfaction with the CPS's decision-making. This raises concerns over how well the CPS is communicating information about the VRR process and victims' rights to victims, which stands contrary to the purpose of the reform and undermines the provision of information to victims, which is a key element of addressing victims' procedural justice needs.

Problems with the data

In addition to identifying the number of decisions reviewed, the quantitative analysis found that, of the 2863 cases reviewed between 1 June 2013 and 31 March 2015, 2491 cases (or 87 per cent) were found to be correct. This left 372 decisions being overturned, which accounts for only 13 per cent of all reviewed decisions and 0.16 per cent of all qualifying decisions (*n*=230,506) made by the CPS in this period. When analysing the quantitative data over a four-year period – between 5 June 2013 and 31 March 2017 – of the 449,560 qualifying decisions the CPS made, requests for review were made in 6743 cases (1.50 per cent of all qualifying decisions). Of these, 765 decisions were overturned, accounting for 11 per cent of all reviewed decisions and 0.17 per cent of all qualifying decisions. This means that while the number of qualifying decisions (*n*=449,560) and requests for review (*n*=6743) continued to rise four years post the VRR's implementation, the number of overturned decisions decreased from 13 per cent (*n*=372 overturned cases of *n*=2863 reviews) in the 2013–15 period to 11 per cent (*n*=765 overturned cases of *n*=6743 reviews) in the 2015–17 period.

An examination of patterns in the offence types proceeding through the VRR found that 60 per cent of requests were for decisions made at the pre-charge stage – that is, when the prosecutor's decision that no further action will be taken is made before the offender is charged by the police.[10] A major limitation of the review process in light of this finding is that, where a prosecutor decides not to lay charges, they are not asked to determine or record what the charge(s) might have been. This means that there is no data to accurately identify which offences are not being proceeded with in the first instance. The only recorded data on offence types are those involving offences dropped post charge – that is, once the case has proceeded beyond the police investigation. Similar to the concerns raised regarding the practice of plea negotiations (Flynn 2016; Rakoff 2014), for which there is limited data recorded on the types of offences that are withdrawn or altered, the absence of this information hinders our capacity to understand or critique prosecutorial pre-charge decisions. It also limits the opportunities to identify any patterns that might exist in prosecutorial decision-making regarding offence types, or situational or victim factors, and whether there may be any untoward biases that influence or shape prosecutorial decisions not to proceed with a case. This may be particularly relevant in relation to police and prosecutor charging decisions in connection with sexual offences, which have been strongly criticised for being influenced by rape myths and outdated stereotypes (Heenan and Murray 2004; Jordan 2004a, 2004b; Lievore 2005a, 2005b; Powell et al. 2013). In this regard (and as discussed earlier), Heenan and

Murray's (2004: 5) examination of 850 reports of sexual assault offences made to Victoria Police (Australia) between 2000 and 2003, for example, found that a charge was more likely to be laid when the victim was 'physically injured; medically examined; not influenced by alcohol or drugs at the time of the offence; subject to other offences alongside the rape; and raped by offenders well known to the police for previous sexual offending'. These findings demonstrate the potential dangers of not recording data on prosecutorial charging decisions at an early stage, which could reduce our capacity to understand whether patterns of decision-making based on stereotypes and rape myths still exist. The impacts of this extend beyond reducing public transparency to include failing to meet victims' procedural justice needs, as the lack of data can further undermine victims' confidence in a criminal justice system that initially let them down, yet which claims to be 'open' and 'transparent' in its decision-making processes.

Numerous studies have linked limited understanding of prosecutorial decision-making with reduced public confidence in the legal system (Flynn 2016; Stubbs & Tolmie 2008; Victorian Community Council Against Violence 1997; VSAC 2006); and if victims' understanding of the VRR does not align with the operation of the system in practice, concerns will arise around what motivates prosecutorial charging decisions. Such questions will likely highlight the possibility of the influence of negative stereotypes on prosecutorial decisions, as well as the pressures prosecutors face to 'save money, expedite cases and reduce caseloads' (Flynn 2016: 573). Put simply, without information about these decision-making processes, it is impossible to accurately identify what types of cases are failing to reach the charge stage, or the contexts in which such decisions are made.

This was a key issue identified by Eva, a rape crisis support worker, who noted that, with at least 85 per cent of women still not reporting their victimisation, often for fear of being disbelieved or because of the traumatic nature of the criminal justice process, there is a demonstrable need to ensure that prosecutorial decision-making processes are not being influenced by 'ideal' victim and 'real' rape stereotypes (Bows & Westmarland 2016; Christie 1986; Estrich 1987). She explained that this is important not only to protect those who come forward, but also to encourage others to feel safe in reporting these crimes. Without accurate data on these processes, questions remain over the extent to which prosecutors may be continuing to make decisions informed by stereotypes and rape myths.

In relation to sexual offences, the quantitative data shows that the CPS reviewed 365 sexual offence cases (out of 2863 decisions) between 1 June 2013 and 31 March 2015, and the decisions in 305 of these cases were found to be correct. In the 60 sexual offence cases in which the decision was found to be incorrect, all the decisions were reversed. Sexual offences therefore constituted fewer than 13 per cent of all cases reviewed in the two-year period (2013–15). Additionally, figures in relation to sexual offences between 1 April 2015 and 31 March 2017 show that 826 review requests were made – more than double the number of requests made in the prior two-year period. Of these 826 sexual offence cases referred for review, the wrong decision was found to have been made in 77 decisions, which means that 91 per cent of decisions were deemed to be correct. Sexual offences therefore comprised 22 per cent of all cases reviewed in this two-year period (2015–17), representing a significant increase on the prior two years. However, these figures are unlikely to be representative of all sexual offence decisions that go through the VRR process because the CPS is not required to record data on offence types that do not proceed with charges. Additionally, these figures were not reflective of the experiences of the interview participants in this study, who noted that the majority of the matters they had observed through the VRR involved sexual violence victims.

Raising hopes and expectations

Another concern identified in relation to the data surrounds the potential for the VRR to raise victims' hopes and expectations that the case might proceed as a result of the review. This was a prominent concern identified by the majority of participants when discussing the low percentage of cases that are being overturned and the length of time it can take to review a case.

As noted above, between 1 June 2013 and 31 March 2015, only 372 decisions were overturned (0.16 per cent). Similarly, between 1 April 2015 and 31 March 2017, only 325 decisions were overturned (0.15 per cent) out of the 219,054 decisions that qualified for review. As Olivia, a policy advisor within a victim support organisation, emphasised:

> You could argue that they [victims] are being retraumatised by the sheer fact that they have got their hopes up again about something being reviewed and then … the same decision is made.

Olivia clarified that 'it's not a victim's right to overturn the decision, it's a victim's right to review', which means that ultimately the decision rests with the CPS. This statement is significant in acting as a reminder that the VRR operates within an adversarial system, where the interests of the state override those of individual victims. Yet this may be unclear to some victims, who may believe that their view will be the primary factor influencing the VRR, when in fact the decision is based solely on the evidence, not on the victim's perspective. Similar concerns were raised in Chapter 2 in relation to Flynn's (2012) study of victims and plea negotiations following the introduction of the *Victims' Charter Act 2006* (Vic) in Victoria, in which some prosecutor participants noted that the new statutory obligations on them to keep victims informed may lead to victims misunderstanding the adversarial nature of the justice system. Likewise, David, a key policy and government stakeholder in the present study, noted how the VRR could give the victim 'false hope' that the original decision would be overturned, when it is likely that the decision will be upheld.

In raising such concerns, several participants highlighted the important role specialist support agencies play in managing victims' expectations. As Eva, a rape crisis support worker, explained, 'I think it does raise expectations and hopes but I think if they are engaged with specialist support then they know that they are supported through that whole process'. Sophie, a victims' rights advocate and campaigner, similarly commented:

> To be the most positive experience, they [victims] would continue to need some sort of support, whether it's an ISVA [Independent Sexual Violence Advisor] or a counsellor, and they would need to understand the process. So these external agencies would also need to manage expectations rather than maybe presenting that it's something it's not, so it kind of needs everyone to be working together.

However, even with such support mechanisms in place, the very low number of overturned decisions may result in victims feeling traumatised twice – initially by the prosecutor's decision not to proceed with charges, and then in the second instance by someone else not believing them.

Victim satisfaction with the VRR

As it currently stands, there is no publicly available data on victims' satisfaction with the VRR process. This may be due to its recent implementation. However, based on the interviews with those working directly with victims who have gone through the VRR process, it appears that the VRR has not significantly improved victim satisfaction with the criminal justice system. While the VRR may meet some of the needs of victims, depending on the individual victim and their experience, it is limited in its ability to consistently respond to victims' procedural justice needs – namely, those around information, validation, voice and control – through the criminal justice process, and this is likely to result in victim dissatisfaction with the reform.

Although the participants did not have any published data upon which to draw regarding victims' satisfaction levels with the VRR, several participants referred to feedback they had received from victims who had been through the process. These participants primarily made reference to the length of time a review takes and the failure to provide victims with correspondence in a timely manner – that is, within the timeframes specified by the CPS. This was identified as a major issue given that it prolongs a process with which victims are already dissatisfied, and that the burden of having to wait a considerable amount of time for a review can exacerbate the trauma victims experience, both from the crime itself and the criminal justice process. In this regard, Kate, a managing lawyer in the CPS, stated:

> Sometimes people [victims] don't like the time it takes, but that's partly because … we actually look at the other evidence, especially when it's recorded on a video, that can take … literally hours to look over at what a person is saying on a recording [and] because our evidence is done by video recording in sexual offence cases … it does take a bit of time.

Kate also observed that, 'for some victims, it will only be right if we prosecute'. This comment acts as a reminder that victims' expectations vary according to a range of factors; and despite the similarities in their procedural justice needs, victims may desire different substantive outcomes.

Emily, a sexual assault clinical lead counsellor, similarly reflected on whether victims are generally satisfied with the VRR scheme and stated:

> No, because of the length of time and … from the two [victims] I have worked with and from their experience, their decisions were negative so I think they came to the conclusion that the decision was made from the [outset], but lip service was being paid to the idea that somebody else might have a look and it might be different.

Similarly, Georgia, a policy researcher working within a victim support organisation, cited an example where a victim was not given a response within the specified timeframe as promised by the CPS, which resulted in increased anxiety for the victim. Extensive waiting periods can also raise victims' hopes that something might change, which could exacerbate their disappointment if the outcome remains the same. The length of time the review takes therefore appears to be an issue. The VRR may indeed cause further delay within a system that is already backlogged.

Significantly, the VRR can also reduce a victim's prospects of recovery, as victims are not able to move on with their lives while waiting for the outcome of a review. Emily explained that 'the longer that [the review] goes on, the longer a client might be in a situation where they can't access the right sort of therapy to improve their life' because specific trauma therapies cannot be practised until a case has been finalised. This means that victims who are suffering from post-traumatic stress disorder, for example, may continue to experience it for at least as long it takes to finalise the case. As Emily described:

> For my client who had a review, the decision was made in October and then in February she got the final decision, so there's another great big time gap … She was living in false hope really, and again it was the time delay, so it was another four months before she was able to access specific therapy to support her.

Interestingly, even in cases where decisions have been overturned as a result of a review, according to those interviewed, victims have still expressed dissatisfaction with the criminal justice system on the basis of not having faith in prosecutorial decision-making. For instance, Georgia, a policy researcher working within a victim support organisation, reflected on a historical sexual abuse case in which the original decision was to not proceed with charges on the basis of insufficient evidence. The VRR process was then pursued and the 'second decision found that there was enough evidence to proceed and inadvertently that sort of undermined their [the victim's] confidence in the original decision' (Georgia).

Georgia explained that, while 'the victim still appreciated the fact that they were going to get their chance to see justice done', they were dissatisfied with the process that led to the original decision and consequently lost confidence in the criminal justice system.

The above discussion demonstrates that there are a range of issues that can impact a victim's satisfaction with the VRR. Despite a primary aim of the reform being to increase victims' confidence in the criminal justice process, the length of time the review takes, alongside issues around a lack of transparency, accessibility and accountability, may hinder the VRR's capacity to address victims' procedural justice needs (information, validation, voice and control), thereby reducing its effectiveness.

Concluding remarks

Although the majority of the interview data identified the potentially positive outcomes of the VRR's introduction, some observations indicated that such outcomes were not always reflective of the VRR in practice. In particular, the absence of data surrounding pre-charge decision-making and the lack of independence of the review process itself mean that the provision of transparent information about the decisions made in a case may still be inadequate for some victims, despite the VRR's implementation. Due to the significant amount of time a review can take, the VRR may also unnecessarily raise the hopes and expectations of some victims, which can lead to further disappointment and anguish when the decision is not overturned.

Without question, the VRR is a unique reform that allows victims to challenge prosecutorial decision-making, and it helps to overcome some of the foremost limitations of the prosecution process for victims whose cases do not proceed to trial. For example, by allowing for decisions to be reviewed and potentially overturned, it not only ensures that victims receive information on the original decision, but also that an explanation is provided as to why this decision was made, which may reduce a victim's feelings of alienation and disempowerment. Importantly, and as demonstrated by the CPS letter presented in Figure 4.1, additional explanations of why the decision was made can potentially redress victim perceptions of not being believed. However, having the review conducted 'in-house' reduces the level of accountability associated with the VRR, and the fact that no data is recorded on the prosecutor's pre-trial decision-making means that we cannot know whether outdated stereotypes and problematic myths around rape and the 'ideal' victim continue to shape prosecutorial decision-making.

While in theory the VRR presents major benefits for victims, the data suggests that the reform's shortcomings may limit its ability to meet victims' procedural justice needs. In addition, the limitations pertaining to accessibility and accountability indicate that the way the VRR operates in practice may undermine its capacity to achieve its stated objectives around transparency and victim satisfaction. This therefore limits the prospect of the VRR creating a more inclusive environment for victims – a key issue that continues to impact on victims' experiences with and perceptions of the justice system. In this regard, the VRR may unfortunately attract criticisms similar to those directed at many other victim-focused law reforms, particularly those involving sexual offences, insofar as the reforms are limited in their ability to achieve their intended aims in practice.

Notes

1 A version of this chapter was published as Iliadis, M. and Flynn, A. (2017). 'Providing a Check on Prosecutorial Decision-Making: An Analysis of the Victims' Right to Review Reform', *British Journal of Criminology*, 58(3), 550–68, doi.org/10.1093/bjc/azx036. The quantitative analysis presented in this chapter extends upon the analysis in this published article.

2 See Kirchengast (2016a: 103) for a doctrinal analysis of the implementation of the VRR and the High Court's decision in *Killick.*

3 *R v Killick* [2011] EWCA Crim 1608, [2012] 1 Cr. App. R. 10 [48].

4 The VRR exists in addition to the victim's right to seek a judicial review of the prosecutor's decision. A judicial review involves a court proceeding in which a judge reviews the lawfulness of a decision or action made by a public body. It is not concerned with the outcome of that process, but rather focuses on whether the correct procedures were followed (UK Judiciary 2017).

5 *Directive 2012/29/EU of the European Parliament and of the Council of 25 October 2012, Establishing Minimum Standards on the Rights, Support and Protection of Victims of Crime, and Replacing Council Framework Decision 2001/220/JHA.*

6 In England and Wales, a victim is defined as someone who has suffered harm, 'including physical, mental or emotional harm or economic loss which was directly caused by a criminal offence' (Ministry of Justice 2015).

7 If a legal bar exists on bringing a new charge (for example, the suspect has been formally acquitted or there is a statutory time limit) and the only remedy if the original decision is determined to be incorrect is an apology, the case is handled by the Area Chief Crown Prosecutor. All other requests are sent to the Appeals and Review Unit for review.

8 This letter was provided by a participant during data collection. It is not a sexual assault case.

9 As part of this research, Kate, a managing lawyer in the CPS, provided access to previously unpublished statistical data on the VRR.

10 In England and Wales, prosecutors are involved in the police's charging decision, which is different from the process that operates in Victoria where police charge and prosecutors simply receive a copy of the charges and evidence brief (see *The Code for Crown Prosecutors 2013* (UK) & *Public Prosecutions Act 1994* (Vic)).

5 Separate legal representation for victims under section 34 of the *Sex Offenders Act 2001* (Irl)[1]

Introduction

> Although the representation in Ireland is limited, it represents an important recognition that there are times during the trial process where victims must be allowed to participate in the trial as more than witnesses – in order to protect their rights and interests.
>
> (Stern Review 2010: 98)

Concerns over procedural (in)justice for sexual assault victims have underpinned Ireland's shift towards increased consideration and involvement of victims in the legal process, beyond that of their witness status. In 2001, Ireland contentiously introduced a limited form of pre-trial ILR for sexual assault victims. Constituting a form of victim participation, this reform is distinct within adversarial systems in allowing a unique level of victim input. Section 34 of the *Sex Offenders Act 2001* (Irl) (henceforth, section 34) inserted a new section (4A) into the *Criminal Law (Rape) Act 1981*[2] that allows sexual assault victims to access state-funded legal representation[3] to oppose a defendant's application to introduce a victim's sexual history evidence in court. This is a significant right in light of the parameters of adversarial legal systems, which have traditionally excluded victims. It also enables victim interests to be acknowledged and included alongside those of the accused and the state, thereby recognising the 'triangulation of interests' (*Attorney-General's Reference (No 3 of 1999)* [2001] 2 AC 91: 118). The ILR thus arguably helps to address some of the main criticisms pertaining to the prosecution process for sexual assault victims, particularly in relation to the cross-examination stage.

Initial proposals for ILR for sexual assault victims in Ireland

In Ireland, initial proposals for ILR for sexual assault victims were put forward by rape crisis centres, women's organisations, and members of the Joint Oireachtas Committee in 1987.[4] These groups lobbied for increased recognition of sexual assault victims' rights throughout the criminal prosecution process in light of major criticisms related to the conflicting interests among the victim, the accused and the prosecution (the triangulation of interests), and the ill-treatment of sexual assault victims within the criminal justice process generally (Irish Law Reform Commission [ILRC] 1988). These criticisms were focused in particular on the cross-examination of victims, during which it was common for prosecutors to refrain from objecting to certain lines of questioning, such as questions related to the victim's previous sexual history. In an attempt to address these shortcomings, it was proposed by the Joint Oireachtas Committee, along with other victim support bodies, that sexual assault victims be granted ILR throughout criminal justice proceedings. In this context, the legal representative would be entitled to intervene throughout the trial to protect the victim's interests whenever they considered it appropriate to do so (ILRC 1988, 1987). In making its recommendation, the Joint Oireachtas Committee (cited in the ILRC 1987: 69) argued that:

> [A] defendant in a rape case ... can apply for legal aid and receive free legal representation. The complainant however is denied access to discussion or consultation with the legal representatives of the State. Indeed it is normal for a complainant to meet the State prosecutor for the first time in court on the day of the hearing. This practice is unacceptable, ... having regard particularly to the special and unique circumstances that apply in rape and sexual assault cases.... Victims of rape should be able to consult with the State's legal representatives before the court hearings and ... be fully briefed on court procedures, including the type of questions likely to be put to them by defending counsel. State counsel in prosecuting a case does not ... officially represent a complainant and ... complainants in cases of serious sexual assault, and particularly rape, should be granted free legal representation.

This recommendation was initially rejected by the Irish Law Reform Commission (ILRC) on the basis that it would be 'constitutionally suspect' if proceedings for sexual offences were conducted upon 'fundamentally different principles from those applied in all other criminal proceedings' (ILRC 1987). Furthermore, the ILRC believed that such a radical change would tilt the balance of the criminal trial in favour of the prosecution as it would result in dual representation for the victim, despite the fact that the prosecution represents the state and, as such, does not routinely prioritise the victim's interests. In support of its argument, the ILRC (1987: 69) claimed that permitting dual representation would be 'hostile to the interests of the accused' and jeopardise their right to a fair criminal trial.

Although the ILRC (1987) rejected the proposal for ILR for sexual assault victims throughout the entire trial, a modified version of this proposal was put forward to the Commission by the Joint Oireachtas Committee in which a victim would be entitled to ILR where a defence application is made to the judge for leave to cross-examine the victim on their prior sexual history. However, this proposal was also rejected by the ILRC (1987: 69) on the grounds that:

> The implementing of this suggestion would make a substantial change in criminal procedure, which would … probably have far-reaching consequences. In practice, representation would be unlikely to make any difference to the judge's ruling.… Correspondents may not have appreciated that judges have a duty to protect all witnesses from unfair cross-examination by counsel … they do not need counsel appearing for witnesses to remind them of it.

The ILRC (1987: 69) cited other potential consequences of such a proposal:

> If representation of witnesses in rape cases were allowed, it would be difficult to refuse it in other cases. Cross-examination about previous sexual behaviour … is not the only kind of cross-examination about past conduct which may cause distress to prosecution witnesses.

Concerns also arose about the possibility of legal representatives 'coaching' victims by advising them on how to answer questions in cross-examination, or to downplay or highlight certain aspects of their evidence (ILRC 1987: 70). The ILRC (1987) stated that such 'coaching' would not only distort the course of justice but would also undermine the principles upon which the adversarial criminal trial is based. Additionally, it raised concerns about funding victim ILR, suggesting that it would need to include means testing such as is applicable to accused people applying for legal aid (ILRC 1987). The Commission argued that this could place some victims in a more vulnerable position by leaving them unrepresented (ILRC 1987). At this point in time, therefore, the proposal was rejected.

Introducing ILR for sexual assault victims under section 34

Ireland revisited the idea of separate ILR for victims 10 years after the ILRC (1987, 1988) rejected the Joint Oireachtas Committee's recommendations (Raitt 2010). The issue of ILR re-emerged due to consistent pressure being placed on the government by the Dublin Rape Crisis Centre. In particular, the centre drew upon empirical research findings from a report by Bacik, Maunsell and Gogan (1998), which presented a comparative analysis of the impacts of the laws and legal procedures that provided assistance, representation and support to victims of rape across 15 Member States of the European Union. In this study, every jurisdiction, except England and Wales, and Ireland, offered victims some form of ILR throughout proceedings (Bacik, Maunsell & Gogan 1998). In light of their findings, Bacik, Maunsell and Gogan (1998: 18) recommended ILR for victims, arguing that 'such a right should extend from the reporting stage, through to the trial', to ensure that victims are kept informed of the case's progress and pre-trial procedures. Bacik, Maunsell and Gogan (1998: 18) further argued that the victim's prospective legal representative could also be present at trial to 'intervene on behalf of the victim, for example, to request that certain protective measures be adopted, and to prevent unduly hostile questioning of the victim', such as questions relating to their previous sexual history.

Given Ireland's conservative history of law reform in the area of victims' rights, the eventual introduction of separate ILR – via section 34 – marked a unique and contentious legislative response. Section 34 allows a victim to access state-funded ILR to oppose a defendant's application to introduce a victim's sexual history evidence in court. The amendment to the *Criminal Law (Rape) Act* under section 34, subsection 4A(1), states:

> Where an application under section 3[5] or 4[6] is made by or on behalf of an accused person who is for the time being charged with an offence to which this section applies, the complainant shall be entitled to be heard in relation to the application and, for this purpose, to be legally represented during the hearing of the application.

A victim's legal representative can challenge an application by the defence to seek the leave of the judge as outlined in section 3(1) of the *Criminal Law (Rape) Act*. This right is significant as it marks the first attempt within an adversarial criminal law jurisdiction to grant sexual assault victims the right to have ILR in this context. It also represents legal recognition of the trauma associated with sexual assault victims giving evidence in court, under cross-examination in particular. This form of ILR could thus help to reduce the likelihood of secondary victimisation resulting from criminal procedures and attend to victims' key procedural justice needs, as explored in the next section.

Increased victim participation meeting victims' procedural justice needs

As stated above, the introduction of section 34 marks a significant milestone in the area of victims' rights. The participants in this research identified that ILR has strong potential to address victims' procedural justice needs for information, voice, control and, arguably, validation. In relation to *information*, the victim's representative can *test* the rationale for the application to cross-examine the victim on their prior sexual history and force the defence to *justify* the application, to a greater extent than would be possible were the victim not legally represented. ILR also provides the victim with information that enables them to better *understand* the rationale for both the application and the outcome of the case, as their legal representative acts as an interpreter of the law and criminal prosecution process. In terms of *voice*, the victim's legal representative has the ability to *oppose* the legal argument underpinning the application and its relevance to the case. In this way, the representative can be seen as accountable to the victim as they *defend* the victim's interests and right to privacy. This is an important benefit of section 34 as it gives a voice to victims, who have traditionally had very limited input into their case due to their role as a witness. Section 34 may also enhance victims' *control* in the process, as their legal representative can *counteract* the argument to include the victim's sexual history evidence; and if the counter-argument is upheld by the judge, the victim will be more likely to feel a sense of *agency* and control in the process. However, even where the defence's argument to adduce the victim's sexual history is accepted, the victim's perception of being heard through their representative will in turn enhance their sense of *autonomy* and control throughout proceedings. With regard to *validation*, David, a principal officer working within a national gender-based violence organisation, argued that the victim may feel validated if the case results in a *guilty verdict*, but that 'the system is not really geared to validating them [victims] otherwise'.

This all suggests that victim participation through the provision of ILR has the potential to address some of the main criticisms of the prosecution process in relation to victim experiences, particularly as it may contribute towards the victim's sense of achieving procedural justice, and allow them to feel like genuine participants rather than mere witnesses. This is an important consideration in light of the findings emerging from Payne's (2009: 22) report on the perceptions and experiences of rape victims in the criminal justice system:

> Victims frequently expressed anger that their place in the criminal justice system is effectively as a witness in their own case. Many were disappointed that the prosecution represents the Crown, rather than the victim, in contrast to the defendant who has his [sic] own legal representation.

The broader implications of Payne's (2009) findings are therefore that, prior to the introduction of section 34, the absence of ILR for sexual assault victims in Ireland meant that victims did not feel supported or confident that their privacy, including in relation to their prior sexual history, would be protected. In this regard, the provision of ILR has the potential to enhance victims' procedural justice experiences and address the objectives of the An Garda Síochána *Victims' Charter* (Irl), which include that priority be given and commitment made to protecting victims' dignity, concerns and needs.

On this note, the participants in this research agreed that Ireland has come a long way in relation to protecting sexual assault victims' privacy and procedural justice needs (David, principal officer, national gender-based violence organisation; Joanna, CEO, sexual violence support centre). Indeed, David described section 34 as providing a necessary protective barrier between the victim and the arbitrary use of previous sexual history questioning:

> The experience was that, in looking at sexual history, there was a general trolling through a woman's sexual history [experiences].... She's trolled by the fact that she's had lots of partners and then to imply that she was … 'wildly promiscuous' and … 'careless' as to who she slept with.

Bearing in mind such concerns, Bacik et al. (2010) reflect on the beneficial role of ILR in this context:

> Victims groups were delighted to see the introduction of section 4A, enabling the victim in a rape or sexual offence trial to have legal representation to enable her or him to argue against the introduction of evidence relating to sexual experience.... This represented some improvement on the old law, and might contribute to making the trial process a less traumatic experience for the victim.

Section 34 can thus act as a legislative safeguard to shield victims from these sorts of questions, or at least challenge the perceptions that lead to such questioning. As David noted, the ILR 'protects the victim from an incursion into their private life', which may prevent secondary victimisation and go some way towards addressing victims' procedural justice needs, as victims are more able to challenge, control and prevent the introduction of their sexual history evidence in court.

Victim inclusion in and satisfaction with the criminal justice process

The significance of enhanced victim participation rights through ILR has been emphasised by Bacik, Maunsell and Gogan (1998: 17–18), who discovered that:

> A highly significant relationship was found to exist between [victims] having a lawyer, and overall satisfaction with the trial process. The presence of a victim's lawyer also had a highly significant effect on victims' level of confidence when giving evidence, and meant that the hostility rating for the defence lawyer was much lower.

Within this context, section 34 could increase victims' confidence during the cross-examination stage, and thereby enhance the likelihood of victims reporting and mitigate the high rates of attrition in sexual assault cases. For the DPP, this equates to potentially securing more convictions, which would demonstrate success in meeting its stated aims of prosecuting in the public's interest and providing protection from sex offenders (Rape Crisis Network Ireland [RCNI] 2012).

Victim participation in the criminal justice process is important even in cases that do not result in conviction. Most participants in this research shared this view in line with procedural justice theory, which posits that the attainment of a conviction is not the *only* factor determining what is perceived to be a 'just' outcome (Clark 2010; Tyler 2007). As Emily, a sexual assault clinical lead counsellor, observed:

> Initially if somebody is found not guilty, there is ... immediate ... distress, anxiety, anguish ... disbelief and anger.... When people have had a little time to reflect, they can reflect on at least the fact they have got to court,

> because not many cases get to court.... Lots of people ... say, 'I'm not even thinking about the verdict, I just want my case to be heard, I just want charges to be brought'; ... they have held the person who perpetrated the offence accountable, they haven't just ignored it, or not reported or dropped out. That in itself is an achievement, being able to face the person that did this in a courtroom setting is very powerful.... People have said to me, 'I think they believed me, but I think they believed him too'.... People will say beyond reasonable doubt is a very high level of proof ... because you can doubt anything. Or they will say, 'It's easier to believe that I was a fibber, than that he was a rapist'.

This comment demonstrates that, for some victims, reporting the crime and taking the case to trial represents a victory in itself, and signifies the importance of ensuring that the offender is held morally accountable, even when the crime cannot be proven in a court of law. It also highlights the significant role that procedural justice plays in shaping victims' perceptions of just outcomes.

Problems with the application of section 34

Notice of intention to cross-examine on prior sexual history

One of the concerns regarding the practical application of ILR for victims relates to section 4A(2), which deals with 'notice of intention' (otherwise known as applying for 'leave'). Section 4A(2) states:

> Notice of intention to make an application under section 3 or 4 shall be given to the prosecution by or on behalf of the accused person before, or as soon as practicable after, the commencement of the trial.

Additionally, it states:

> Subsections (3), (4) and (5) set out the obligations of the prosecution to notify the victim of the application and his/her right to be legally represented, the judge's obligation to ensure subsections (2) and (3) have been complied with, and the judge's obligation to postpone or adjourn the trial if, 'in his [sic] opinion', the period between the complainant's being put on notice of the application, and the application itself, is not long enough to 'have afforded [the victim] a reasonable opportunity to arrange legal representation' – respectively.
>
> (RCNI 2012: 6)

The participants in this research noted that it is common for defence lawyers to apply for leave to cross-examine well after the commencement of the trial, which limits the time available to the victim to prepare for court and arrange ILR (Emily, sexual assault clinical lead counsellor; Joanna, CEO, sexual violence support centre). As Joanna argued, 'prior to setting the court date, one would hope that the defence would make the request before the trial, but sadly sometimes it happens that the defence doesn't make the request until during a trial'. Not only does this have emotional and psychological consequences for the victim, but, as Joanna explained, it can also impact on the victim's confidence when testifying, which can delay their recovery.

In a recent submission tendered by Ireland's Legal Aid Board to a Review into the Investigation and Prosecution of Sexual Offences,[7] the Board stated that defence counsel generally notify the prosecution of their intention to make an application 'close to, or after the commencement of the trial, [and] sometimes shortly before the complainant is due to give evidence' (Legal Aid Board 2019: 4). This limits the time available to source counsel who are sufficiently briefed on the case. It also diminishes any opportunity for meaningful consultation between the victim and their legal representative. In fact, it is common for victims to meet their legal representatives 'outside the courtroom door' on the day of the hearing (ibid. 5). When considering that the rate of Legal Aid uptake by victim-applicants increased by 81 per cent from 2014 to 2018 (26 applicants in 2014 compared to 47 applicants in 2018), resourcing issues will continue to impact victims' experiences of procedural justice and will likely diminish the quality of the evidence they provide in instances where the judge decides to accept the defence's application to cross-examine the victim's prior sexual history.

In a study conducted by Bacik et al. (cited in RCNI 2012), they found that notice of intention to apply for leave to adduce sexual history evidence is usually issued by the presiding judge, regardless of whether the application was made before or during the trial. Further, they state that '[the] defence may be giving notice of intention to make a section 3 application even where there is little or no real prospect of them doing so' (ibid. 6). Bacik et al. argue that section 3 applications were thus being made (late or otherwise) as a basis from which to 'intimidate' the victim and 'discourage' them from continuing with the prosecution (ibid. 6). Bacik et al. (2010)and Hanly, Healy and Scriver's (2009) studies also draw attention to the wide range of 'apparent bases' for granting section 3 applications. They found significant discrepancies among judges in the exercise of their discretion to permit section 3 defence applications in the trial to not only adduce previous sexual history evidence, but also to cross-examine the victim (Bacik et al. 2010; Hanly, Healy & Scriver 2009; RCNI 2012).

These issues have been observed in other adversarial jurisdictions. For example, a UK-based study conducted by Kelly, Temkin and Griffiths (2006: 77) identified that safeguards on the admission of victims' sexual history in rape trials were overwhelmingly 'evaded, circumvented and resisted'. The study found that, in practice, in two-thirds of the trials sampled applications to admit sexual history evidence were approved without adhering to procedural rules. Furthermore, similar to the findings of the present research, Kelly, Temkin and Griffiths (2006) identified that applications were not commonly made at the pre-trial stage and two-thirds of the applications made at trial were admitted.

Additionally, there was a strong correlation between an application to permit sexual history evidence and a defendant's acquittal.[8]

Comparative trends are also notable in Scotland. Research conducted by Burman et al. (2007), for example, reveals that, despite amendments to the *Sexual Offences (Criminal Procedure) Act 2002* (Scot) intended to prevent the arbitrary use of sexual history questioning of the victim, defence counsel frequently sought late applications to cross-examine the victim's prior sexual history either as a procedural step or as a basis for intimidating the victim. Burman et al.'s (2007: 2) study examined 231 sexual offence cases that were indicted to the High Court over a 12-month period (1 June 2004–31 May 2005) and found that almost three-quarters of High Court sexual offence trials (72 per cent) included section 275[9] applications to adduce sexual history evidence under the revised Act. This figure stands in stark contrast to the findings of their initial study in which applications for leave were only observed in one-fifth of trials (21 per cent) (Burman et al. 2007). Their study also found that 'lodging of … late application[s] … was not, in itself, a barrier to the success of an application' (Burman et al. 2007: 78).

These findings suggest that the perverse rationale to include a victim's sexual history evidence, late or otherwise, is not unique to Ireland, but rather is indicative of a broader global problem across adversarial systems. At the same time, the findings highlight issues in regard to judicial decision-making, which tie in with other concerns identified by the participants around the limited nature of the legal representative's role in Ireland.

The limited role of the legal representative

The ILR provided for victims under section 34 only applies to the application stage. This means that if the judge allows the application, the victim has no further legal assistance and must go on to endure the cross-examination about their prior sexual history without representation. As demonstrated in the discussion above, applications to cross-examine the victim on their prior sexual history are commonly admitted by the judge. For example, Bacik et al.'s (2010) study found that, between 2003 and 2009, 70 per cent of applications to allow prior sexual history evidence were granted by the Central Criminal Court across a sample of 59 cases of rape and/or aggravated sexual assault. This raises questions as to the relevance and value of the legal representative, given their limited role and input.

David, a principal officer working within a national gender-based violence organisation, argued that the extent of the representative's role in the trial is dependent upon the judge's discretion. While the victim is entitled to have ILR in the event of an application, such representation is only supposed to apply for the part of the hearing that involves the legal argument as to whether the victim's past sexual history should be allowed in evidence. In reflecting on this issue, David explained:

> The representation is around the ordeal in the absence of the jury [and] the legal argument [as to] whether the evidence is admissible or not. Now there

> may be some pre-hearing of the evidence for the judge to assess what is at issue, but the trouble then is that the legal aid is for the ordeal only and not for the subsequent questioning, and the practice there I think varies. Sometimes the court asks the person [the legal representative] to wait for the questioning to see that it follows the spirit of what was agreed in the legal argument and sometimes, conversely, the judge will ask the legal representative to leave.

The problem here is that this judicial discretion leads to inconsistencies in victims' experiences with the criminal justice system, including their perception of procedural justice and fairer substantive outcomes. Such inconsistencies are likely to increase attrition rates and dissatisfaction levels with the criminal justice process. Significantly, this discussion highlights problems pertaining to judicial discretion and (in)consistency in legal procedure. It also points to a need to expand the legal representative's role so that they can be present during the cross-examination of the victim if the judge decides to accept the defence's application. This may help to address issues of consistency in judicial decision-making and potentially reduce feelings of anxiety and stress experienced by sexual assault victims who are cross-examined. This is an important consideration in light of one of the key objectives of the reform, which is to assist victims throughout the cross-examination – a stage in the criminal trial that is identified as one of the most harmful for sexual assault victims.

A limitation of section 3: supporting myths about rape and sexuality?

Although section 34 has increased the scope for victim participation through ILR and for supporting victims' interests and right to privacy about their previous sexual experiences, section 3(1) of the *Criminal Law (Rape) Act* creates a possible limitation. Section 3(1) states that 'no question shall be asked in cross-examination at the trial, by or on behalf of any accused person at the trial, about any sexual experience of a complainant with a person *other than that accused*' (emphasis added, *Criminal Law (Rape) Act*). This means that questions may still be asked in relation to the victim's previous sexual history with the accused. What is problematic about this is that research has shown that most rapes and sexual assaults are perpetrated by someone who is known to the victim, such as an intimate partner (Daly & Bouhours 2010). In addition, while section 3(1) is supposed to offer a protective measure to victims, section 3(2)(b) maintains that judges can permit questioning or evidence relating to a victim's sexual history if they are convinced by the defence's application that such evidence or questioning has relevance and significance to the case, insofar as the jury might be persuaded to believe that the accused person was guilty were that evidence not adduced (*Criminal Law (Rape) Act*). James Hamilton (2010: 2), former Director of the DPP, supported this legislative provision, claiming:

> What is important is to have a legislative scheme which will allow evidence of previous sexual history to be admitted where it is properly relevant, as will frequently arise where a rape is alleged to have been perpetrated by a person who is, or has been, in a sexual relationship with the complainant.

What is concerning about this is that the legislation fails to recognise the complexities surrounding rape investigations and prosecutions, as the admission of any evidence relating to a victim's prior sexual history can reduce the likelihood of successful conviction. This is especially so considering that consent (or lack thereof) is difficult to prove in rape cases, particularly in the context of intimate relationships, in relation to which misconceptions surrounding sexual assault remain prevalent (Kelly, Temkin & Griffiths 2006). For example, considering that rape in marriage was not defined as a crime in many common law jurisdictions until the late 20th century, it is not uncommon for the myth that rape cannot occur in marriage to infiltrate social and legal discourse, as many people still believe that marriage (or an intimate relationship) implies ongoing consent – thus upholding the myth that only 'stranger' rape is 'real' rape (Hasday 2000). Other rape myths in relation to intimate relationships revolve around the idea that women maliciously fabricate claims to seek revenge (Easteal & McOrmond-Plummer 2006; Estrich 1987). Such problematic beliefs have been proven to distort the pursuit of justice, from as early as the initial reporting of a crime through to the trial (Easteal & McOrmond-Plummer 2006; Estrich 1987). This is especially so in relation to jury deliberations, where preconceived (but false) notions based on gendered prejudice have been known to influence the verdict (Taylor 2007). Despite a breadth of research that counteracts these myths and false claims, such beliefs persist among criminal justice personnel and the general public (Easteal & McOrmond-Plummer 2006; Estrich 1987).

The Irish legislation thus does not provide sufficient protection from these misconceptions. The legislation does acknowledge that, traditionally, these prejudices have impacted on trials; but by allowing applications and giving the judge discretion in *exceptional* circumstances, it allows prejudice to continue to shape the outcomes of cases and the experience of victims in relation to procedural and substantive justice. This is evident in Bacik et al.'s (2010) study in which they found that the most common bases upon which applications were made were when there existed consensual sexual relations between the accused and the victim before the crime, alleged promiscuity or routine display of suggestive behaviour by the victim, and previous allegations by the victim of sexual crime. As mentioned above, their research also identified that nearly three-quarters of applications to allow such evidence were granted by the court in 59 cases of rape and/or aggravated sexual assault (Bacik et al. 2010). While the percentage of cases in which the victims consented to the application to cross-examine is unknown, this proportion of successful applications is problematically high; and it can be presumed that, given the damaging effects of cross-examination for victims, it is unlikely that many victims (if any) would have consented to the application (RCNI 2012). In light of these findings, Bacik et al. (2010) raise 'strong criticisms of the rule [allowing the admission of previous sexual history evidence in certain circumstances] which can perpetuate outdated and sexist myths about rape and sexuality' (cited in RCNI 2012: 5).

As noted above, these findings are not unique to Ireland, but reflect a trend in other adversarial jurisdictions where counsel exploit the loopholes in safeguards aimed at preventing the introduction of victims' sexual history. For example, in considering the findings of the broader research discussed above, in Australia, the State of Victoria has a statutory safeguard placing limits on the cross-examination of a victim's previous sexual history unless, 'because of special circumstances, it would be likely materially to impair confidence in the reliability of the evidence of the complainant' (*Criminal Procedure Act 2009* (Vic) s 352(b)). As in Ireland, Victoria problematically admits sexual history evidence in circumstances where the judge deems that:

> It has got substantial relevance; ... if someone is saying it's rape and they subsequently allegedly had sex with the perpetrator, that would be relevant.... It doesn't sit that one minute you're saying you're raped and the next minute you're consensually having sex with him.
>
> (Natasha and Ashley, judges of the Victorian County Court)

Discussing more contentious scenarios, Ashley cited instances in which she would consider permitting a victim's sexual history evidence in court, particularly where there had been a separation in a marriage and the woman claimed that she would have 'never' had sex with the accused subsequent to the separation. Ashley described how, in such cases, women may claim that they were sexually assaulted in a position to which they had not consented, while the defence may claim that, because this position was a normal part of the victim's prior 'sexual history ... and repertoire ... [that] she did do these things beforehand with consent ... that is an issue you might then want to seek to cross-examine her about'. Other Australian-based studies have also found that, in practice, many Australian jurisdictions still frequently use evidence of a victim's sexual history and reputation in court (Heath 2005; Heenan 2003).

According to McGlynn (2017), the situation in England and Wales reveals similar failures in the law's response to the perceived 'relevance' of sexual history evidence. The Court of Appeal judgement in *R v Ched Evans* held that evidence of the victim's sexual history with persons other than the accused (third-party evidence) should have been considered in accordance with the 'similarity exception'[10] under section 41(3)(c)(i) of the *Youth Justice and Criminal Evidence Act 1999* (UK) because the complainant had: (i) 'been drinking', (ii) 'instigated certain sexual activity', (iii) 'directed her sexual partner into certain sexual positions', and (iv) 'used specific words of encouragement' (*Judge v UK, Application No 35863/10, 2011 SCCR 241 at 28*; McGlynn 2017). McGlynn (2017: 391) argues that these judgements 'undermine the principles of autonomy and free choice which should underpin any notion of consent to sexual activity' and serve to construct highly 'prejudicial assumptions about women's passivity in sexual activity' (ibid. 382). Permitting defence applications in these circumstances also problematically serves to render women responsible for their victimisation and offers legal impunity to perpetrators for their crimes.

The experiences in comparable international jurisdictions therefore shed light on the weak legislative frameworks governing restrictions on the admission of victims' sexual history evidence insofar as these frameworks allow for the infiltration of rape myths and stereotypes in the courtroom in 'exceptional' circumstances. Similar to Bacik et al.'s (2010) argument of the dangers of allowing for these exceptions, such examples also highlight that, in practice, the legislation in place does little to protect victims' rights and interests and 'hinders them [victims] from giving their best evidence' (McGlynn 2017: 391). This can leave victims equally as vulnerable as they would be if the legislation did not exist.

Concluding remarks

The provision of separate ILR for sexual assault victims in Ireland represents a significant shift towards enhancing victims' rights in adversarial criminal justice systems. It allows a unique level of victim participation in the legal process, enabling victims to access government-funded ILR to oppose a defendant's application for the admission of their sexual history evidence in court. The introduction of this reform demonstrates that Ireland has sought to redress the trauma associated with sexual assault victims giving evidence in court, and being cross-examined in particular. As noted by the Stern Review (2010: 98):

> Although the representation in Ireland is limited, it represents an important recognition that there are times during the trial process where victims must be allowed to participate in the trial as more than witnesses – in order to protect their rights and interests.

This chapter has explored the significance of the reform within this context, drawing upon the ways in which increased victim participation through ILR can enhance sexual assault victims' experience of procedural justice, specifically by offering victims a voice, a degree of control and information during the process. If a case results in a guilty verdict, it may also offer victims validation.

However, the shortcomings of the reform, such as those revolving around the delayed notice of intention, the legal representative's limited role and inconsistency in judicial discretion, raise doubt as to the extent of the positive impacts of this reform for victims. The findings presented throughout this chapter demonstrate that, even since the introduction of this reform, a high volume of applications to adduce victims' sexual history have been granted, which suggests that there appears to be minimal preclusion of victims' sexual history evidence in criminal trials in practice. And 'despite compelling justifications for restrictions on the use of sexual history evidence', the failed safeguards point to the 'erroneous purposes' for which it is frequently admitted in court (McGlynn 2017: 373), many of which stem from the 'resilience of cultural mythologies about women and sexuality' (Stubbs 2003: 23).

Against this backdrop, while noting the potentially beneficial impacts of ILR for sexual assault victims in the context of section 34, particularly in terms of fostering victim participation within the legal process and protecting victims' from further harm, the findings presented in this chapter suggest that the implementation of ILR has had a counter effect of retaining sexual history evidence in trials. This issue is not unique to Ireland, but rather, as demonstrated throughout this chapter, is commonplace across common law jurisdictions even amid reforms to rape shield legislation designed to preclude victims' sexual history evidence being used in court.

Ultimately, the shortcomings of section 34 lend further support to research that has critically analysed women's experiences of procedural injustice following the introduction of victim-oriented reforms intended to improve victims' status, rights and treatment (see Chapter 2). The gaps between the theoretical aims and practical outcomes of section 34 limit the prospect of sexual assault victims attaining procedural justice through the restricted form of ILR offered in Ireland. While one solution may involve the extension of ILR beyond the application stage, there is also a need to 'challenge [the] deeply embedded practices … that result in women's sexual history and character influencing determinations of responsibility, blame and guilt' (McGlynn 2017: 392), and that underpin the frequency and rationale of applications to adduce sexual history evidence.

Notes

1 A version of this chapter was published as Iliadis, M. (2019), 'Victim representation for sexual history evidence in Ireland: A step towards or away from meeting victims' procedural justice needs?', *Criminology and Criminal Justice*, https://doi.org/10.1177/1748895819851848.

2 Section 4A of the *Criminal Law (Rape) Act*, as inserted by section 34.

3 Section 28(5A) of the *Civil Legal Aid Act 1995* (Irl) provides for a complainant, who is the subject of an application under section 3 of the *Criminal Law (Rape) Act 1981* (Irl), to be granted legal aid in relation to such an application.

4 The Joint Oireachtas Committee is responsible for contributing to legislative and policy areas of justice, security, the rule of law and equality (Houses of the Oireachtas 2016).

5 *Criminal Law (Rape) Act* s3(1):

> If at a trial any person is for the time being charged with a rape offence to which he pleads not guilty, then, except with the leave of the judge, no evidence shall be adduced and no question shall be asked in cross-examination at the trial, by or on behalf of any accused person at the trial, about any sexual experience of a complainant with a person other than that accused.

6 *Criminal Law (Rape) Act* s4(1):

> Where a justice of the District Court conducts a preliminary examination of a charge of a rape offence, then, except with the leave of the justice, evidence shall not be adduced and a question shall not be asked at the examination which, if the examination were a trial such as is mentioned in *section 3* (*1*), could not be adduced or asked without leave in pursuance of that section.

7 The Review was chaired by Tom O'Malley BL, who is a senior lecturer in law, a member of the ILRC and a practising barrister specialising in judicial review (Department of Justice and Equality 2018).

8 The acquittal rate was 90 per cent where an application was accepted, compared with 52 per cent where no application was made.

9 Section 275 of the *Sexual Offences (Procedure and Evidence) Act 2002* (Scot) was amended in response to the perceived failure of sections 274 and 275 of the *Criminal Procedure Act 1995* (Scot).

10 The 'similarity exception' pertains to section 41(3)(c) of the *Youth Justice and Criminal Evidence Act 1999* (UK) whereby evidence of the complainant's past sexual behaviour is deemed to be 'so similar' that the 'similarity cannot reasonably be explained as a coincidence'.

6 Victim participation through the SACVR[1]

Introduction

> I passionately believe that there should be greater clarity about the victim actually having their own standing in criminal proceedings and if a court objective is to assist the victim to regain control and to allow them to be actively engaged in decision-making that affects them, then there is a strong argument that it should be [that] they [victims] have the right [to participate] in the first place and a commissioner is a person you go to when your right is not being upheld. At the moment in South Australia, it tends to be the Commissioner having the priority and the victim being able to sort of follow on the shirt tail of the Commissioner, and I am not sure whether that ultimately achieves the ongoing objective that … [the Commissioner] has which is about procedural justice for the victim … I think that can be achieved by sort of tilting it that way; I suspect that it's a process of evolution.
>
> (James, leading victims' rights authority)

Recent Australian commissions of inquiry, including the VLRC (2016), the RCIRCSA (Cth, 2017) and the RCFV (2016), have focused much needed attention on the rights of crime victims. These inquiries have shed light on the plight of crime victims but have also raised awareness of the lack of rights victims are afforded. Institutional arrangements as to who should manage, regulate or enforce the rights of victims have also been the subject of these inquiries. Since the VLRC final report in 2016, reform has been encouraged regarding the range of powers held by the Office of the Commissioner of Victims' Rights[2] in order to help consolidate victims' rights under a statutory power that can protect and advance the interests of victims as important constituents in the justice system. A question arises, however, as to whether the existing limitations of the adversarial system for sexual assault victims can be addressed through a third party or intermediary, such as a Commissioner for Victims' Rights. Arguably, the Office of Commissioner of Victims' Rights provides an appropriate means of improving victims' experiences in the criminal justice system without undermining the traditional structure of the adversarial system, based as it is on the contest between the accused and the state.

An Office of the Commissioner of Victims' Rights is presently constituted across most Australian states and territories, albeit under various titles.[3] Victim representation through such an office has precedence in South Australia, with rights and powers that allow the Commissioner to intervene in proceedings where victim interests become compromised or to investigate any alleged departure from the state's *Victims' Rights Charter* framework.

In NSW, although the Commissioner lacks any specific power to represent victims, ss 11 and 12 of the *Victims' Rights and Support Act 2013* (NSW) provide the Commissioner with the power to make enquiries and conduct investigations, and to compel evidence, respectively. While such powers may be conventionally used to seek discovery of evidence required to determine routine compensation claims, the joint powers to investigate and compel evidence give the Commissioner the capacity to look into complaints where charter rights have been denied to victims, including, potentially, the right to be kept informed and consulted with regard to pre-trial prosecutorial decisions, such as the rights provided in support of victims of sexual violence under cl 6.5(2) of the *Victims Rights and Support Act 2013* (NSW).[4] Such powers arguably allow the Commissioner in NSW to take up a victim's cause, where they decide to investigate a failure to maintain a right provided under the charter. In this respect, the NSW Commissioner's role can be somewhat likened to the functions of the Commissioner in South Australia. However, South Australia is presently the only state where such rights to victim representation are explicit in statute.

This chapter explores the unique powers of the South Australian Commissioner for Victims' Rights (SACVR – also referred to as the Commissioner). It considers the extent of the Commissioner's powers and in what circumstances the Commissioner can exercise their powers to intervene in cases where victims' rights and interests have not been adequately represented. By examining a range of de-identified cases relating to victims of sexual offences, this chapter illustrates how the Commissioner can utilise their powers to represent victims and intervene in certain matters. In discussing these cases, the chapter considers whether the appointment of legal representation through the Commissioner's powers has impacted on victims' capacity to access procedural justice. It also considers whether victim representation through the Commissioner has positively contributed to victims' substantive justice experiences. Following the case study analysis, the chapter discusses some of the limitations of the Commissioner's powers and functions.

The emergence of the SACVR

The movement towards acknowledging victims' rights in South Australia can be traced back to the 1980s, when the rise of the global victims' rights movement gained prominence. In the same year that the UN adopted the *Declaration of Basic Principles of Justice for Victims of Crime and Abuse of Power* (1985), South Australia promulgated Australia's first declaration on victims' rights. This was shortly followed by the introduction of the VIS in 1989, which granted victims a limited participatory right in criminal proceedings through the use of a VIS (*Criminal Law (Sentencing) Act 1988* (SA)). South Australia's commitment to crime victims continued to develop and in 2006, for the first time in Australian history, the Department of the Premier and Cabinet appointed Michael James O'Connell to the position of Interim Commissioner for Victims' Rights for a period of one year, commencing on 19 October 2006 and expiring on 18 October 2007.[5] Then, in 2008, the South Australian Governor in Executive Council constituted the first Office of Commissioner of Victims' Rights by renaming the South Australian Victims of Crime Coordinator – Michael O'Connell – as the Commissioner for Victims' Rights.[6] This appointment was made due to the perceived failure of the criminal justice system to adequately respond to victims' procedural justice needs and expectations from the prosecution process. In reflecting on the capacity of the Commissioner to represent and protect victims' rights and interests, Xavier, a criminal justice professional interviewed for this research, explained:

> In certain specific situations, both in and out of court, the role of a Commissioner of Victims' Rights or some similar role to represent the victim's interest, and if necessary, to secure legal representation, is not just desirable but I would say necessary.

Views such as this one prompted the introduction of the SACVR to strengthen victims' rights and address victims' concerns regarding their role and treatment in the criminal prosecution process.

Section 16 of the *Victims of Crime Act 2001* (SA): the Commissioner's powers and functions

The SACVR is an independent statutory officer whose role is likened to a crime victim ombudsperson. Their functions are stipulated under section 16 of the *Victims of Crime Act 2001* (SA), which mandates that 'the Commissioner must not be a member of the Public Service … [and] is entirely independent of direction or control by the Crown or any Minister or officer of the Crown' (*Victims of Crime Act 2001* (SA) s 16(2) & 16(E)(1)). In consultation with the Commissioner, the Attorney-General may provide directions and make recommendations to the Commissioner as to the undertaking of their role; however, these must be published in the Gazette and be laid before each House of Parliament within six days after they have been given (*Victims of Crime Act 2001* (SA) s 16(E)(2)).

The Commissioner can receive a victim's grievance about their treatment in the justice system and then consult any public official or agency to resolve the issue or dispute. If the Commissioner believes that the public official or agency has violated the declaration governing the treatment of victims, they can recommend that the offending official or agency provide a written apology to the aggrieved victim. The Commissioner has also utilised other avenues to pursue systemic change when confronted with a series of like complaints. For example, the Commissioner has appointed legal counsel to represent bereaved families during coronial inquests and has been heard on issues pertaining to child protection.

The SACVR also carries out functions that are not conventionally associated with an ombudsperson. As stipulated under section 16(3), the powers of the Commissioner include: advising the Attorney-General on how to marshal available government resources to effectively and efficiently help crime victims, assisting victims in their dealings with prosecuting authorities and other government agencies, consulting with prosecutors in the interests of victims and in particular cases about matters including VISs and plea negotiations, consulting with the judiciary about court practices and procedures and their effects on victims, monitoring the effect of the law on victims and victims' families, making submissions either personally or through legal counsel to protect victim interests, and making recommendations to the Attorney-General on matters arising from the performance of these functions.

This means that victims can contact the Commissioner for legal assistance in negotiating the justice system in a range of matters in South Australia. James, a leading victims' rights advocate, defined these provisions as both 'explicit and implicit entitlements'. The explicit entitlements refer to those that are clearly and precisely defined in the legislation. For example, section 32A of the *Victims of Crime Act 2001* (SA) states that victims may exercise their right through an appropriate representative,[7] such as the Commissioner, to deliver a VIS on their behalf during sentencing guideline hearings (*Criminal Law (Sentencing) Act 1988* (SA)). This clause makes this right very transparent. In contrast, implicit rights have been described as rights that are specified in statute but vaguely or ambiguously defined. This can be seen in section 16(3)(b), which states that the Commissioner can 'assist victims in their dealings with prosecution authorities and other government agencies' (*Victims of Crime Act 2001* (SA)). This clause does not make clear *how* the Commissioner may assist victims in this context. In reflecting on this section of the Act, James argued that this right 'is silent [as to] ... what that might imply'. Robert, a manager of a Witness Assistance Service (WAS), similarly described the Commissioner's powers as 'the broadest that I see in the country'. The SACVR's broad powers thus give them scope to utilise their functions to justify various (undefined) legislative interventions. As described by the former SACVR, Michael O'Connell (2012: 7), this has included giving victims the opportunity to be active participants in decision-making processes:

> I have provided direct legal representation for individual victims in consultation with prosecution, in criminal and civil proceedings and coronial inquests, as well as initiated legal matters that affect victims in general.

The SACVR, or legal counsel engaged by them, enables victim participation in a variety of ways. As mentioned earlier, section 32A of the *Victims of Crimes Act 2001* (SA) provides that '[r]ights granted to a victim under this, or any other, Act may be exercised on behalf of the victim by an appropriate representative chosen by the victim for that purpose'. Where appropriate, the Commissioner consults with a victim to determine whether intervention is warranted and, if so, makes an independent determination to exercise representative rights to:

- determine if criminal proceedings should commence;
- attend plea negotiation meetings with prosecutors;
- request a review of plea negotiation decisions;
- submit individual victim impact statements; or,
- draft and submit neighbourhood impact statements for collectives of victims or social impact statements for the public at large.[8]

The Commissioner may also appoint counsel to assist victims during criminal proceedings, for example, to apply for a suppression order, to express views on protected communications, and to respond to a defence request for access to a transcript of evidence given at a Royal Commission. In addition, the Commissioner can appear in sentencing proceedings before the District Court to answer the questions of the judge, such as whether there was a chance for reconciliation between victims and defendants.

The SACVR may therefore intervene in proceedings in instances where victims' respective state charter rights are not upheld or where disputes may arise between public officials, or between victims and service providers or officials. The Commissioner's ability to intervene in proceedings with cognate powers to represent victims is thus a unique function of the Commissioner in South Australia. As will be demonstrated by the case examples discussed below, this has made victims' rights in South Australia both actionable and enforceable (see O'Connell 2015b).

Within the context of sexual assault cases specifically, Zoe, a sexual assault crisis response and counselling coordinator, shed light on the potential benefits for sexual assault victims of having legal representation provided to them by the SACVR:

> One of the challenging things for sexual assault victims is to often feel that their needs are not well understood by the criminal justice process … [It's important] … to understand the criminal justice process … and why certain decisions might be made in a certain way or things are interpreted in a certain way. Any provisions that do assist people [victims] to feel that they understand and have a level of participation in the process … [are] a very good thing to have.

The Commissioner's authority to intervene in proceedings, both in person or through counsel, therefore enables court-based intervention in the interests of the victim, and represents a major development insofar as the requirements of adversarial justice are concerned. Contrary to their witness status, section 32A of the *Victims of Crime Act 2001* (SA) grants victims de facto standing in proceedings from which they would otherwise be excluded. As demonstrated by the four case examples considered below, through representation by or on behalf of the SACVR, the interests of the victim shift from peripheral to integral, despite the victim not gaining personal party status to proceedings.

Intervention by the Commissioner: the cases[9]

The provision of legal counsel for victims has resulted in court decisions and interpretations of law that have favoured victims' interests without unduly impacting the rights of accused people. This can be seen in the following cases.[10]

Case A

As explained in Chapter 2, prosecuting authorities encounter difficulties in prosecuting sexual offence cases because the quest for a verdict often comes down to one person's word against another. Case A involved an alleged sexual assault against a young woman by a taxi driver in his car. While the victim was adamant that she had not consented, questions arose about the victim's level of intoxication, which the defence argued was perceived by the accused as indicative of giving consent. Despite the police and prosecutors maintaining the view that the offence had occurred, they questioned the realistic prospect of conviction due to issues surrounding proof of consent, which would need to be substantiated beyond reasonable doubt in a court. These concerns led to a decision to engage in plea negotiations.

Leading victims' rights advocate, James, described the victim in this case as feeling like 'a tennis ball between these two perspectives, going backwards and forwards'. As a result of the victim's frustration with the process and the DPP, the Commissioner intervened to provide the victim with legal representation. The victim's legal representative was not permitted to sit in on the plea negotiations, but they were able to engage in separate discussions with the police and prosecution in order to gain an understanding of the case and the reasons for the decisions being made. The victim's lawyer was thereby able to provide the victim with a comprehensive understanding of how the decisions were reached, so that when the prosecutor asked for the victim's view, the victim was able to:

> enunciate her own personal views about the issue, not the views that had been stirred up by the police, or not the views that she held because she thought that the prosecution, who had already made it clear they were not her lawyer, appeared to be part of the enemy as well.
>
> (James)

Having legal representation therefore enabled the victim to have more of a voice and involvement in her case. Despite the charges ultimately being withdrawn, the presence of the victim's lawyer allowed the victim to gather advice and information independent of the normal criminal proceedings, and this assisted her to obtain an intervention order against the accused. The Commissioner elected to cover the costs of that application and the defendant agreed to the conditions of the intervention order. Therefore, despite the accused not being tried, the victim in this case can be seen as having some 'success' in her substantive justice outcome as her safety and security concerns were addressed. This impacted positively on the victim's emotional and psychological recovery. James observed that the victim's lawyer 'gave her this stronger sense of engagement [and] a stronger voice ... with a sounder knowledge [of] what was happening'. He further explained:

> The victim is still aggrieved by the fact that she didn't get her day in court [in relation to the sexual assault], but very thankful that (a) she had a voice, (b) she had a point of reason to talk to [a legal representative], and (c) she got an intervention order. So, we got three out of four things that she wanted that she may not have got if she had not got counsel.

These outcomes demonstrate how the victim's representative in this case was able to positively contribute to the victim's procedural justice experience in terms of providing information, voice and a degree of control. Significantly, this case reveals how, although the victim was not able to attain validation via a trial or guilty verdict, as James's observations suggest, the processes underpinning the decisions made were perceived as fair by the victim.

Case B

The second case involved a sexual assault of an adolescent by her mother's male partner. On one occasion, the mother left the adolescent in the care of her partner at the family home. The partner used a laptop to show the adolescent a pornographic video before sexually assaulting her. Prior to trial, counsel for the accused applied for a copy of all of the material stored on the laptop's hard-drive. The stored material included private information belonging to the mother and the adolescent. The Commissioner, through legal counsel, asked to be heard on the defence application. Counsel for the Commissioner argued that international and domestic law, including the *Universal Declaration of Human Rights 1948*, the *Convention on the Rights of the Child 1990*, and the *Children's Protection Act 1993* (SA), afforded all people, especially the adolescent victim, the right to privacy; and, although that right was not absolute, the court should be mindful of it in its decision on what material should be disclosed to the accused and to the court. After considering the victim's representative's views, the judge called a voir dire, which allowed the legal representative and Commissioner to gather witnesses to explain the issues relating to the case. The outcome was that the judge concluded that the defence could have access to electronic records related to any activity that occurred on the laptop within 24 hours before the offence and 48 hours after the offence, but that all other records were not to be accessible.

The Commissioner's functions in this case thus allowed the legal representative to protect the victim's right to privacy. The legal representative gave the victim a greater opportunity to experience procedural justice, as the victim was able to regain a sense of control over an incursion into her private life. The victim was given a voice, which could challenge the defence's application for access to her private information. The representative also provided information to the victim in acting as an interpreter of the law and legal process. Significantly, this case demonstrates how procedural justice can be achieved for both parties simultaneously (victim and offender). James argued that this case is a good example of 'where you can have a parallel system of justice and protect the rights of the accused to discovery, but at the same time, protect the rights of the victim to privacy'. In other words, this case exemplifies how all interests within the *triangulation of interests'* framework can be met.

Case C

In this case, a prosecutor notified several adult victim-survivors of child sex offences perpetrated by the same individual that charges were unlikely to proceed. Some of the victims felt that they were merely informed of the decision and the reasons for it, rather than being consulted before the decision was made. The Commissioner appointed legal counsel to assist the victims to attain a review of the prosecutor's decision to withdraw charges – similar to the VRR process in England and Wales. As a result, the prosecutor's decision pertaining to one of the victims was overturned and their case proceeded to trial. Although a guilty verdict was not reached, the victim felt that the legal counsel provided them with a means to hold the prosecutor accountable for their charge decisions. The victim's legal representation also gave the victim an opportunity to be heard and to have their views considered more than would have been the case without the representation, thereby enhancing the victim's perceptions of procedural justice.

Case D

In a similar vein to Case C, in this case, an adult victim of an alleged sex offence struggled to understand and navigate the justice system due to differences of opinion between police investigators and the prosecution staff on whether criminal charges should proceed. Therefore, the Commissioner employed legal counsel with whom the victim consulted, and the counsel accompanied them to the adjudication meeting to discuss the evidence and likelihood of securing a conviction. Counsel helped the victim to articulate their views but also to negotiate access to information to assist with a private application for an intervention (protection) order. After the meeting, the victim, although disappointed with the decision to withdraw all charges, still believed that they had been heard, which was a belief they had not held prior to retaining counsel. The assistance provided to the victim by legal counsel in this case enhanced the victim's sense of safety and procedural justice.

The benefits of enforcing victims' rights through an Office of Commissioner for Victims' Rights

The Commissioner's capacity to address and represent victim interests in South Australia has indeed drawn greater attention to victims' rights in that state. Police officers, prosecutors, magistrates and judges, and defence counsel, despite their initial wariness, and even opposition, have recognised the potential to improve the administration of justice by having a 'third voice' actively involved in decisions that affect victims (see Beloof 2005). The Commissioner, through legal counsel, has empowered victims by providing them with access to procedural justice and, arguably, by giving victims an equitable voice, while reducing the likelihood of secondary victimisation. The SACVR has thus become a significant point of reference for the reform of law and practice, and has increasingly been cited as influencing like reforms throughout Australia.[11] South Australia's experience appears to reject the notion that victims ought to be relegated as witnesses for the prosecution and instead reflects a significant step towards victims gaining more comprehensive participatory rights as stakeholders of justice.

The limits of the Commissioner's powers

Resources

Notwithstanding the significant benefits arising for victims from the Commissioner's powers, the participants in this research also identified various limitations of the role. One of the limitations identified by three-quarters of the South Australian participants pertained to resources. These participants argued that insufficient resources limit the Commissioner's powers from being exercised to full effect, which could leave some victims unrepresented (James, leading victims' rights advocate; Robert, manager, WAS; Xavier, criminal justice professional). As Xavier observed, 'sadly, instructing legal counsel is incredibly expensive'.

In 2015, the Commissioner's legal budget began at $250,000 and was increased to $300,000 in the same year in line with Consumer Price Index (CPI) adjustments (James). Although this appears to be a significant rise, James argued that it did not represent an increase in real terms, given the CPI-based increases in the cost of many things. James cited a case where the Commissioner intervened in a coronial inquest, which cost approximately $90,000 – comprising a substantial 30 per cent of the Commissioner's legal budget. Given the very limited budget, the Commissioner is often more constrained by a lack of resources than by their powers within the law, as James commented. This raises questions about the extent to which the Commissioner is able to intervene in cases, what sorts of cases gain priority over others, and what factors the Commissioner takes into account when deciding whether to intervene. This limitation therefore has the potential to create a hierarchy of victimisation, as the Commissioner's intervention may be justified on the basis of the perceived seriousness of each case, leading to some cases gaining prominence over others. This could also lead to some victims having greater opportunities than others to experience procedurally just outcomes.

Legislative limits and the DPP

All the South Australian participants noted the significance of the Commissioner's powers, with Robert arguing that the 'state benefits greatly from having a Commissioner of Victims' Rights'. Robert also claimed that the Commissioner is 'an important tool of accountability … keep[ing] prosecution, … judges, … [and] defence lawyers honest'. However, despite the strengths of the Commissioner's powers in statute (*Victims of Crime Act 2001* (SA)), their powers are somewhat limited insofar as they are not authorised to take civil action against the prosecution if the prosecution fail to uphold their statutory requirements to victims. This is evident in section 5(3)(a) of the *Victims of Crime Act 2001* (SA), which states that the principles stipulated in the Act governing the treatment of victims by public agencies and officials 'are not enforceable in criminal or civil proceedings'. Therefore, if the Commissioner suspects that a public agency or official has failed to comply with the requirements in Part 2 of the Act governing the treatment of victims, they may only 'recommend that the agency or official issue a written apology to the relevant victim' (*Victims of Crime Act 2001* (SA) s 16A(2)). In reflecting on this clause, Robert commented, 'there's no civil action [if the prosecution fail to uphold victims' rights] … [therefore], although his powers are procedurally effective, I think they're quite weak in some ways'. He further explained:

> We have a public service agenda to provide good public services … what are the consequences of not doing that or not doing that really well? … Probably not much really – a slap on the wrist and [the Commissioner] writing to the Director and saying, 'This victim wasn't provided to', and we just go, 'Well we're sorry'. Do you know what I mean? So, in some ways … is it important? Yes. Do [the Commissioner's] powers have impact? Yes. Does it have legal clout or that real kind of … [impact on] … civil action … [being pursued] … by not abiding or adhering to the Victims of Crime Act? Is there a real consequence? … Not really. I think it's … a little bit weak in that sense.

What is evident from Robert's comments is that, while the legislation at once provides the Commissioner with powers to protect and uphold victims' rights, it simultaneously safeguards public agencies and officials from civil action if they fail to meet their statutory obligations to victims. Therefore, the legislation essentially protects the same individuals who might be failing to uphold victims' rights in the first instance, and around whose work the legislation is aimed at ensuring accountability. This allows for the persistence of unfettered and potentially biased decision-making by the DPP, which raises significant concerns in relation to sexual assault cases in particular, where misconceptions surrounding sexual violence commonly exist. Although such decisions may be subject to the

Commissioner's scrutiny to some degree, they are not punishable by law, as the Commissioner (or victim) is precluded from taking formal action against the DPP if the victim's rights or interests are not upheld. This issue was also identified in Chapter 2 in regard to section 22(1)(a) of the *Victims' Charter Act 2006* (Vic), which essentially safeguards the prosecution from being held accountable for not adhering to their statutory requirements (Flynn 2012).

Prolongs the process

A third potential limitation of the Commissioner's powers emerged from the data when the participants were asked to reflect on whether these powers could unduly interfere with the traditional adversarial system, or whether they would further delay an already drawn-out process. Most participants contended that the Commissioner's powers do not undermine the principles of adversarial justice. As Julie, a criminal justice professional, claimed:

> It doesn't intrude … on the adversarial process or the trial itself, in particular before the jury, but [it] allows the individual victim to have their … rights protected … if there's enough money to get a lawyer … and to have the system explained to them and be supported. There's certainly value in that.

In relation to prolonging the process, Robert maintained, 'I have seen the introduction of legal representatives that have got in the way [of the process]', suggesting that there is the potential for this to impact and prolong a victim's recovery. Robert argued that, in order to avoid delays in finalising a case, the inclusion of a victim's legal representative should only take place during pre-trial processes:

> I've seen that introduction [of legal representation] happen quite late in the process and for that independent legal representative [to have] be[en] given status to appear [in court] and … take us back to a much earlier point in the process.

The impacts of this extend to 'tak[ing] [the DPP] back to very early debates that were argued and decided', leading to what Robert describes as judicial frustration:

> Why are we going back to all this just now because you've got representation? We're now going back to a very fundamental debate that the DPP has a position on, we've made some rulings on, and now the independent lawyer's coming in and kind of got a different agenda.

Robert provided an example of a case involving an alleged offender who had a mental impairment. He explained that the victims in this case were frustrated with certain aspects of the proceedings and, as a result, the Commissioner intervened to provide legal representation to them. An unintended consequence of the Commissioner's intervention, however, was that the process was prolonged and there were heightened levels of frustration for those involved, 'probably including the people [victims] who had that lawyer' (Robert). The potential for the Commissioner's intervention to prolong an already drawn-out criminal prosecution process would be undesirable from the point of view of a victim as it can interfere with their recovery in the aftermath of the crime. In some cases, it may also be seen to undermine the integrity of the DPP's decision-making as the legal representative may hold a different view to the prosecution – a view that is more reflective of the victim's interests.

Although this finding is significant in highlighting the impacts of a prolonged process for both the criminal justice system and victims, perhaps it should not simply be seen as a limitation given that one of the Commissioner's key functions is to intervene in situations where victims' rights have not been adequately upheld. Indeed, some victims may prioritise having their rights and interests protected at the cost of a drawn-out process. Considering that the Commissioner can 'assist victims in their dealings with prosecution authorities and other government agencies' (*Victims of Crime Act 2001* (SA) s 16(3)(b)), the need for such intervention may only or specifically arise at later stages of proceedings. For example, a situation that lends itself to a need for intervention by the Commissioner during the trial may arise if defence counsel seeks leave to subpoena a victim's sexual history evidence during the trial. In this instance, the Commissioner may justifiably intervene to protect the victim's interests and privacy concerns. Additionally, it would simply be beyond the scope of the Commissioner's role to intervene at the early stages of the process if there were no legitimate basis to do so.

Concluding remarks

Drawing on data relating to the Office of the SACVR, this chapter has explored the unique powers held by the Commissioner as stipulated in the *Victims of Crime Act 2001* (SA). The expansion of representative rights and the right to intervene in proceedings through an independent Commissioner appears to be justified to meet the at times competing needs arising from the victim's rights, the independent prosecution interests of the state, and the due process rights of the accused. Housing such powers in an Office of Commissioner represents a measured response that limits victims' private access to the criminal trial, yet extends their ability to participate in criminal justice. Importantly, expanding the powers held by the Office of Commissioner does not grant victims' standing in a criminal court, but it also does not detract from those few instances where this is already provided by law; for example, in relation to the delivery of a VIS. Indeed, as demonstrated by Cases A–D, such an approach facilitates the competing triangulation of interests between the state, the accused and the victim, and its merits warrant further consideration in light of the recommendations set out in key Australian commissions of inquiry to develop the powers and functions of Commissioners in other Australian states and territories, such as

Victoria (VLRC 2016). While there is some evidence to suggest that cost and resource limitations, as well as delays, may hinder the potentially beneficial outcomes arising for victims, as could legislative limits on the Commissioner's role, most of the participants supported the view that the SACVR provides a means for addressing victims' procedural justice needs. As explored in the next chapter, expanding the powers of the Victorian Commissioner may therefore arguably be an appropriate 'next step' for victim inclusion, but also an incremental and mindful step that maintains the integrity of adversarial processes.

Notes

1 Sections of this chapter were published as Kirchengast, K, Iliadis, M & O'Connell, M. (2019), 'Development of the Office of Commissioner of Victims' Rights as an Appropriate Response to Improving the Experiences of Victims in the Criminal Justice System: Integrity, Access and Justice for Victims of Crime, *Monash University Law Review*, 45(1), 1–28.

2 The Office of Commissioner of Victims' Rights is variously defined across Australian states and territories. In South Australia, the position is termed 'Commissioner for Victims' Rights', whereas in Victoria it is termed 'Victims of Crime Commissioner'.

3 Similar powers to that of an Office of Commissioner of Victims' Rights may be exercisable under a departmental head or director of victim services in the Northern Territory, Queensland and Tasmania.

4 *Victims Rights and Support Act 2013* (NSW) s 6, cl. 6.5(2):

> A victim will be consulted before a decision referred to in paragraph (b) above is taken if the accused has been charged with a serious crime that involves sexual violence or that results in actual bodily harm or psychological or psychiatric harm to the victim, unless: (a) the victim has indicated that he or she does not wish to be so consulted, or (b) the whereabouts of the victim cannot be ascertained after reasonable inquiry.

5 This appointment was pursuant to section 68 of the *Constitution Act 1934* (SA).

6 The Department of the Premier and Cabinet appointed Michael James O'Connell to the position of Commissioner for Victims' Rights in South Australia for a period of five years commencing on 17 July 2008 and expiring on 16 July 2013, pursuant to section 16 of the *Victims of Crime Act 2001* (SA). Michael James O'Connell served as the state's first Victims' Commissioner for 12 years, from October 2006 to June 2018.

7 An *appropriate representative* in relation to a victim includes:

(a) an officer of the court
(b) the Commissioner for Victims' Rights or a person acting on behalf of the Commissioner for Victims' Rights
(c) an officer or employee of an organisation whose functions consist of, or include, the provision of support or services to victims of crime
(d) a relative of the victim

or

(e) another person who, in the opinion of the Commissioner for Victims' Rights, would be suitable to act as an appropriate representative. (*Victims of Crime Act 2001* (SA) 32(A)(3))

8 *Sentencing Act 2017* (SA) s 15.

9 The case examples discussed in this section were provided by the research participant, James, a leading victims' rights advocate.

10 These cases have been anonymised to protect the identity of the victims. The details of each matter lie with the SACVR. All cases (A–D) are based on actual matters in which the Commissioner intervened based on his statutory powers under s 32A of the *Victims of Crimes Act 2001* (SA).

11 See, for example, the recommendations in the VLRC's (2016) final report to enhance the powers of the Victims of Crime Commissioner.

7 The prospect of ILR for sexual assault victims within Victoria's criminal prosecution process

Introduction

> The form of the adversarial criminal trial has changed considerably over time. These changes have related to shifting ideas about the nature and meaning of crime, and what it is that the criminal justice system should achieve for victims, offenders and society generally.
>
> (VLRC 2015: 10)

> The twenty-first century criminal trial is increasingly reconceived in form and substance, yet victims remain controversial and contested participants of justice, despite being increasingly connected to the criminal trial.
>
> (Kirchengast cited in VLRC 2016: 23)

In 2015, the inception of the VLRC's consultation paper on *The Role of Victims of Crime in the Criminal Trial Process* arose out of recognition of the need to reconceptualise the role of victims as participants in the criminal trial process. In noting the inadequacies of the criminal justice system for victims of crime to date, the paper recommended numerous discrete reforms to address victims' procedural and substantive justice concerns. The *Victims' Charter Act 2006* (Vic) was identified as the source through which such reforms ought to take effect. The VLRC delivered its final report in 2016 in which it set out an ambitious reform agenda to improve the status, role and treatment of victims in the criminal justice system. In the same year, the Victorian Government agreed to implement all 227 recommendations emerging from the RCFV (2016), and then, in 2017, the RCIRCSA made whole-of-system recommendations to improve prevention efforts and responses to victim-survivors of sexual violence.

Collectively, these inquiries identified the imperative to formalise victims' rights through reforms that have precedence in other Australian and international jurisdictions – namely, those examined throughout this book. Reforms were centred around establishing a right for victims to seek an internal merits review of a decision by the DPP to discontinue a prosecution or to proceed with a guilty plea to lesser charges, as well as robust internal audit processes to review compliance with policies for governing decision-making and consultation with victims and the police (Kirchengast, Iliadis & O'Connell 2019; VLRC 2016: xxii). Likewise, reform was encouraged regarding the range of powers held by the Office of the Victorian Victims of Crime Commissioner (VoCC). The VLRC (2016: xxi), for example, recommended developing the Office of the VoCC to empower them to review the outcome of victims' complaints regarding compliance with *Victims' Charter* principles. The questioning of a victim's sexual history was also raised by all three inquiries as a significant ongoing issue (RCFV 2016; RCIRCSA 2017; VLRC 2016). Somewhat more contentiously, the prospect of introducing ILR for victims of sexual violence was also raised in the VLRC (2016) and the RCFV (2016) final reports. While the VLRC (2016) did not support this recommendation, the RCFV (2016: 62) recommended legal representation for applicants and respondents within Magistrates' Court of Victoria headquarter courts and specialist family violence court divisions (see Iliadis, Fitz-Gibbon & Walklate 2019 for an analysis of recommendation 60).

The notion of introducing ILR for victims of sexual violence in criminal justice proceedings has gained significant traction internationally, yet empirical analysis documenting the perceived benefits and potential implications of such a reform has been largely absent from these debates. Drawing upon the perceptions of participants interviewed in this research, this chapter seeks to advance understandings of the potential benefits, limitations and role of ILR for sexual assault victims within Victoria's criminal justice system, taking into account the various contexts in which ILR may conceivably operate. It also explores whether there is scope to introduce a victim-focused reform in Victoria akin to any of the three reforms operating in the focus jurisdictions – England and Wales, Ireland and South Australia – as recommended by the VLRC (2016), RCFV (2016) and RCIRCSA (2017).

ILR for sexual assault victims: fitting or undermining the adversarial framework?

Victims' rights and interests continue to be highly contested across adversarial systems. While there has been an increasing emphasis on acknowledging and supporting crime victims, such as through the provision of social services and victim-focused law reforms, there is an ongoing reluctance to enhance the role and status of victims through ILR so that they are officially considered a party to proceedings. This opposition primarily stems from concerns relating to the potential implications of such changes for the adversarial criminal justice system and the accused. For example, in drawing from the UK context, Doak, Henham and Mitchell (2009: 653) observe that 'victims' participatory rights are inherently foreign to the normative parameters of the English criminal justice system' and 'the idea of conferring *procedural* rights on victims of crime (i.e. the notion that they should be allowed to participate in the criminal process) has always proved much more contentious [among legal stakeholders]'. Similar views predominate within Victoria's legal system. The VLRC's (2016: 28–9) latest report on *The Role of Victims of Crime in the Criminal Trial Process*, for instance, determined that ILR for victims cannot be justified because 'the legitimate rights of the accused should be protected and fulfilled', and that increasing victims' participation rights through ILR would interfere with the accused's rights to a fair trial.

Despite such resistance, there continue to be pressing concerns arising from sexual assault victims' persistent dissatisfaction with the prosecution process, which support arguments for enhancing victims' rights in order to better respond to their procedural justice needs. The challenges victims face in negotiating the adversarial system are discussed extensively in Chapter 2, and arise at all stages of the process, from reporting the crime and dealing with prosecuting authorities, to testifying in court and being cross-examined. In some of these contexts, it has been suggested that the use of ILR for sexual assault victims could help to alleviate the potential for (or extent of) secondary victimisation.

It has also been argued that the implementation of victim ILR could benefit sexual assault victims' procedural justice experiences (Braun 2014, 2019; Iliadis 2019; Iliadis, Fitz-Gibbon & Walklate 2019). For example, ILR has the potential to address problems caused by a lack of: consultation and *information*; involvement and input into the process, thereby diminishing victims' *voice* and *control*; and support and representation, which can help victims to feel *validated.* Contrary to the role of the state prosecutor, ILR could also offer a mechanism to safeguard victims' interests and procedural rights, which are often overlooked (Braun 2014, 2019; Raitt 2010). Indeed, ILR for sexual assault victims has been recommended by international commissions of inquiry in response to the criticisms of current reforms for failing to adequately address victims' procedural justice needs from the criminal prosecution process.

The analysis presented in this chapter indicates that there appears to be almost as many potential benefits as there are limitations to introducing ILR in Victoria's adversarial system. Of the 26 participants, 24 were asked to consider whether 'there is prospect for legal representation for victims of sexual assault in a common law jurisdiction'. Of these respondents, 38 per cent (n=9) opposed the idea; 25 per cent (n=6) supported the idea; 21 per cent (n=5) believed there is some prospect but only in limited circumstances; and 17 per cent (n=4) initially rejected the idea but then changed their view during the course of the interview to potentially consider it within a limited scope or context. In total, 63 per cent (n=15) of the participants approved of the implementation of ILR for sexual assault victims, whether it be in a limited context or not. However, most of these participants believed that the potential limitations of victim ILR would curtail some of the positive benefits arising for victims from the introduction of this reform.

The potential benefits of implementing ILR for sexual assault victims

The arguments in support of enhancing sexual assault victims' rights through ILR largely relate to the flaws of the adversarial system in adequately responding to victims' procedural justice needs, such as the failure of current reforms to increase victims' satisfaction with the justice process. When examining the participants' perceptions of the potential for ILR for sexual assault victims in Victoria, an abundance of responses highlighted the benefits that such a reform could offer victims. The participants who supported the notion of some form of victim ILR ($n=15$), whether in a limited context or not, indicated that it could lead to victims experiencing a more 'just' process, regardless of the substantive outcome. Oscar, a leading victims' rights advocate, described justice as being 'a right not a privilege', arguing that 'it's got to be the way the system works [because] at the moment it's the other way around'. James, another leading victims' rights advocate, justified his support for victim ILR by drawing on a procedural justice lens, arguing that:

> Fairness is about giving people an opportunity to have a fair, open, frank voice or expression, that not only is … allowed to be said, but … must be heard … There are lots of entitlements that victims have … but very few are … written in a way that generally recognises the obligated to the obligatee relationship … I argue that a victim is an obligatee and that the state's institution, whether they be police [or] prosecutors … are obligated. Unfortunately, in terms of fairness, the way our current principles and rights are written and then applied is more like a customer standard charter, or customer service charter, and our measures that we use to determine whether there has been compliance are more around intrinsic things like 'are you satisfied?' [rather] than whether the procedural process … was in fact fair in the context of what the law obligates those people to do.

In further elaborating, James claimed:

> At the moment, the state has a lawyer [and] the defendant has a lawyer. The victim, the person actually harmed, who has to live with all of these effects for the rest of their life [as a result] of the choice made by the offender, has no equitable voice … What I would like to see is that they actually get invited to sit at the justice table itself and, like everyone else at the table, they have an equal and equitable voice. That images a way of thinking about it.

Chloe, a leading victims' rights authority, also defended the prospect of victim ILR with reference to procedural justice theory when she questioned:

> Why shouldn't they have a victims' lawyer? … We have such an adversarial system that is so indoctrinated … we have got to work towards changing the culture of this because it's very important for victims … Procedural justice is balanced at the very beginning, it's balanced in the middle, and it's balanced in the end, and what I mean by that is there is a victim and there is a defendant and the process works for both. The outcomes are going to be maybe what one didn't want, and what the other didn't want, but it starts off … at the baseline and works through because it is the only way you will rehabilitate victims … That's how I see the procedure working.

A similar view was held by Adelle, a policy researcher working within a victim support organisation, who maintained:

> The victim not being a party for a case … [is] an uncomfortable place for them to be, because on the one hand we do say that the state takes responsibility [but] on the other hand we have got all of these shifts towards acknowledging victims' rights … so on the one hand we are saying they are not a party to the case, but then on the other hand we are saying, 'Oh actually they should have all of these things and they should be important' … It's kind of an almost in-between spot they're in … What is their role? Are they just a witness? Are they something more? … They [victims] feel they are the most important person in the case, [as] it's happened to them, and yet we take that away from them and we say, 'No, it's the state's case, it's not your case'. [Whereas] for them, it is their case.

This comment reiterates the complex and ambiguous position of victims, as they are placed at the nexus between the state's interests and their own. Georgia, a policy researcher working within a victim support organisation, and Adelle added their view on this nuanced issue, stating that victims are often disappointed upon discovering that the case is considered to be an offence against the state as well as them, and these feelings become exacerbated when they realise that the prosecutor they have been referring to as 'my lawyer' does not actually 'do what they want'. Georgia also explained that victims are often 'not given enough detail and information about how the system works itself'. This points to another potential benefit of victim ILR, as the representative can solely advocate for the victim's interests and provide them with timely information. This is an important benefit because, as Oscar, a leading victims' rights advocate, claimed:

> A prosecutor can't do it, they're too busy … they'll meet with you [the victim] … at breaks and dinner time, before and after the court, but they just don't have the time to go into it … they can't really sit down and explain it [the process].

In a similar vein, Chloe pointed to the benefits of victim ILR because:

> The prosecutor doesn't have enough time to build a relationship with that victim [and] to give them encouragement … [for example], when they … are cross-examined by the defence, so coldly and brutally … they [victims] look at the prosecutor to protect them. I have met many victims who wanted the prosecutor to say, 'You shouldn't be asking that'. I think that's the challenge for sexual assaults, because it's very personal … [but] that's not good enough … that's not balancing the scales. It's actually doing injustice to victims who are going through such horrendous times.

These views indicate that victim ILR could potentially provide victims with more of a voice, and more information and control than they currently receive.

In terms of validation, David, a principal officer working within a national gender-based violence organisation, stated that 'the system is not really geared to validating them [victims] … but [h]aving the case go to court [may be] a victory for them, [even] … if it falls [through] because of evidence or legal argument'. Olivia, a policy advisor within a victim support organisation, similarly reflected on substantive case outcomes, noting:

> Generally speaking, through our analysis and through the surveys we have done, we know that even an outcome that wasn't to their [the victim's] liking is made a lot more palatable if they have the feeling that they were listened to [and] that the whole process was communicated in a timely fashion in a way that they understand … Victims want to be treated like people, they don't want to be treated as a sausage in a sausage factory that [merely] has to go through a process.

Enhancing victims' participation rights may not only empower victims, but also 'bolster the legitimacy of the criminal justice system as a whole' (Walker & Telford 2001 cited in Doak, Henham & Mitchell 2009: 653). As Walker and Telford (2000: 10) contend:

> Participation is clearly an important concept in criminal justice as an instrument for assisting in the achievement of other ultimate objectives. For example, without the involvement of the public in reporting crime, the criminal justice system would be fatally handicapped in its pursuit of the security objective. Similarly, participation in the criminal process also serves to legitimise the system by engaging interested, and often aggrieved parties in resolving a dispute, or as a form of external audit to help equitable procedures.

However, even in light of the perceived benefits of participating in justice processes, the principles governing the administration of justice in common law systems are based on adversarial exchange between the state prosecutor and the accused, which raises a pertinent question as to whether (and indeed how) victim ILR could conceivably be integrated into adversarial systems.

ILR for sexual assault victims: at what stages?

For the participants who identified the benefits of state-funded or privately administered ILR for sexual assault victims ($n=6$), most were of the belief that the role of a victim's representative should not be limited to certain procedural stages. For example, Oscar, a leading victims' rights advocate, stated that 'it should be throughout the whole trial'. Emily, a sexual assault clinical lead counsellor, also held this view but acknowledged that this 'would be very difficult' to officially implement. James, a leading victims' rights advocate, similarly maintained:

> My preference would be not to limit [ILR] and to allow victims to have counsel pre-chamber, or pre-trial, during charge bargaining, during proceedings, where and if it's appropriate, and that could be around certainly any time there is a decision that directly affects the victim and the victim feels that they need to have that counsel … I believe that there are, for the purposes of equity … many people who are disenfranchised, who are illiterate, who, due to their psychological [and] emotional wellbeing at that point in time, are not able to clearly articulate how they are feeling for the purpose of victim impact statements … I believe that having … counsel then … will be important and it could also be a moderator in a sense that it would help to ensure that the victim [has] got good guidance on the content of their statements and therefore [can] assist the court.

James supported his argument by making reference to the current levels of dissatisfaction with the process among victims, who feel that their voices are not always considered:

> We find situations where victims have … great emotional outpourings … [for example, on occasion] … there are either accusations that the judge didn't hear [or] … edited the victim's [impact] statement … If the victim was assisted better in that process, then we might not have some of the anger that we have … My preference would be to go across the board [with victim ILR] … My ultimate goal is to say we should have a publicly funded … justice system [that] should comprise police, courts, corrections, a public defender's office fully funded by the state and a public victim's office fully funded, and we should … [conceptualise justice as does] … Lord Steyn … [according to] the notion that there is a triangulation of interests, rather than just two parties.

James's view therefore supports the idea that victim ILR should be implemented throughout the entire prosecution process, as it could help sexual assault victims to achieve their key procedural justice ideals, leading to greater overall levels of satisfaction with the process. His stance also suggests that justice would be better served if victims were conceptualised as a party to proceedings within a tripartite system of justice that takes into account the interests of victims alongside those of the state and the accused.

Despite some marked support from the participants for victim ILR throughout the entire duration of proceedings, the VLRC (2016: 118) ultimately concluded that:

> victims should not be a party or have a general right to participate in court during the criminal trial process. However, there are particular aspects of the criminal trial process in which victims can or should be able to participate.

In particular, submissions to the VLRC (2016: 145) included strong support for victim ILR that enables victims to access advice and information and to contest confidential communications applications:

> Victims need legal representation, independent of the prosecution, to ensure that they do not lose the right to protect their confidential communications in a situation where their interests conflict with the prosecution's. Sometimes prosecutors may be reluctant to oppose an application, even where the victim objects. Sexual assault counsellors told the Commission that conflicts between the interests of the prosecution and the victim can arise frequently.

Likewise, other participants in this research reflected upon the 'legitimate and necessary role for limited legal representation for victims in a variety of specific circumstances', including, for example, when private communications such as medical or sexual history is sought (Xavier, criminal justice professional). Chloe also suggested piloting ILR in order to distinguish 'which [stage] is worthy' and 'whether victims want to see a legal representative at such [a] stage'. She highlighted the potential for victim ILR at an appeal court, stating, 'I think it would be very important to have that [prospective] victim's legal representative there … [so the victim] understand[s] what is going on because it is very piecemeal'.

The victim-focused reforms operating in the three focus jurisdictions were also a focal point of discussion among the Victorian interviewees, and this helped to inform some of their responses when contemplating the feasibility of victim ILR within Victoria. For example, Georgia discussed the positive impact ILR could have during the cross-examination stage, similar to the reform operating in Ireland, as it could provide a degree of 'intervention … [into] any inappropriate, intrusive and digressive questioning'. She also considered the potential for limited representation during the plea negotiation stage, when the impact of the crime upon the victim is often neglected (see also Flynn 2012; Flynn & Freiberg 2017). Other participants suggested implementing a system of review similar to the VRR operating in England and Wales, and having victim ILR available in that process. As Natasha, a member of the Victorian judiciary, stated:

> I would see a very big role for [victim] representation here because you would want someone with legal knowledge to … say, 'Well, what about this? Have you looked at this? … Has this person been followed up?' I mean sometimes police procedure isn't that good, they might have been slack. A fresh eye wouldn't hurt at all and, in fact, I would have thought it would be very difficult for a complainant to have a meaningful review without representation – you would want someone really pushing them and demanding to see exactly what … [is going on] … I do think complainants should have a right to review and I do think it would be important for them [to have representation within that context]. I could imagine that, for many of them, it would be very difficult to undertake this exercise [seeking a review] without representation.

When the participants were asked to reflect upon which of the victim-focused reforms discussed would be justified or most viable in an adversarial setting like Victoria, some were not able to readily decide and concluded that all reforms could be effective. As David, a principal officer working within a national gender-based violence organisation, explained:

> Which is a better fruit, an apple or an orange? I mean they're different … We're very concerned about attrition and the right to review might help in attrition in a marginal way, but it's a different part of the procedure. If your case is not prosecuted, you will never get access to legal representation, so it is a case of apples and oranges. As an official, I'm always trying to analyse problems and I would never be balancing the two, saying will we give them one or the other? Well, you might. You might say, if both were on the table, 'Well we could get away with one but can't get away with the other – at the moment it's possible to do one, it's not possible to do another' – but I think both are desirable.

David's response highlights the inherent differences between the reforms. Having a system of review, such as the VRR, represents a provision for information, whereas providing ILR to victims constitutes a form of participation. This may mean that, while these reforms are not really comparable in terms of their objectives, they both still have the capacity to address key elements of victims' procedural justice needs. Thus, although both reforms may be desirable, they may not be equally justifiable within Victoria's adversarial legal system. In contemplating radical changes to adversarial systems, David emphasised that 'incremental change' in 'due course' is the approach usually taken by bureaucrats 'given the traditions surrounding courts' and the criminal justice process generally. Bearing that in mind, Xavier, a criminal justice professional, claimed that 'the adversarial system is … not frozen in time. It evolves with changing social attitudes'. James similarly stated that 'innovation', and its 'capacity to adapt over a period of time', is one of the key features of the common law itself. Within this context, Victoria's legal community may be more willing to accommodate an incremental step reform (such as the VRR) than ILR for victims, as it would not have as significant an impact on the way the adversarial system operates. The potential for a VRR-style reform to be introduced within Victoria will be discussed at more length later in this chapter following the discussion below on the potential limitations of ILR for sexual assault victims.

The limitations of ILR for sexual assault victims

Nine of the 24 participants did not support the introduction of ILR for sexual assault victims, arguing that it would not be compatible within an adversarial setting. The participants who opposed ILR cited the structure of the adversarial system, which has not traditionally accommodated victim participation rights in the form of ILR, and argued that ILR would undermine the core adversarial principles upon which the system is based. In particular, three key limitations of ILR emerged from the data. First, adding a 'third player' was considered to impact the 'equality of arms', thereby undermining the traditional operation of the adversarial system and potentially duplicating the role of the prosecutor. Second, the question of who would fund victim ILR was commonly asked, and in a system already lacking in funds and resources, many participants claimed that securing funding for ILR would be difficult. And, finally, the likely withdrawal or reduction of state-based victim support services was identified as a potentially negative consequence of introducing ILR because the victim's legal representative could be seen as duplicating some of the support offered by the state. For these reasons, and as addressed more extensively in the subsequent sections, some participants were not supportive of ILR in any capacity.

Problems with adding a 'third player'

One of the key limitations that arose in the data in relation to the prospect of ILR for sexual assault victims was the notion that it would disrupt the equality of arms and unbalance the criminal justice system. As David, a principal officer working within a national gender-based violence organisation, stated, victim ILR in a common law system:

> would upset the equality of arms … [it would be] unbalanced because there would be two sets of counsel against him [sic] [the defendant] … It would be the state's legal team prosecuting and … the victim's legal team who would want prosecution as well … It would be a re-engineering of the adversarial system, and while that may be very desirable from the point of view of the victim, it will be a very radical step and extremely difficult to bring into being … You have got to look at the unintended consequences and the unforeseen. Cases might become much longer and more contentious … which would be counter to the interests of the victim.

Xavier, a criminal justice professional, similarly stated, 'across the board or general trial … you would have a third wheel. It just wouldn't work'. The creation of what would essentially be a third party to proceedings was thus perceived as unfairly disadvantaging the accused by having both the prosecution and representation for the victim. In this regard, Adelle, a policy researcher working within a victim support organisation, explained:

> Part of the reason why we are even interested in it [ILR for sexual assault victims] … is that victims often are dissatisfied by the fact that the defendant does have their lawyer and obviously the victim doesn't. So the victim already feels that there is an imbalance … [but by] … giving them a lawyer as well … it might be seen that they have two lawyers on their side and one for the defence.

Likewise, Georgia observed:

> It could raise expectations unnecessarily … most victims don't understand the system … it's a very complex system, there's no reason why they

> should be expected to understand it, but they will find it very difficult to understand the different roles which are being played. So they might actually believe that they have got two lawyers prosecuting for them … [and] it might seem that that power imbalance has actually gone the other way now, in their eyes.

This issue was also identified by the VLRC (2016: 121), which stated that 'a new legal service might inflate expectations about what independent lawyers can achieve for victims in circumstances where they have no substantive rights'. Along similar lines, Sean, a member of the Victorian judiciary, argued that, by 'making it a three-way contest … when you get three legal representatives in the one situation, the level of complication is tripled'. According to these views, adding another legal player might actually further complicate the process for sexual assault victims, which could be counteractive in meeting their needs and expectations with regard to the legal process.

The impact on the due process rights of the accused

The participants also drew attention to the ways in which the potential power imbalance produced by the introduction of ILR could unduly impact upon an accused's due process rights to a fair trial. As Julie, a criminal justice professional, observed:

> Giving victims an incredibly active role through a lawyer … changes the balance and we know that most accused people can't afford representation themselves, let alone representation from legal aid, and to be faced with two prosecutors just tips that balance even further.

Kate, a managing lawyer in the CPS, also raised the potential for 'vengeful' victims imposing their 'punitive' views upon offenders if victims were to be given ILR:

> I've got no problem with people instructing lawyers but a victim doesn't have any legal right in the criminal process because we don't allow any sort of revenge. It has to be independent and it's the state taking over and saying that behaviour is unacceptable.

In contrast, however, James argued that:

> There is nowhere in any of the literature that … demonstrates in inquisitorial systems where victims do have their own legal standing, that the outcome is any less fair, or that the offenders are treated less justly [or] that there are more violations of their rights … I firmly believe that you can have a parallel system of justice [in an adversarial process] … imagin[e] … two tram lines running parallel to one another … there are things that we

> can do to make the journey for the victim a better, legally, justly speaking, experience and that doesn't require us to unduly impact on the rights of the other person [the defendant].

Other participants held similar views to James insofar as they believed that ILR would not imbalance an adversarial system or impact negatively on the rights of the accused. As Chloe claimed:

> If you're looking at a victim's advocate with practised directions and would only get involved to a degree, [it] wouldn't have an imbalance such that it would be outweighing [the rights of the accused] … [The prosecution] doesn't represent the victim, it represents the state … The victim's advocate would represent the victim … They [the victim's advocate] could be the team player to build the relationship [with the victim]. This would encourage more victims coming to court to give evidence. I have to say I think the professionals would go against it, but I think victims' advocates would have a role to play [in the prosecution process].

Chloe's views suggest that there could be scope for ILR for sexual assault victims, even in a limited context, without infringing upon the rights of the accused. Chloe argued that a victim representative would hold a very significant place in the criminal justice system as they could help to address the perceived gap between victims' rights and offenders' rights, which is exacerbated by the fact that the prosecution does not formally represent the victim. The problem remains, however, of how to fairly test the victim's accusation in a way that upholds the accused person's right to cross-examine the victim in support of their defence. Considering that a fundamental feature of the adversarial criminal trial involves the capacity for an accused to defend themselves against a criminal charge by cross-examining prosecution witnesses, then a victim's access to ILR may not necessarily limit potentially harmful questioning. Yet ILR may counteract the degree to which the defence are given licence to such questioning.

Duplicating the role of the prosecutor?

Some participants raised concerns around a victim representative potentially duplicating the role of the prosecutor, and as a consequence could not foresee a legitimate role for ILR. Sean, a member of the Victorian judiciary, questioned what sort of role a victim representative would have if they were to become involved in the trial process because 'they can't be objecting in terms of cross-examination – that's a prosecutor's role'. Adelle, a policy researcher working within a victim support organisation, also expressed concern about the victim representative's role:

> It would be hard to see quite where they fitted in. What are they actually doing in the system we have which isn't designed for that role? … There

> would be overlaps [between the victim representative and the prosecutor] and then what if there's conflict between the victim's lawyer and the state prosecutor?

The potential for duplication between a prosecutor and victim representative could also lead to what Bianca, a manager working within a victim support agency, described as a 'lack of clarity of [their] roles'. In this regard, Robert, a manager of a WAS, questioned from whom the victim's lawyer would be taking instructions. He maintained that, inevitably, the victim's lawyer would be obliged to take instructions from the victim, 'regardless of whether they think that's a good idea or not' (Robert).

Establishing ILR for sexual assault victims may also 'remove the incentive for prosecution lawyers to communicate regularly and effectively with victims' (VLRC 2016: 121). Yet victims report wanting to feel included, informed and supported throughout the process (VLRC 2016: 121). There are already obligations on the police, the Office of Public Prosecutions (OPP) and victim service agencies to address the needs of victims in this regard. And the VLRC (2016: 121) states that if such obligations are complied with, there is no perceived need to place a 'burden on victims to obtain legal assistance'. Many victims also do not want to deal with another agency and lawyer (VLRC 2016: 121). In this regard, if prosecutors regularly met their statutory obligations to victims in accordance with the *Victims' Charter Act 2006* (Vic), the perceived need for ILR may be less relevant.

Overall, the participants raised concerns relating to the equality of arms and the traditional operation of the adversarial system, which made them reluctant to consider the introduction of victim ILR throughout the trial. However, despite this resistance, some participants were more supportive of the possible introduction of victim ILR during pre-trial processes associated with defence applications for the discovery of private communications or sexual history evidence, as explored later in this chapter.

Funding ILR

Another key limitation emerging from the data revolved around the issue of securing funding for ILR for sexual assault victims. Some participants raised their concern over who would be able to fund victim ILR, particularly in a period of fiscal restraint during which there have been extensive cuts to funding legal aid for accused people (see, for example, Flynn & Hodgson 2017). Reductions in funding legal aid for both users and providers are notable in Flynn and Hodgson's (2017) edited collection, *Access to Justice and Legal Aid: Comparative Perspectives on Unmet Legal Need*. In England and Wales, for example, Flynn and Hodgson (2017: 2) observe a gradual 'de-investment in legal aid … since the mid-2000s', with 'the most devastating cuts [occurring] … in 2013 following the introduction of the *Legal Aid, Sentencing and Punishment of Offenders Act 2012* (LASPO)'. LASPO was aimed at reducing the legal aid budget by £350 million (AU$615 million) (Flynn & Hodgson 2017: 2). To highlight the extent of the impacts, data by the Ministry of Justice indicates that, after the introduction of LASPO, 62 per cent of individuals 'entitled to access legal aid in 2012 were no longer entitled to access that same assistance in 2013' (Howard 2014 cited in Flynn & Hodgson 2017: 2).

In Australia, there have been similar trends in reducing legal aid assistance. For example, the federal budget cut 'AU$6 million … from community legal centres, AU$15 million … from legal aid commissions, and AU$43 million … from advocacy services over a four-year period [2014–17]' (Flynn & Hodgson 2017: 4). These cuts have impacted services that provided legal assistance to some of the most disadvantaged accused people, such as those with Indigenous Australian and Torres Strait Islander backgrounds (Flynn & Hodgson 2017: 4). This situation presents a significant limitation to the possibility of introducing ILR for sexual assault victims in that 'resourcing equitable access [to ILR] is difficult to justify when victims are not a party to proceedings' (VLRC 2016: 121).

The participants argued that careful consideration would be required when contemplating such a reform, in light of the cost implications for the criminal justice system and potentially for victims. Xavier, a criminal justice professional, drew attention to the financial implications, noting that 'the logistics of how it [ILR] is to be secured, particularly in a time of fiscal restraint and austerity, are not straightforward'. Given such financial constraints, Mark, a criminal justice support officer, proposed that if victim ILR were to be introduced, '[it] would have to be for an identified group of victims that need this service the most'. Kate, a managing lawyer in the CPS, also claimed:

> What lies behind [the introduction of ILR] is obviously finance … In this country, they are cutting back legal aid for defendants, so there's no prospect of any public money being made available for victims … In that case, you would have [a situation which meant that] … if you have got the money, you could afford a lawyer as a victim, and if you haven't got the money then you can't, and I think that is very, very wrong in a justice system … that's a very dangerous road to go down.

Similarly, Robert, a manager of a WAS, stated:

> If the state is there representing the state, the state is not going to fund (I don't think) an independent lawyer … that is someone you pay for … The other aspects that bother me a little bit about that is, what does it mean to run a criminal jurisdiction like a civil jurisdiction? … I would feel worried that if we start to run a criminal jurisdiction like a civil jurisdiction, which is user pays, that means that those [who] can afford independent [legal] representation get far better outcomes than those who can't.

Julie, a criminal justice professional, expanded on Kate's and Robert's views, arguing that 'while it [ILR] might on the face of it sound empowering, I think it has the real potential to say that there are different classes of victims'. In explaining her view, Julie drew attention to the impacts the introduction of ILR may have on women who are economically dependent or disadvantaged compared to women who are financially stable, and discussed whether a means- or merits-based test would be applicable for public funding. This points to another potential limitation of restricting ILR to sexual assault victims, in that other vulnerable victims would not then have access to the same support. This could create the perception of a 'hierarchy of victimisation' (Carrabine et al. 2004; see also Iliadis, Fitz-Gibbon & Walklate 2019), whereby the experiences of some victims are taken more seriously than others. At the same time, considering the difficulties around securing funding, 'it would be difficult to resource a service so that *all* victims who expect to access legal advice and assistance do so' (VLRC 2016: 121, emphasis added).

In contrast, the participants who did not identify funding as an issue argued that 'it [a lack of funding] is not an excuse' to avoid administering justice fairly, citing the need to balance the triangulation of interests (Xavier, criminal justice professional). Chloe, a leading victims' rights authority, similarly claimed:

> We are not making a special law for a victim; we are making a balanced law that has an offender's rights [considered] as well as a victim's rights ... There is an argument [for ILR for sexual assault victims] and it's a very important stage here ... If you look at defendants' rights, there is legal representation ... and we need to look at placing that in the same line [for victims] ... I would argue ... there is funding available. We have to look at the legal aid system to make it better to protect everyone who is vulnerable ... We have got to make sure they [victims] are represented because the cost to the state ... if a [victim requires] health [services], housing [and other essential needs in the aftermath of the crime, could ultimately] ... outweigh the cost of giving them an advocate to protect them. It's part of their rehabilitation ... I think it's going to be quite challenging [securing victim ILR], and one that I'm prepared to challenge for victims.

Chloe's argument reflects a cost-benefit analysis – although victim ILR would be a greater financial investment initially, the potential benefits of its introduction could extend to a reduction in demand for state services, thereby lowering the long-term costs to the state. Chloe also highlighted the potential benefits of this for a victim's recovery, as well as increasing the likelihood of victims reporting satisfaction with the criminal justice system.

Withdrawal of state support services

The third key limitation that arose in the data relates to the potential withdrawal of state support services if ILR were to be introduced for sexual assault victims. This was identified as a key concern by Robert, a manager of a WAS, who argued that providing ILR for sexual assault victims (or victims more generally) would diminish the need for victim services provided by the state, such as the WAS in the OPP.[1] Robert cited an example in which ILR was provided by the SACVR to a family in a homicide case because the primary victim's family[2] felt that the prosecution was not thoroughly representing their rights and interests. As a result of the imposition of victim ILR in this case, the WAS and social work services withdrew their support to the victims, in order to avoid interfering with the support and advice provided by the victim representative. In discussing the impacts of this, Robert explained:

> I'm not suggesting that that's a reason not to have independent [legal] representation, but I think what you actually encourage, potentially, is that states withdraw from procedural support and also from the other kinds of support [mechanisms] that [are offered to] victims … I think part of people's satisfaction with the justice system … [relates to] … not only … the outcome, but … the procedure … Independent lawyers might have more influenc[e] [over] the outcome … but I'm not convinced that they will have good procedural support. I'm not sure they're trained, and they don't have a set of support structures to provide good, grounded, ongoing emotional and practical [support] … that a state must provide as part of public service.

Victim ILR could therefore impact upon the state's willingness to provide and fund support services to victims. Indeed, this was evident in the VLRC's (2016) latest report when it made reference to existing victim support agencies that provide general and tailored procedural information and support, such as the OPP WAS, Child Witness Service, Victims Assistance Program providers, Centres Against Sexual Assault and Victoria Police.[3] The VLRC (2016: 121) claimed that there is no need for victim ILR and that any additional funding targeting victims would be better placed within the state's existing support services. However, these views strongly contrast with the literature examining sexual assault victims' needs from and experiences of the criminal justice process, which suggests that state-based procedural supports do not consistently meet victims' procedural justice needs (Clark 2010; VLRC 2001, 2003, 2004). This then leads to victims wanting to pursue alternate support mechanisms, in order for their interests and rights to be upheld.

Other participants supported the notion that if the prosecution and state-based services were operating as they should, there would be no need for ILR for sexual assault victims. Olivia, a policy advisor within a victim support organisation, argued that 'if prosecutors spoke to victims and did their bit, rather than seeing themselves as [solely] agents of the Crown … then I don't see the need for it [victim ILR]'.

Sophie, a victims' rights advocate and campaigner, agreed with this view, and believed that this could avoid the resourcing issue arising from having to 'stick another layer of fixing things on top' of what already appears to be a convoluted system. Her comment relates to this issue as being more about the 'quality' of the state's existing services than about seeking alternate avenues of support, such as ILR, for sexual assault victims. She argued that a shift to victim ILR could create the perception that victim-focused reforms are a 'tick-box' exercise, and that this could further delay what she perceives as the changes needed in the existing state mechanisms aimed at improving victims' procedural justice experiences. This observation raises pertinent points for consideration as it questions whether the perceived need for victim ILR arises from the inadequacy of current mechanisms, processes and reforms designed to protect and uphold victims' rights and to meet victims' needs, or whether ILR is a necessary part of cultural change by way of reconceptualising and enhancing the role of sexual assault victims within Victoria's criminal justice process.

The aforementioned limitations therefore suggest that careful consideration is needed in contemplating a reform such as victim ILR, which has not traditionally been utilised in adversarial systems. Even where the participants saw the potential benefits of ILR for sexual assault victims' procedural justice experiences, many perceived the limitations as ultimately outweighing these benefits.

Could reforms similar to those in the focus jurisdictions enhance victims' rights in Victoria?

VRR

The VRR has provided a platform for victim recognition within an adversarial criminal justice process in which the interests of the state have traditionally overridden those of victims. The participants from all interview locations saw value in the VRR from the point of view of both the criminal justice system and the victim. It was identified as providing a way to ensure accountability and transparency in prosecutorial discretion, as well as improving the consistency of such decision-making. It also allows the prosecution to identify what they are doing well, so that they can continue to maintain good practice.

In describing how the VRR enhances a victim's status, Sophie, a victims' rights advocate and campaigner, claimed that, 'from a police and crime commissioner's perspective, this is all about the general move towards giving victims a greater voice throughout the process'. Similarly, Emily, a sexual assault clinical lead counsellor, observed that the VRR is 'really important because it has given them [victims] the opportunity to say, "I am not happy with your decision, I want you to think again" '. In reflecting on whether the VRR is a positive reform for victims, Chloe, a leading victims' rights authority, commented:

> I welcome the CPS doing this VRR. I think it's really important for victims to have … questions answered for them because when there is a prosecution, they are … not closely involved because they [the CPS] don't represent the victims, they represent the state. So I think it's a very important initiative the CPS did and I welcome the opportunity for victims

> to [use the VRR]. Speaking to some victims, they have managed to get … a conviction in court, which wouldn't have happened without the VRR, so I think it's a … very important stage for victims' rights.

This comment demonstrates that the theoretical underpinnings and practical application of the VRR carry great significance as the reform has increased victims' rights in ways unprecedented in other common law jurisdictions.

Despite the shortcomings of the reform, as discussed in Chapter 4, the participants from all interview locations identified value in introducing a VRR-style reform in other common law jurisdictions. In particular, the participant responses drew upon procedural justice elements when explaining why the VRR would benefit victims in other adversarial systems. For example, Chloe stated:

> I think in any country it's welcoming because it's victims' rights … I do think that victims should have a right in any country to be represented [and] to have a voice, so I would welcome that because there could be miscarriages of justice for victims.

Some participants believed that there would be scope for a VRR-style reform in other common law jurisdictions provided that the criminal justice systems therein operated in a similar way to that of England and Wales. Participants also saw value in a VRR on the basis that it would provide external support mechanisms to help victims through the criminal justice process. For example, Olivia, a policy advisor within a victim support organisation, argued that even in jurisdictions where there are gaps in the system in terms of responding to victims' specific needs, the VRR 'aims to bridge a lot of those gaps through increasing the communication [and] making sure victims fully understand what their rights are'. She further claimed that a VRR needs to be accompanied by other support systems that guide victims through the criminal justice process. Olivia explained that, without specialist support in place, a potential issue arising from the introduction of a VRR in other common law jurisdictions would be that victims could become revictimised by the process were they to request a review on the basis of unrealistic expectations.

Another potential issue related to introducing a VRR in a common law jurisdiction like Victoria is that it may be used as a solution to the lack of communication and transparency for victims (Olivia, policy advisor, victim support organisation). Olivia hypothesised that if there were a criminal justice system with adequate support services in place and prosecutors who were trained to specialise in sexual assault cases, then there ought not to be a need for a review system. In this sense, Olivia expressed concern that a VRR could be seen and used as a 'sticking plaster' for much broader systemic issues inherent to the criminal justice system.

In reflecting on whether there is scope for a VRR in other common law systems, including Victoria's, some participants from England and Wales cited the VRR's limitations. For example, Emily, a sexual assault clinical lead counsellor, claimed that 'if it worked as it should, yes, because any additional opportunity for a victim to have their voice heard would be worthwhile, but it needs fine-tuning [and] it needs to be more than a paper exercise in my opinion'. Eva, a rape crisis support worker, argued that a VRR would be viable in other common law jurisdictions 'as long as the reviewer is independent', as this would make the process sufficiently transparent and accountable. Interestingly, however, the RCIRCSA (2017: 105) final report recommended that:

- Each Australian Director of Public Prosecutions should establish a robust and effective formalised complaints mechanism to allow victims to seek an internal merits review of key decisions;
- Each Australian Director of Public Prosecutions should establish robust and effective audit processes to audit their compliance with policies for decision-making and consultation with victims and police; and
- Each Australian Director of Public Prosecutions should publish the existence of their complaints mechanism and internal audit processes and data on their use and outcomes online and in their annual reports.

This recommendation is supported by the VLRC (2016: 74), which proposed that the state government consider 'establish[ing] a right for victims to seek internal review of a decision by the Director of Public Prosecutions to discontinue a prosecution or to proceed with a guilty plea to lesser charges'.

While there thus appears to be significant support for the introduction of a VRR-style scheme in Australian jurisdictions, Iliadis and Flynn (2019: 30) argue that if such a reform were to be introduced, 'there is strong[er] merit in having an external system independent of the prosecution offices – much like Victoria's Independent Broad-Based Anti-Corruption Commission, which operates for allegations of police misconduct'. Iliadis and Flynn (2019: 30) also note that care would need to be taken to avoid the potential shortcomings, such as those evident in England and Wales (as discussed in Chapter 4). Indeed, Iliadis and Flynn (2019: 30) suggest that an external review has 'greater potential to unpick gaps in decision-making processes, to create public confidence and better recognise the needs and interests of victims who wish to challenge the "justice" they receive'.

VRR: a move towards ILR?

The VRR reform in England and Wales is significant as it gives victims the opportunity to pursue and challenge prosecutorial decision-making in cases where they believe that the wrong decision has been made. While technically constituting a provision for information, it also enables victims to feel more involved in the process.

When the participants across all jurisdictions were asked to consider whether the VRR represents a movement towards ILR for victims, many drew attention to the structure of the adversarial system, which does not traditionally accommodate victim interests (see Chapter 2), and therefore renders the notion of ILR for victims problematic. For example, Chloe, a leading victims' rights authority, spoke of the notable differences between the VRR and ILR, arguing that:

> It's still part of the CPS, it's a scheme that's available for victims but they [the CPS] don't work for the victims ... they work for the Director of Public Prosecutions ... While it says the 'Victims' Right to Review', it's an access to get information ... It is a formula that is based on the ... management of the CPS ... It's opening up that communication for victims, but it's still very much in the environment [and] in the establishment of the CPS.

Georgia, a policy researcher working within a victim support organisation, similarly maintained that the VRR resembles 'a slight shift' towards 'restoring the balance', but that adversarial systems are still a 'long way off with a thing like ... [ILR]'. She further explained that 'the victim is still very much marginalised within the system – they are still considered a witness in the case by definition', and claimed that the 'whole language and ... approach ... would have to change to [that of] a civil jurisdiction in order to achieve that [ILR for victims]'. Adelle, a policy researcher working within a victim support organisation, reflected that, 'I wouldn't say it would never happen', but she did not identify ILR as a feasible option within the current constraints of the adversarial system.

Other participants completely rejected the idea of the VRR constituting a step towards ILR for victims, arguing that victims should not be allowed to actively participate in decision-making through ILR and that having a VRR is an adequate mechanisms for determining whether a decision is right or wrong (Kate, managing lawyer, CPS).

However, while some participants could see the benefits of a VRR-style reform, they also argued that the VRR has not gone far enough in addressing victims' procedural justice needs:

> To get equal balance would [be to] have a victim's advocate that works purely for the victim and applies to the CPS to look at the case if there is legal imbalance ... It [the VRR] is the right approach for a victim to get an answer to something they didn't understand in the courtroom, [but] ... we need that conduit that speaks for the victim ... somebody that they build a relationship up [with], because they don't build a relationship up with the CPS ... they have no relationship [with the CPS]. They [the CPS] are just asking questions, whereas that victim's advocate speaks for the victim and works for the victim ... [a] victim's lawyer ... will be tremendous for victims.
>
> (Chloe, leading victims' right authority)

While Chloe identified value in the VRR, she argued that, for a triangulation of interests to be truly acknowledged, ILR is needed so that victims can feel that their interests are being taken into account. Eva, a rape crisis support worker, similarly explained:

> The feedback from the ISVAs [Independent Sexual Violence Advisors] here said, 'In our experience, victims do not feel this is a step towards legal representation, but victims would welcome any steps that may provide access to legal representation, for example, [to] challeng[e] [a] victim's sexual history [evidence] being disclosed in court'.

Based on the participants' responses, the VRR reform can be seen as a significant step towards enhancing victims' rights in an adversarial system. However, none of the participants were of the opinion that the VRR signifies a necessary shift in the direction of ILR. Thus, although the VRR offers greater inclusivity of victims and thereby to some extent meets victims' procedural justice needs, the participants did not believe that the logical progression from a VRR is the implementation of ILR.

Separate legal representation for sexual assault victims

Many participants supported introducing ILR for sexual assault victims in Victoria in a restricted way, similar to the reform operating in Ireland. David, a principal officer working within a national gender-based violence organisation, stated that it should be 'seriously considered because it … [has] a very strong benefit for the victim in a very difficult case'. Other participants similarly identified a place for such a reform in Victoria, arguing that it could empower victims in circumstances where the defence attempts to discredit the victim's character by drawing upon outdated myths and stereotypes about sexual assault. As James, a leading victims' rights advocate, maintained, the introduction of this reform in Victoria would be:

> A very important step, particularly for women as victims who already often are in a position of disempowerment as a consequence of the broader structures in our community. So, I think it's a wonderful counterweight for notions of patriarchy that not only pervade our society as a whole, but also in our legal justice system because of the dominance of men in prominent positions. But, most importantly, it helps empower the victim and puts her (because most of the cases have involved a 'her') into a position where they can feel for … once that they have some genuine voice, and I think that's really important. And it is also important for one other thing, and that is that so often when matters involving sex offences go to trial, the primary method for defence involves two facets: that is, trying to demonstrate that the victim has a motivation for making up the story, and … try[ing to] destroy the victim's character by making a whole range of suggestions … There has to be some way of helping the victim navigate that quite horrible experience, and prosecution has shown consistently a reluctance to do it.

While some participants cited the benefits of such a reform in Victoria, one participant argued that:

> In Victoria, there's a pretty strict legislative test before previous sexual history of a complainant [can be admitted] … I'm not sure that having a victim representative to argue [against] it, if you've [already] got a tight enough legislative framework, is necessary.
>
> (Simone, member of the Victorian judiciary)

Simone further claimed that 'you'd hope that, in an ideal world, that is actually what the prosecution should be doing [opposing the defence's attempts to submit the victim's sexual history as evidence], and that the legislative criteria for restricting the right to use it … should be sufficient'.[4] Several participants also noted that, in Victoria, the judge already has the capacity to restrict the admission of sexual history evidence in exceptional circumstances. Because of this, David (principal officer working within a national gender-based violence organisation) asserted that it would be 'counterproductive to bring in Victorian legislation' that introduces ILR. However, several participants argued that the cultural factors embedded within the criminal justice system mean that prosecutors do not consistently uphold victim interests by opposing the inclusion of such evidence. In this regard, Simone acknowledged that 'there could be a role for a victim representative' in this context.

Legal representation by a Commissioner for Victims' Rights

The participants were asked to consider the prospect of enhancing the powers of the Victorian VoCC in line with those of the SACVR. In contemplating this, Robert (manager, WAS) reflected on the limited rights of victims and how the SACVR offers support in this context:

> [The South Australian Commissioner] provides victims with an avenue to address their concerns, issues, grievances, their need to change the law … He [sic] can have a good insight into policy and practice … of a prosecution office and about where that works for victims and where it doesn't. Some states don't have any of that … So, in some ways … he [sic] is … a very good public voice … who provides lots of practical financial assistance and other assistance to victims to make sure their rights are [upheld] … Certainly I think other states [outside South Australia] have far less than we have as a state in relation to a Commissioner of Victims' Rights.

In this way, Robert identified the potential benefits of extending the VoCC's powers to align with those of the SACVR. Although Victims of Crime Commissioners are currently constituted across all Australian jurisdictions except for the Northern Territory, Queensland and Tasmania, as discussed in Chapter 6, the SACVR's powers are far greater in scope (see also Kirchengast, Iliadis & O'Connell 2019).

This comparison is notable with Victoria, where the VoCC was appointed for the first time in October 2014. As stated under section 13(1) of the *Victims of Crime Commissioner Act 2015* (Vic), the VoCC has the following functions:

a to advocate for the recognition, inclusion, participation and respect of victims of crime by government departments, bodies responsible for conducting public prosecutions and Victoria Police

b to carry out inquiries on systemic victim of crime matters

c to report to the Attorney-General on any systemic victim of crime matter and

d to provide advice to the Attorney-General and government departments and agencies regarding improvements to the justice system to meet the needs of victims of crime.

A comparison between the functions of the SACVR and the VoCC reveals that both bear responsibility for advocating victims' rights and interests, and making recommendations on how victims' concerns can be addressed. The VoCC, however, primarily undertakes investigatory and advisory work, whereas the SACVR has a far more active role, including intervening and participating in cases at various stages of the prosecution process. Recently, however, the VLRC (2016: xxii) recommended that the VoCC should be:

- Empowered to review the outcome of complaints regarding compliance by investigatory, prosecuting and victims' services agencies with the *Victims' Charter Act 2006* (Vic) principles, on application by the complainant, if the complainant is not satisfied with the agency's response to the complainant; and
- Required to report annually to Parliament on the implementation of the *Victims' Charter Act 2006* (Vic) by all investigatory, prosecuting and victims' services agencies, including information about the number of complaints made and processed about compliance with the *Victims' Charter* principles.

Other changes to the VoCC role were also recommended by the VLRC (2016) that may arguably help to make victims' rights enforceable. In reflecting on the potential benefits of enhancing the VoCC's powers in line with those of the SACVR, some participants saw immediate benefits, while others highlighted certain limitations. The primary limitation involved resources, which is indeed a key problem in South Australia in relation to funding for the SACVR. Considering the South Australian experience, James, a leading victims' rights advocate, explained that:

> [The Commissioner is] constrained by the resources more so in many ways … than by the law. So, I would argue that not only does … the Commissioner in Victoria need to have the … authority … but [also] needs to have the adequate resources to be able to do it.

James also pointed to the adverse reactions that might arise from Victoria's legal community were the VoCC to be granted the power to appoint ILR because, 'if Victoria tries to go from (a) to (c) without taking a step in the middle, … there will be a great deal of opposition'. Similar views were expressed by some other participants, who stressed the need for incremental change as opposed to overly ambitious reforms within the criminal justice system.

Notwithstanding the benefits arising from the SACVR's powers, James questioned whether the functions of this role represent the most appropriate remedy for the disempowerment victims experience within the adversarial system. In particular, he raised this in relation to the Commissioner's core objective, which is to seek procedural justice for victims:

> I passionately believe that there should be greater clarity about the victim actually having their own standing in criminal proceedings, and if a court objective is to assist the victim to regain control and to allow them to be actively engaged in decision-making that affects them, then there is a strong argument that it should be they have the right [to ILR] in the first place and a Commissioner is a person you go to when your right is not being upheld. At the moment in South Australia, it tends to be the Commissioner having the priority and the victim being able to sort of follow on the shirt tail of the Commissioner, and I am not sure whether that ultimately achieves the ongoing objective that … [the Commissioner] has, which is about procedural justice for the victim … I think that can be achieved by sort of tilting it that way. I suspect that it's a process of evolution.

This comment suggests that, although the SACVR's powers are influential, and may contribute to positive procedural outcomes for victims, they have not enhanced or altered the structural position of victims within the adversarial system. As Julie, a criminal justice professional, explained,

> whilst the [South Australian] Victims of Crime Commissioner can access funding to give victims a lawyer, he [sic] still has to rely on either common law principles or what exists in the legislation for the victim's lawyers to have standing.

This acts as a reminder that victims continue to occupy the same position within the adversarial system – as witnesses to proceedings. It also reinforces the fact that it is the Commissioner who is afforded additional rights, not the victim.

There is no doubt that South Australia has taken a significant step through the establishment of the SACVR to improve formal responses to victims in the adversarial system, particularly as the Commissioner has the capacity to offer ILR in some circumstances. Indeed, the established Office of the SACVR provides an expansion of representative rights to victims. Arguably, as illustrated by the participants' observations, the right to victim ILR might best proceed through an independent Office of Commissioner for Victims' Rights in order to simultaneously meet the needs of victims while having regard to the due process rights of the accused and prosecution interests of the state. Within the Victorian context, housing such powers and reforms within the VoCC's Office may help to ensure a measured response to victims that limits their private access to the criminal trial, yet extends their ability to participate in proceedings. However, changes to the VoCC's role do not come without their limitations, and, as noted by the participants in this research, if the VoCC's powers are to be enhanced, it will be vital to also increase the resources available to them. Enhancing the powers of the VoCC in Victoria would also not grant victims 'party' status in a criminal court, but it would provide a remedy that goes some way towards meeting victims' participatory and procedural justice needs.

Concluding remarks

This chapter explored the prospect of introducing ILR for sexual assault victims in Victoria's adversarial system, by examining the potential benefits and limitations that emerged from the interview data. Based on an analysis of the participants' responses that supported the idea of ILR for sexual assault victims, varied opinions were evident in relation to the stages of the legal process for which ILR would be appropriate. While some participants argued that it would be feasible to include ILR throughout the entire process, others argued that ILR would only be likely to empower victims at certain stages of the process – for example, to restrict the introduction of private communications such as medical or counselling records, or of prior sexual history as evidence. According to the data, victim ILR would also be less contested if the representation were limited, preferably to the pre-trial stage, rather than provided throughout the entire prosecution process as this may unduly complicate the trial process. Some participants also supported the introduction of a system of review, similar to the VRR reform operating in England and Wales, and having ILR operate only as part of such a review process.

The main objections to ILR that emerged in the data related to the idea of an equality of arms within the adversarial process, as the participants argued that ILR may create the perception that there are two lawyers prosecuting for the victim – the state prosecutor and the victim's representative. Concerns also arose around the potential for ILR to interfere with the due process rights of the accused. In addition, the participants highlighted fiscal constraints, arguing that there would be great difficulty funding ILR for victims in a period that has already seen significant cuts to legal aid funding for accused people. Furthermore, some participants highlighted the potential for a withdrawal of assistance via state-based services if victims were to be independently represented. These participants maintained the view that the state already provides quality procedural support to victims, for example, through the WAS division of the OPP and various state-funded victim support groups, which ILR would not be able to offer. The various potential benefits and limitations of ILR suggest that there may be scope for consideration of this reform, albeit it within a limited capacity.

The chapter also considered whether there is scope to introduce reforms in Victoria that are similar to any of the three reforms operating in the focus jurisdictions, taking into account the potential implications for Victoria's adversarial system. Of the three reforms, the data indicates that the greater potential for positive impacts would arise from a VRR-style reform. Significantly, a VRR-style reform would not interfere with the adversarial principles of the Victorian legal system, according to the participants. And if it were carefully planned, it could help to improve victims' procedural justice experiences. While the participants expressed marked support for introducing a system of review in Victoria, it appears that there may be stronger merit in an external system of review in order to avoid the criticisms raised in relation to the VRR in England and Wales.

Finally, the VRR was not considered to be part of a general shift towards the introduction of ILR. Instead, the participants understood the VRR to be more about the provision of information than about active victim participation. In this regard, introduction of a VRR-style reform was not considered to mark a radical change to the victim's role in an adversarial process, and instead was seen as an 'incremental step' towards integrating victims' needs. Accordingly, this chapter found that, at the present time, a VRR-style reform appears to be the most viable reform to introduce in Victoria – a finding supported by the VLRC (2016) and the RCIRCSA (2017). And if ILR were to be introduced, it would need to be within a defined and limited context, such as is available to victims in Ireland or through the SACVR, to ensure that the fundamental principles underpinning the adversarial system are maintained.

Notes

1 The WAS 'supports victims and witnesses of serious crime through the court process' (OPP 2017). This includes the provision of information relating to the prosecution process, case progress and specialist support services. The WAS is part of the Victims Strategy and Services Directorate of the OPP (OPP 2017).

2 According to the Victims of Crime Assistance Tribunal ([VOCAT] 2016), 'a primary victim is a person who is injured or dies' as a result of a violent crime. The family of the deceased victim are considered to be 'related victims'.

3 The Child Witness Service 'is a specialist service for children and young people who are witnesses in criminal proceedings' (OPP 2017). Its services include the provision of psychologists and social workers who provide tailored support and information to children and their families during the prosecution process (OPP 2017). The Centres Against Sexual Assault provide information to victim/survivors about their legal rights and the services available to them, as well as counselling support (CASA House 2010).

4 Questions pertaining to a victim's sexual history or experience are restricted in all Australian jurisdictions, including within Victoria. See, for example, *Crimes Act 1914* (Cth) ss 15YB–15YC; *Criminal Procedure Act 2009 (Vic)* ss 343–345, 352.

8 Concluding comments

Introduction

> 'What do we want? Incremental change. When do we want it? In due course'. That's the kind of way that bureaucrats see things, incremental change ... Given the traditions surrounding courts ... you do need to take incremental steps ... It could be counter-productive to come in with ... [a] very draconian ... approach.
>
> (David, principal officer working within a national gender-based violence organisation)

> Reforms of criminal laws and procedures concerning sexual assault remain vital but insufficient. They have an important symbolic value but are likely to be limited in effectiveness ... One source of the failings of law reform efforts to date has been the resilience of cultural mythologies about women and sexuality.
>
> (Stubbs 2003: 23)

The late 20th and early 21st centuries have witnessed a shift towards increased consideration of the rights, status and treatment of victims of sexual violence in adversarial justice systems. In 2001, Lord Steyn stated:

> The purpose of the criminal law is to permit everyone to go about their daily lives without fear of harm to person or property. And it is in the interests of everyone that serious crime should be effectively investigated and prosecuted. There must be fairness to all sides. In a criminal case, this requires the court to consider a triangulation of interests. It involves taking into account the position of the accused, the victim and his or her family, and the public.
>
> (Lord Steyn cited in R v H [2004] 2 AC 134, 145–6)

Following Lord Steyn's statement, major changes to the ways in which victims are perceived and treated in criminal justice systems began to take effect, and an emphasis was placed on the development of charters or declarations that recognise and enforce victims' inherent rights and interests.[1] Significant changes to criminal law and procedure also arose out of the need to protect vulnerable victims of sexual offences from adversative court processes. Reforms to rape law likewise encouraged the need to further support and protect victims of these significant social and legal harms, while changes to the role of victims in the criminal justice system sought to recognise victims as important stakeholders of justice, rather than mere witnesses to proceedings. Despite such changes, profound concerns relating to how sexual offences are investigated and determined continue to permeate social, legal and political discourse.

Sexual crime has been labelled as 'one of the worst violations of human dignity … [insofar as] it can deeply traumatise … victims, their family and even whole communities' (Sir John Gillen 2019: i). It is a gendered crime that is predominantly perpetuated by men against women and children who are known to them (Australian Institute of Health and Welfare [AIHW] 2019). It is difficult to discern the full extent and types of sexual violence occurring as these crimes are significantly under-reported by victims for a range of reasons stemming from shame, social and cultural pressures, fear of being disbelieved, and fear of the perpetrator and legal system (AIHW 2019).

As explored throughout this book, particularly in Chapter 2, for victims that do report, intrusive court practices (Smith 2018) and police cynicism towards victims of sexual violence (Jordan 2004a, 2004b) can heighten the risk of secondary victimisation for victims and increase the likelihood of their withdrawal (Sanders & Jones 2007). Recently, the Gillen Review also alluded to the procedural challenges impacting victims' engagement with justice processes – many of which lead to 'improper' attrition – such as aggressive and humiliating questioning at trial that is spurred by outdated myths and stereotypes relating to rape and sexuality (Sir John Gillen 2019). These challenges, combined with a victim's limited role in proceedings, create a hostile climate in which victims often feel denied access to both procedural and substantive justice, rendering them reluctant to pursue prosecution. Considering that 'the integrity of criminal prosecutions and the justice system more broadly rests upon victims' confidence that the reporting of offences will not cause further harm, or exacerbate existing harm' (Kirchengast, Iliadis & O'Connell 2019: 2), the need to conduct research into the rights, role and status of victims of sexual violence in criminal justice systems is eminently justified.

In Australia, most notably within Victoria, numerous major inquiries, including the VLRC's (2016) report on *The Role of Victims of Crime in the Criminal Trial Process*, the RCFV (2016) and the RCIRCSA (2017), have considered matters affecting victims of sexual violence and their recourse to justice. Concerns over victims' procedural and substantive justice experiences have similarly gained traction internationally, including in the UK, with the Gillen Review inquiring into *The Law and Procedures in Serious Sexual Offences in Northern Ireland* (Sir John Gillen 2019). These inquiries have all considered how sexual assault victims' rights can be enhanced, as well as better managed, regulated and enforced in order to improve victims' standing, protection and access to justice.

Collectively, these inquiries highlight the imperative to respond to victims' procedural and substantive justice concerns through reforms that address the particular needs of victims (including sexual assault victims) and that provide victims with an opportunity to feel included, heard and protected within adversarial justice processes, thereby reducing the likelihood of secondary victimisation. Despite their recommendations varying in nature and scope, a common theme to emerge from these inquiries is the need to enhance victims' information and participation rights.

In Australia, sexual assault victims' rights, treatment and standing is comparable to that of other adversarial jurisdictions, where victims are not generally afforded standing in proceedings and retain limited participatory rights. Indeed, a consistent finding of these Australian commissions of inquiry is that victims continue to report dissatisfaction with their rights and treatment, and feel denied of access to both procedural and substantive justice (RCFV 2016; RCIRCSA 2017; VLRC 2016). In 2016, the VLRC set out a reform agenda, largely unrealised as of 2019. Its proposed reforms centred around developing the Office of the Victorian VoCC to enhance its representative powers and functions, and the *Victims' Charter Act 2006* (Vic) was identified as the source through which such reforms ought to take effect. The RCIRCSA (2017) criticised victims' charter frameworks across Australia more broadly for being 'largely unenforceable', except in New South Wales and South Australia where the Office of Commissioner for Victims' Rights can 'receive, and attempt to resolve, complaints about breaches of their charters'. Various reforms have therefore been recommended to address the failures of Victoria's criminal justice system in relation to victims, including 'establish[ing] a right for victims to seek internal review of a decision by the Director of Public Prosecutions to discontinue a prosecution or to proceed with a guilty plea to lesser charges' (VLRC 2016: 74). In this vein, the RCIRCSA (2017: 105) proposed the introduction of a reform that would provide victims with a formal complaints mechanism to allow victims to request an internal merits review of key decisions – specifically, to 'establish robust and effective internal audit processes to audit their [DPP] compliance with policies for decision-making and consultation with victims and police', and to render such complaints mechanisms publicly accessible.

Although the RCFV (2016) did not address changes to the Office of Commissioner specifically, or propose the implementation of a VRR-style reform, it did consider the need for reforms akin to those explored throughout this book, including the representation of victims in the justice system within specialist family violence courts (see, for example, Iliadis, Fitz-Gibbon & Walklate 2019). However, in contrast to the recommendations made by the VLRC (2016) and RCIRCSA (2017) in relation to the development of a VRR-style reform and the powers of the Victorian VoCC, the RCFV (2016) did not comment on how ILR can be achieved for victims or the contexts in which it could conceivably operate. This has led scholars such as Iliadis, Fitz-Gibbon and Walklate (2019: 8) to argue that:

> In the absence of prescribed detail addressing how this recommendation should be brought to life, and reflecting the breadth of resistance accompanying this recommendation, … there is a pivotal need to pilot this reform in varying contexts.

This could include providing ILR for victims in similar circumstances to those for which it is provided for victims in Ireland in relation to defence applications for the admission of a victim's sexual history evidence or medical or counselling records. As noted by Iliadis, Fitz-Gibbon and Walklate (2019: 8), piloting and monitoring the impact of such a reform also 'affords the opportunity for other Australian state and territory jurisdictions, as well as comparable adversarial jurisdictions internationally, to learn from the Victorian experience'. Likewise, it provides an opportunity for Victoria to learn from the experience in Ireland, where ILR is already provided for in these instances.

As evident throughout these inquiries and the analysis presented in this book, clear consensus has emerged that supports the need to address the inadequacies of justice system responses to victims of sexual violence. This book contributes to contemporary, ongoing debates about the limitations of the adversarial justice system for meeting the procedural justice needs of sexual assault victims. It examines and analyses the impact of victim-focused law reforms introduced in three different locations – England and Wales, Ireland and South Australia – designed to mitigate the harms experienced by women who testify as the primary witness in sexual assault investigations and prosecutions. The book focuses specifically on reforms that increase the level of information and participation available to such victims – for example, granting victims the right to challenge prosecutorial discretion (England and Wales) and being afforded ILR at certain stages of the legal process (Ireland and South Australia).

An analysis of these reforms provides an opportunity to consider how they are positively and/or negatively impacting victims' procedural justice experiences and whether they are influencing substantive justice outcomes. A major finding emerging from this book is that the reforms have fallen short of adequately enhancing victims' procedural justice experiences because of broader socio-structural issues inherent to adversarial legal systems, including the yielding culture that continues to promote rape myths and stereotypes as a basis for intimidating and blaming victims, and discouraging them from pursuing prosecution. Considering that a key aim of the criminal justice system is to detect and prosecute dangerous offenders and to keep people safe from harm, it is clear that adversarial systems are failing to uphold both their moral and legal obligations to victims who report and testify in their capacity as survivors of sexual violence in the first instance, and as witnesses for the prosecution in the second.

The approach adopted in this book reflects a commitment to exploring how existing adversarial systems can be more victim-friendly in order to better safeguard the rights and interests of sexual assault victims, alongside those of the state and the accused, thereby recognising a triangulation of interests. One of the central arguments of this book is that, while reform is needed to improve sexual assault victims' experiences and perceptions of procedural justice, such reforms must be situated within wider efforts to address certain underlying issues in adversarial systems, including the myths and stereotypes that underpin responses to sexual violence and the need to reconceptualise victims' role and level of involvement in proceedings. This means that broader attempts for reform would need to recognise victims as 'participants' in proceedings, which requires reconceptualising the adversarial criminal trial as implicating a triangulation of competing interests between the state, the accused and the victim. By analysing whether the three victim-focused reforms examined in this book address (or neglect) sexual assault victims' needs and expectations of procedural justice within an adversarial system, the book also considers whether there is scope for introducing similar models of reform, including ILR for sexual assault victims, in Victoria's adversarial system.

The research findings presented in this book are informed by 26 semi-structured interviews conducted with high-level criminal justice professionals; key policy and government stakeholders responsible for creating, implementing and working with the reforms; and victim support workers. The qualitative data was supplemented by a quantitative analysis of a statistical dataset unique to this study on the VRR reform operating in England and Wales. This dataset included information on the number of review requests and reviews undertaken, the outcomes of reviews, and the types of cases referred for review. Case study and primary source document analysis also informed the research findings. This methodological approach provided a rich dataset from which to conduct a thematic analysis that revealed that sexual assault victims experience ongoing procedural justice challenges in adversarial systems, which have not traditionally accommodated victim involvement given the emphasis placed on the two-sided contest between the prosecution and the defence. With a particular focus on these challenges, the book considered whether the enhancement of victims' rights through the three victim-focused reforms under study have improved the procedural justice experiences of sexual assault victims, and whether similar reforms, including the prospect of ILR for victims (whether in a limited or any context), could operate within the constraints of Victoria's adversarial system.

This book argues that the limitations placed on the role and status of sexual assault victims within the adversarial system need to be addressed through legal reform. However, careful consideration is required when developing victim-focused reforms in order to ensure that they function effectively and meet their intended objectives of improving victim satisfaction with, and participation in, the criminal justice system. Indeed, as exposed throughout the analysis of the reforms under focus, there remain a number of shortcomings in the way the reforms currently operate, which limit the opportunity for victims to experience procedural justice.

From the analysis of the data, four key findings emerged: (i) there are gaps between the theoretical objectives and practical application of the three victim-focused reforms, limiting the opportunity for victims to experience and gain a sense of procedural justice; (ii) victim-focused reform can be perceived as a sticking plaster for broader systemic issues inherent to adversarial justice systems and their ability to accommodate victims; (iii) incremental change is crucial to introducing victim-focused reforms to the adversarial system in order to avoid disrupting the traditional principles upon which the system is based; and (iv) adversarial systems would better respond to victims' needs and expectations if justice were to be conceived within a triangulation of interests framework. Each finding is discussed in turn below.

The gap between theory and practice

This book reveals significant gaps between the theoretical objectives of the victim-focused reforms under focus and the ability of these reforms to meet their objectives in ways that improve victims' procedural justice experiences in practice. As demonstrated in Table 8.1 below, each reform has the potential to meet various aspects of sexual assault victims' procedural justice needs.

In England and Wales, the findings reveal that the VRR may not always provide an opportunity for victims to experience procedural justice. While the interviews identified the potentially positive outcomes of the VRR's implementation, there remained some concern that these outcomes are not always achieved in practice. This is perceived as resulting from the lack of independence of those conducting the review, which leads to problems with transparency and accountability, as well as the absence of data on pre-charge decision-making, which leaves questions as to whether outdated stereotypes around sexual assault continue to influence police and prosecutor decision-making. The length of time a review can take was also found to raise the hopes and expectations of some victims unnecessarily, which can lead to further disappointment and anguish in cases where the decision is not overturned. Therefore, while the theoretical underpinnings of the VRR represent major benefits for victims, the reform's shortcomings may limit the potential for victims to experience procedural justice.

In Ireland, the ILR to which victims are entitled under section 34 of the *Sex Offenders Act 2001* (Irl) has the potential to enhance victims' procedural justice experiences prior to, and during, the cross-examination stage. This is a significant right given the traumatic nature of cross-examination for sexual assault victims. However, this book found that, in practice, the shortcomings of the reform – such as those associated with the delayed notice of intention, the legal representative's limited role in the process and the inconsistencies identified in judicial discretion – have reduced the extent of the positive impacts of this reform for sexual assault victims.

In South Australia, under section 16(3)(b) of the *Victims of Crime Act 2001* (SA), victims can contact the SACVR for legal assistance 'in their dealings with prosecution authorities and other government agencies'. Significantly, this clause allows the SACVR to provide ILR to victims in matters where the Commissioner believes that victim interests have not been adequately considered or upheld. Notwithstanding the unique nature of this right in an adversarial system,

Table 8.1 The potential for victim-focused reforms to meet victims' procedural justice needs

	England and Wales VRR reform	*Ireland* Separate legal representation for victims under s 34 of the *Sex Offenders Act 2001* (Irl)	*South Australia* Victim representation by the SACVR
Information	If victims request a review, they are provided with a detailed explanation of why the case could not proceed if the original decision is not overturned.	Victims should be informed about the defence's application for the introduction of their sexual history evidence. This information can give victims the opportunity to seek ILR to then challenge the application and its relevance to proceedings.	Legal representation focused on the victim ensures that they are kept up to date and informed on their case.
Validation	Victims can feel validated if the decision is overturned. Victims may feel validated by receiving an explanation about the reason why their case did not proceed and why the decision was not overturned. This is because the reason will highlight that it is not about the victim not being believed, but that the evidence may not meet the high standard of proof required in sexual assault cases.	Victims may feel validated from having ILR – someone who acknowledges their role in proceedings. However, the legal representative's role is limited to the application stage.	Victims may feel validated where the legal representative appointed to the case is able to uphold and support their views and concerns, and present these to the court.
Voice	Victims are given a greater voice as they are able to challenge prosecutorial decisions.	Victims have a limited participatory right and a representative to voice their concerns surrounding the protection of a victim's privacy.	The legal representative can present the victim's voice.
Control	Victims may feel empowered to regain control over their lives if they are provided with a detailed explanation as to why the case was not able to proceed. Victims may feel that they have control from having the decision reviewed, regardless of whether or not the decision is overturned. Victims are likely to experience the greatest feeling of control in situations where the original decision is reversed.	Victims may feel a sense of control from having an independent legal representative who is there to represent them, regardless of the outcome. Victims are likely to feel the greatest level of control if their legal representative is able to successfully oppose the defence's application to adduce the victim's sexual history evidence.	Victims may feel that they have a degree of control in cases where the SACVR is able to intervene to provide legal representation and assistance.

there exist various issues associated with its practical application, which limit the extent of its positive impact for victims of sexual violence. In particular, the SACVR's limited resources curtail the extent of the assistance and representation that can be provided to victims. The SACVR is also limited in their ability to pursue civil action against the DPP, even where the Commissioner maintains a genuine belief that the victim's rights have not been upheld in accordance with the *Victims of Crime Act 2001* (SA). Accordingly, the true impact of the SACVR's powers in enhancing the procedural justice experiences of victims through ILR is diminished.

Despite their different approaches, all three reforms have attracted similar criticisms insofar as there exist disparities between their objectives and their ability to achieve these objectives in ways that attend to victims' procedural justice needs. Concerns over this disparity between the theoretical and practical application of the reforms, as well as their ability to address victims' needs from the justice process, are not exclusive to the VRR scheme or the limited forms of ILR operating in Ireland and South Australia. As explored in Chapter 2, such concerns are commonly raised in relation to other victim-focused reforms operating in adversarial systems, such as the VIS, in relation to which victims report not always being informed of their right to complete a statement, or not receiving encouragement or support to do so. Like concerns have been raised about victims' charters and other victims' rights–based mechanisms introduced to afford greater consideration to victims and provide them with information during the criminal justice process, but which often do not give victims any legal right to:

> pursue civil action following the perceived failure of the [criminal justice agency] to adhere to his or her rights as dictated in the *Charter[s]* … [meaning the Charters] are not infallible in terms of being able to protect victims' interests or ensure they are upheld.
>
> (Flynn 2012: 89)

As this book has argued, sexual assault victims' perceptions of justice are largely shaped by their experiences of procedural justice, which means that the gaps between each reform's theoretical aims and practical application could potentially exacerbate the harm experienced by victims, leading to further dissatisfaction with the process. This finding thus raises questions about the effectiveness, legitimacy and applicability of such reforms. Like other victim-focused reforms that have come before them, it appears that, in the case of the three reforms under study, 'there is still a way to go … to ensure victims' rights are delivered reliably and consistently' (The Honourable Robert Clark 2014).

Victim-focused reform as a sticking plaster

A key finding to emerge from this book is that victim-focused reforms are not the most appropriate means of addressing victims' procedural justice needs in the context of systems that lack transparency and accountability to victims, and that continue to permit the negative treatment of sexual assault victims. This issue arose in all three focus jurisdictions where the participants expressed concern about the role and treatment of sexual assault victims, even subsequent to the implementation of victim-focused reforms.

In England and Wales, some participants argued that the 'VRR is a benefit generally' but that the 'potential pitfalls of the VRR' limit its capacity to improve victims' procedural justice experiences (Olivia, policy advisor, victim support organisation). For example, where the VRR is 'miscommunicated or not explained in the right way', it 'could potentially retraumatise victims' (Olivia). Concerns about transparency and accountability were also raised in relation to the absence of pre-trial data on offence types that proceed through the VRR, which limits understanding as to the sorts of offences that are not being proceeded with. Furthermore, the VRR process itself – which requires an individual working within an organisation to review a decision made by someone from that same organisation – can be perceived as undermining the 'independence' of the review, thus highlighting potential transparency and accountability issues. In reflecting on such issues, Olivia expressed her concern around how the VRR:

> might be seen as a sticking plaster for a much wider issue … [and] used as a kind of solution to our [the criminal justice system's] communication and lack of transparency issues for victims, when actually what is needed is … a real analysis of the gaps of support available for victims of sexual abuse … [and] prosecutors specialised and trained up in … dealing with sexual abuse cases.

In a similar vein, Sophie (victims' rights advocate and campaigner) commented:

> There's a lot of work to be done around rape myths, so around what the victim was wearing and how drunk they were … All of that [makes the victim feel] like they are on trial. There's a lot to be done around awareness-raising with judges and just the whole court system around what is appropriate and what isn't.

As explored in Chapter 2, the impacts of these myths extend beyond the formal stages of criminal prosecution to preventing victims from reporting. Most participants made reference to these issues and expressed concern about the legal system's ability to enable women to feel comfortable and safe in reporting, even since the implementation of the victim-focused reforms. These issues were identified by many participants as 'permeat[ing] throughout the whole judicial system' (Olivia) and as gendered in nature given that men are overrepresented among criminal justice personnel, whether as judges, prosecutors or defence lawyers.

Reflective of the common view among the participants, Olivia suggested that there would be less of a 'gap in the approach [to victims] from a judicial point of view' if the legal system's treatment of sexual assault victims were improved. This could include consistent and clear communication with victims and ensuring that victims fully understand their rights. It might also require better training for criminal justice personnel in relation to sexual offence cases. Considering that the VRR was implemented by the CPS in an attempt to be more transparent and demonstrate greater sensitivity towards victims (CPS 2016), some participants questioned its relevance when the evidence suggests that the treatment of sexual assault victims has not significantly improved since the VRR's introduction.

Despite the introduction of section 34 of the *Sex Offenders Act 2001* (Irl), the findings presented in this book indicate that there still exists widespread negative treatment of sexual assault victims by criminal justice authorities in Ireland. For example, this can be seen in the inconsistencies in judicial discretion, including the circumstances in which they allow applications to be made to adduce a victim's sexual history evidence. Furthermore, while defence applications to adduce a victim's sexual history evidence should be made at the pre-trial stage, as this would allow victims sufficient time to prepare for court and arrange ILR, it is common for judges to approve defence applications during the trial, irrespective of whether the defence are issuing applications as a basis for intimidating the victim. Additionally, as demonstrated in Chapter 5, it is not uncommon for judicial officers to allow questioning of the victim at trial that draws on negative stereotypes and rape myths. These issues can be seen to subvert the intention of the legislation – to safeguard victims against irrelevant and offensive questioning and enhance victims' procedural justice experiences.

In South Australia, the participants spoke of the SACVR's powers to grant ILR to victims as a significant 'tool of accountability' that helps to ensure honesty from judges, prosecutors and defence lawyers (Robert, manager, WAS). However, it is important to note that, while this reform seeks to enhance victims' rights, ultimately it is the SACVR who retains the power to seek ILR, not the victim. This acts as a reminder that victims remain marginalised by their role as a witness within an adversarial setting.

Accordingly, despite the existence of the reforms operating in the focus jurisdictions, and their aim of offering victims increased participation rights (through ILR) or information rights (through the VRR reform), such reforms are not widely perceived as viable in addressing issues relating to:

- the adverse stereotypes and rape myths that infiltrate the decision-making of criminal justice authorities
- the lack of transparency in prosecutorial decision-making and accountability to victims
- the lack of victim consultation and regard for victims' rights
- the lack of consideration for victims' procedural justice needs and expectations from the process.

Within this context, and taking into account the gaps between the theoretical aims and practical outcomes of the three reforms, these reforms could create the impression that the criminal justice system is displaying a greater concern for victims' rights, role and treatment in the criminal justice process, without actually addressing the underlying issues impacting victims' procedural and substantive justice experiences.

This is not to undermine the importance of victim-focused reform. Indeed, reforms to victims' rights should be regarded as a significant step towards enhancing the role of victims, who have traditionally been marginalised by their role as a witness to proceedings. However, in line with the VLRC, this book argues that 'the promise of reforms will not be fully realised without cultural change within the criminal justice system' (VLRC 2016: xiv). Driving this cultural change alongside victim-focused reform will help to reduce 'inconsistencies in how victims are perceived, how they see themselves, their expectations and how they are treated' (VLRC 2016: xiv). It could also foster 'a coherent approach to victim-oriented reform', increasing the likelihood that 'those who work within the criminal justice system … [will] me[e]t the ambitions of the reforms' (VLRC 2016: xiv). Significantly, this could eliminate the perception that such reforms are merely sticking plasters masking the real issues.

Incremental change

Another key theme emerging from this research was the importance of incremental rather than radical change within the criminal justice system. This was identified by the participants as a crucial factor determining the success of victim-focused reforms in adversarial systems. In particular, the participants expressed some concern around introducing reforms that offer victims greater participation rights beyond that of a VIS, such as ILR, as this would require rapid and substantial changes to existing adversarial criminal processes. As explored throughout this book, resistance to victim involvement in adversarial justice systems has stemmed from a concern that the imposition of a *third party* – namely, the victim – would unbalance the two-sided contest between the prosecution and the defence, as well as potentially interfere with the accused's due process right to a fair and impartial trial (McAsey 2011: 115).

This book argues, however, that there is a legitimate basis and need to progressively enhance sexual assault victims' rights within Victoria's criminal justice system (and adversarial systems more broadly), providing that any changes continue to fit within the constraints of the adversarial system. At present, the gradual inclusion of victims' rights could take place through the introduction of a VRR-style reform, which would give victims the right to contest prosecutorial decision-making while not interfering with any stages of the trial process. Several submissions[2] to the VLRC (2016: 71) demonstrated support for introducing a system of review akin to the VRR in England and Wales. For example, Kirchengast (cited in VLRC 2016: 72) explained that a VRR-style reform could 'appropriately' consider victims' interests within the parameters of the adversarial process:

> While the views of victims are considered, those views do not determine the outcome and must be weighed against the public interest at all times. As

> such, although the victim is given substantive rights of participation that may be enforced against the state, those rights never become determinative of an outcome nor usurp the state's right to prosecute. The removal of the process of review from the courts also ensures that the rights of the victim are not conflated with the rights of the accused in the trial context. The accused retains the right to challenge the Crown case without the victim acting as a third party to proceedings, should the matter be brought to court.

Kirchengast thus explains how a VRR-type reform could fit within Victoria's adversarial system without jeopardising the adversarial principles underpinning criminal prosecution processes. The implementation of a review mechanism would also not alter the structural position of victims in the criminal justice system; that is to say, victims would not receive the status of party to proceedings, but would be more likely to feel empowered in the process, leading to increased satisfaction with the criminal justice system. A VRR-style reform would contribute significantly to sexual assault victims' procedural justice needs, particularly in light of the difficulties associated with their experience of the legal process, as discussed in Chapters 2 and 4. However, as noted in Chapter 7, if such a reform were to be introduced in Victoria (or Australian states and territories more broadly, as recommended by the RCIRCSA [2017]), the evidence suggests that it should take the form of an external system of review independent of the DPP's office to 'unpick' gaps in decision-making processes and offer more transparency and accountability to victims (Iliadis & Flynn 2019).

While several participants identified some scope for introducing a limited form of ILR for sexual assault victims during identified stages of the process, akin to the reform operating in Ireland, there was less support for enhancing the rights of the Victorian VoCC to provide victims with ILR. In reflecting on the prospect of any form of victim ILR in Victoria, the participants were primarily of the opinion that such changes to victims' rights would be prone to criticism from the wider legal community and that a VRR-style reform would sit more comfortably within Victoria's criminal justice system as it constitutes a provision for information, not participation. Even where participants identified some benefits of introducing ILR for sexual assault victims, most maintained the view that incremental change would be key to the success of any victim-focused reform and that there is a need to 'tread cautiously' when contemplating the introduction of representative rights for victims in adversarial legal systems at this point in time (Iliadis, Fitz-Gibbon & Walklate 2019: 2).

A triangulation of interests

A significant finding arising from this book is that adversarial systems would better respond to victims' needs and expectations if justice were to be conceived within a triangulation of interests framework. The need to better consider the victim's interests was identified by participants across all jurisdictions. The data overwhelmingly pointed to a major flaw of the adversarial system in that it subordinates victims through their role as a witness. In effect, this has prevented victim interests from being considered, despite the direct impact of the crime on victims. This has exacerbated victims' feelings of alienation and exclusion from the criminal justice process and has had profound impacts by way of further harming vulnerable victims, including those who have experienced sexual victimisation. For sexual assault victims, the participants emphasised the importance of fair processes as being inherently linked to increased satisfaction with the legal process, regardless of the substantive case outcome. Within this context, the findings presented in this book indicate that if sexual assault victims are treated fairly and their interests are considered, they will be more likely to experience procedurally just outcomes.

This book thus argues that victim interests can and ought to be better incorporated into existing adversarial structures in order to strengthen victims' overall satisfaction with the criminal justice system. This can be achieved through systemic cultural change in relation to the ways in which victims are viewed and treated, such as by redefining the victim's role to be more reflective of a 'participant with an inherent interest in the criminal trial process that arises from their victimhood' instead of a mere 'witness for the prosecution' (VLRC 2016: 22). Acknowledging victims as participants within adversarial processes can also help to 'guide future reform', such as a VRR-style reform, which can enable victims to feel more like 'insiders, rather than … outsiders unless invited in' (VLRC 2016: 23). A modern conception of the victim's role will also help to guide future reforms, ensuring that they reflect changing standards with regard to victim expectations, such as the need to experience procedural justice.

Conceptualising victims as participants is possible 'without diminishing the primacy given to ensuring that the trial is fair for the community and the accused as well as for the victim' (VLRC 2016: 22), thus reinforcing the notion that justice can be conceived within a triangulation of interests framework. For sexual assault victims, this reconceptualisation marks a critical step towards enhancing their perceptions of, and experiences with, the criminal justice system.

Future research directions

The research upon which this book is premised examined how three victim-focused reforms operate across three adversarial jurisdictions – England and Wales, Ireland and South Australia – in terms of the extent to which they meet sexual assault victims' expectations of procedural justice. The decision to exclude victim participants from this research and to focus exclusively on attaining the perceptions and views of victim support workers, key policy and government stakeholders, and criminal justice professionals was made to reduce the potential distress the research process may cause victims. While this may be seen as a possible limitation of the research, it also points to the potential for future research. For example, it would be useful to speak with victims who have experienced the three reforms to gain their insights into and experiences of the reforms. For the purposes of this book, however, the participants selected were able to speak in relation to victims' experiences with the reforms and provide a professional perspective on the reforms, thereby in part addressing this limitation. Another potential limitation of the research could be identified in the total number of interviews undertaken (n=26). As explained in the introductory chapter, however, the high level of authority and expertise of the participants interviewed ensured that the data obtained was particularly rich and comprehensive.

In this research, the focus on sexual assault victims was not intended to detract from the vulnerability and needs of other victims, but to acknowledge that sexual assault victims warrant an independent investigation due to the range of unique and complex challenges they face in the adversarial system. The decision to focus on sexual assault victims, and female sexual assault victims specifically, may also be considered a limitation of the research. However, this highlights a potential area for future research – to expand the focus of study beyond that of sexual assault victims, especially considering that some of the reforms explored in this research (England and Wales, and South Australia) are applicable to all crime victims. Future research could also broaden the sample of participants to account for the perceptions of men, women and non-conforming gender people as victims and their experiences with the reforms, as opposed to this study's focus on female sexual assault victims specifically.

Lastly, while this book can be considered timely in light of the recent development of the reforms under focus and the widely recognised need to enhance sexual assault victims' rights in order to address their concerns around procedural and substantive justice, its findings are not static as sexual assault victims' needs and expectations of justice change over time. This highlights a need to re-evaluate the operations and outcomes of these three reforms in relation to how they attend to (or neglect) sexual assault victims' needs and expectations from the criminal justice system over time and in the future. A study of this kind would provide an interesting point of comparison with the findings of this book in determining whether the focus on procedural justice remains relevant when exploring sexual assault victims' needs and expectations of justice.

Concluding thoughts

Victims remain 'controversial and contested participants of justice' (Kirchengast 2016b: 2), despite being inherently linked to the criminal trial; and debates around potential changes to the rights and role of victims of sexual violence in adversarial justice systems remain highly charged. In Victoria, specifically, the VLRC was asked to 'review and report on the role of victims of crime in the criminal trial process' (VLRC 2016: viii), which involved identifying victim-focused reforms operating in other adversarial jurisdictions (VLRC 2016: viii). Some reference was made to the types of victim-focused reforms that exist in other jurisdictions, such as the VRR, and the powers constitutive within the Office of the SACVR (VLRC 2016). Other inquiries, including the RCIRCSA (2017), demonstrated marked support for introducing a VRR-style reform, while the RCFV (2016) somewhat more contentiously recommended the introduction of ILR for victims within specialist family violence courts.

This book is timely in execution as it advances understandings of three victim-focused reforms across three adversarial jurisdictions that offer victims increased information (England and Wales) and participation (Ireland and South Australia) – and all three reforms have been raised in various capacities in recent Australian commissions of inquiry. Specifically, this book offers a detailed evaluation of how the reforms are operating and in what ways they address (or neglect) sexual assault victims' needs and expectations of procedural justice within an adversarial framework. In doing so, this book provides impetus to consider whether similar reforms, including ILR for sexual assault victims, could operate in the Victorian adversarial justice system. While the notion of introducing ILR for victims of sexual violence proved to be contentious as it defies traditional adversarial principles, the participants were still supportive of the prospect of its future introduction. On this basis, and as explained by Sir Owen Woodhouse (1967):

> [even] if there may seem to be a weight of tradition against change, at least it is worth remembering that the apparent heresies of one generation become the orthodoxies of the next. The ultimate validity of any social measure will depend not upon its antecedents but upon its current and future utility.

Therefore, the possibility of ILR for sexual assault victims should not be completely dismissed.

Ultimately, this book contends that victim-focused reforms hold significant value in improving the marginalised position of sexual assault victims within adversarial justice systems. They also have the potential to enhance procedural justice experiences as they can provide sexual assault victims with increased access to information, some degree of voice and control, as well as validation of their victimisation experiences. However, Stubbs's (2003: 23) contention continues to ring true – that reforms for sexual assault victims represent 'symbolic value but are likely to be limited in effectiveness ... [because of] the resilience of cultural mythologies about women and sexuality'. This suggests that law reform alone cannot achieve the ultimate goal of enhancing the procedural justice experiences of sexual assault victims, and that other factors, such as cultural change in the ways in which these victims are perceived and treated, also need attention in the adversarial system. Despite the various shortcomings associated with victim-focused reforms, they still represent a significant shift towards including victims' interests alongside those of the community and the accused, thus recognising the triangulation of interests. While further research is required to evaluate changes to the victim's role and level of recognition across adversarial systems, the reforms operating in England and Wales, Ireland and South Australia represent important progress towards further recognition of victims' rights and provide a pivotal starting point for reconceptualising the role of sexual assault victims within adversarial systems of justice.

Notes

1 See, for example, *Victims of Crime Act 2001* (SA); *Victims' Charter Act 2006* (Vic); *Code of Practice for Victims of Crime 2015* (UK); *Victims' Charter and Guide to the Criminal Justice System 2010* (Irl).

2 See, for example, Submissions 8 (Dr Mary Iliadis), 14 (former VoCC, Victoria), 31 (Professor Jonathon Doak), and 30 (Associate Professor Tyrone Kirchengast).

Appendix A

Interview Schedule A (England and Wales)

Introductory Statement – explain the aims of the research project, reiterate the interview timeframe, and respond to any questions the participant has about the research.

Note to interviewees: my research is primarily focused on sexual assault victims. When answering the questions, where possible, can you please answer the questions in relation to sexual assault victims? If this is not possible in some circumstances, please respond to the questions in relation to victims more generally.

VRR Reform:

1 In your view, should victims have the VRR? Why/Why not?
2 In what ways does the VRR benefit sexual assault victims (or victims more generally)? *(Follow up: Does it empower victims by giving them more of a voice, validation, information, control? – procedural justice elements).* Can you provide any examples?
3 In your experience, are there any disadvantages that can arise for sexual assault victims (or victims more generally) from exercising the VRR? Can you provide an example/s? *(Follow up: Are the proposed time limits for victims to exercise this right appropriate?)*
4 In your experience, are victims satisfied with the way the VRR operates? Why/Why not? Can you provide an example/s?
5 In your experience, do sexual assault victims (or victims more generally) frequently exercise this right? Are victims (generally) successful in challenging decisions when they ask for a review? Why/Why not?
6 There are some notable overlaps with what ILR entails and the VRR reform, particularly as it gives victims the opportunity to challenge prosecutorial decisions. In your view, do you think the VRR is suggestive of a step towards ILR for victims in the prosecution process in England and Wales? Why/Why not?
7 Do you believe that other common law jurisdictions, similar to England's and Wales' legal system (i.e. Victoria), might benefit from the introduction of the VRR for sexual assault victims (or victims more generally)? If so, how?

8 What problems do you foresee might arise if the VRR was introduced in other common law jurisdictions (i.e. Victoria) for sexual assault victims (or victims more generally)?
9 Can you identify any aspects of the prosecution process that would be particularly challenging for sexual assault victims? In what ways?
10 In your view, is there prospect for ILR for sexual assault victims in a common law, adversarial legal system? Why/Why not? (*Prompt*: can you identify any benefits/limitations?)
11 In what ways could a legal representative assist victims with the prosecution process? Can you provide some examples? (*Prompt (if needed)*: Would it empower victims by giving them a voice; assist victims with certain stages of the prosecution process; keep victims well-informed about the progress of their case; enable victims to exercise their rights; help victims to navigate victim services?)
12 In your view, should the legal representative's role be limited to a specific procedural stage? Why/Why not?
13 In your view, which reform might be more beneficial and/or justified in an adversarial setting? The VRR or ILR? Why/Why not?

The VRR and plea negotiations:

14 In your experience, how do victims perceive the plea negotiation process? Is this positive or negative? In what ways? Can you provide some examples?
15 In your experience, do victims support the prosecution's view that a conviction is better than no conviction? Why/Why not?
16 Why can't the VRR be used when charges are altered to allow a guilty plea?
17 In your experience, have there been any criticisms relating to victims not being able to use the VRR during plea negotiations? Can you identify any examples?
18 Are there any alternative avenues available to the victim when plea negotiations occur?

Explain the Irish reform:

Ireland has implemented a form of ILR for sexual assault victims through section 34 of the *Sex Offenders Act 2001* (Irl). Since 2001, this section allows a complainant to have ILR to oppose a defendant's application for the introduction of a victim's sexual history evidence in court.

19 What types of benefits do you think this form of ILR might offer victims? In what ways?
20 What types of limitations do you think may arise for victims from this form of ILR? Can you provide some examples?
21 Do you think this form of ILR could be adopted in other common law jurisdictions? Why/Why not?
22 Does this form of ILR have the potential to conflict with traditional adversarial values? Is this an important consideration?

Explain the South Australian reform:

In South Australia, victims are entitled to apply to the SACVR for ILR in matters that involve 'consultation with prosecution, in criminal and civil proceedings and coronial inquests, as well as initiated legal matters that affect victims in general' (O'Connell 2012: 7). South Australia is the only Australian state or territory to have implemented this form of ILR for victims.

23 In what ways do you think this form of ILR might benefit victims, particularly sexual assault victims?
24 In your view, would there be any potential limitations arising from this form of ILR for victims?
25 Do you think this type of ILR could be adopted in other common law jurisdictions? Why/Why not?
26 Does this type of ILR have the potential to conflict with traditional adversarial values? Is this an important consideration?
27 In your view, which reform is more justified in an adversarial setting, the VRR reform or ILR as offered by the SACVR?

Procedural justice:

28 How would you define procedural justice?

Notify interviewee: for the purpose of this research, procedural justice will mean that the process leading to a decision (the *how*) is as important as the outcome itself (the *what*) (Barsoux & Manzoni 1998: 2). In the context of this research, procedural justice is conceptualised as the actions and processes governing a criminal trial within adversarial legal systems and ensuring that the role and treatment of both parties (victim and offender) is fair and consistent, and that their rights are simultaneously upheld. Clark's (2010) study has found that four key elements are crucial in understanding sexual assault victims' procedural justice needs. These are:

Information – victims want to be informed about the progression of their case;
Validation – victims need justice system officials to acknowledge the seriousness of their victimisation experience and its impact on their life;
Voice – victims need a forum to narrate their story to a supportive and receptive audience; and,
Control – victims need representation and consultation, and decisions to be made within their interests, including having the capacity to challenge decisions.

29 Based on this definition of procedural justice, in your experience, do sexual assault victims (or victims more generally) feel like they experience procedural justice in criminal justice proceedings?
30 In which areas are they most likely to experience procedural justice?

31 In which areas are they most likely not to experience procedural justice?
32 In your experience, what do sexual assault victims want most from the criminal justice process?
33 How much does the outcome of the case play a role in determining whether a sexual assault victim feels they experience justice?
34 In your opinion, do you see the VRR as providing sexual assault victims with a greater opportunity to experience procedural justice? Why/why not? In what ways?

END INTERVIEW

Appendix B

Interview Schedule B (Ireland)

Introductory Statement – explain the aims of the research project, reiterate the interview timeframe, and respond to any questions the participant has about the research.

ILR for sexual assault victims under section 34 of the *Sex Offenders Act 2001* (Irl):

1. What motivated the introduction of this form of ILR for sexual assault victims?
2. Why is the ILR limited to this specific procedural stage?
3. Do victims frequently exercise this right?
4. In your experience, has this form of ILR been beneficial for victims? In what ways?
5. In your experience, are there any limitations associated with this form of ILR? Can you provide some examples?
6. The judge has the ability to dismiss the victim's legal representative from further participating in proceedings if they accept the defendant's application – is this a usual occurrence? What impacts does this have for victims? Why was this safeguard introduced?
7. In your opinion, could the role of the ILR be expanded? Why/Why not? If so, to what stages of the trial should the legal representative's role be expanded to? What would the benefits and limitations of this be?
8. Do you think there is prospect to have victim ILR throughout the entire proceedings? Why/Why not?
9. In your view, could this or any other form of ILR for sexual assault victims be used in other common law, adversarial legal systems? Why/Why not?
10. Was there any perceived conflict with the implementation of this form of ILR in Ireland and the traditional adversarial system? How were these responded to? Are there still concerns that this form of ILR undermines the traditional adversarial process?

Explain the VRR reform in England and Wales:

Following the decision of the English High Court in Killick (*R v Killick [2011] EWCA Crim 1608*), in which the court considered the right of a victim of crime to seek a review of the CPS not to prosecute, victims in this jurisdiction now have the opportunity to challenge the prosecutor's decision not to proceed with a prosecution (CPS 2016). This process, referred to as the VRR, allows victims to challenge prosecutorial decisions not to proceed with a prosecution. The resulting outcome either includes the CPS providing a full explanation detailing the original decision to the victim, or in some cases, they may decide to overturn the original decision without going through the full review process.

11 What types of benefits do you think the VRR reform might offer victims? In what ways?
12 What types of limitations might be associated with the VRR reform?
13 There are some notable overlaps with what ILR entails and the VRR reform, particularly as it gives victims the opportunity to challenge decisions made by the prosecution. In your view, do you think the VRR is suggestive of a step towards ILR for victims in the prosecution process? Why/Why not?
14 In your view, which reform is more justified in an adversarial setting, the VRR or ILR? Why/Why not?
15 Do you think a VRR reform could be adopted in Ireland or other common law jurisdictions? Why/Why not?
16 Does the VRR have the potential to conflict with traditional adversarial values? Is this an important consideration?

Explain the South Australian reform:

In South Australia, victims are entitled to apply to the SACVR for ILR in matters that involve 'consultation with prosecution, in criminal and civil proceedings and coronial inquests, as well as initiated legal matters that affect victims in general' (O'Connell 2012: 7). South Australia is the only Australian state or territory to have implemented this form of ILR for victims.

17 In what ways do you think this form of ILR might benefit victims?
18 In your view, would there be any potential limitations arising from this form of ILR?
19 Do you think this type of ILR could be adopted in Ireland or other common law jurisdictions? Why/Why not?
20 Does this type of ILR have the potential to conflict with traditional adversarial values? Is this an important consideration?

Procedural justice:

21 How would you define procedural justice?

Notify interviewee: for the purpose of this research, procedural justice will mean that the process leading to a decision (the *how*) is as important as the outcome itself (the *what*) (Barsoux & Manzoni 1998: 2). In the context of this research, procedural justice is conceptualised as the actions and processes governing a criminal trial within adversarial legal systems and ensuring that the role and treatment of both parties (victim and offender) is fair and consistent, and that their rights are simultaneously upheld. Clark's (2010) study has found that four key elements are crucial in understanding sexual assault victims' procedural justice needs. These are:

Information – victims want to be informed about the progression of their case;
Validation – victims need justice system officials to acknowledge the seriousness of their victimisation experience and its impact on their life;
Voice – victims need a forum to narrate their story to a supportive and receptive audience; and,
Control – victims need representation and consultation, and decisions to be made within their interests, including having the capacity to challenge decisions.

22 Based on this definition of procedural justice, in your experience, do sexual assault victims (or victims more generally) feel like they experience procedural justice in criminal justice proceedings?
23 In which areas are they most likely to experience procedural justice?
24 In which areas are they most likely not to experience procedural justice?
25 In your experience, what do sexual assault victims want most from the criminal justice process?
26 How much does the outcome of the case play a role in determining whether a sexual assault victim feels they experience justice?
27 In your opinion, do you see this form of legal representation as providing sexual assault victims with a greater opportunity to experience procedural justice? Why/why not? In what ways?

END INTERVIEW

Appendix C

Interview Schedule C (South Australia)

Introductory Statement – explain the aims of the research project, reiterate the interview timeframe, and respond to any questions the participant has about the research.

Note to interviewees: my research is primarily focused on sexual assault victims. When answering the questions, where possible, can you please answer the questions in relation to sexual assault victims? If this is not possible in some circumstances, please respond to the questions in relation to victims more generally.

ILR by the SACVR:

1 What rights do victims have to contact the SACVR for legal assistance?
2 In what criminal matters can ILR be appointed to represent the interests of victims in court proceedings?
3 At what stages of the process is the legal representative able to assist victims? (*Follow on:* is the legal representative limited in their capacity to offer assistance to victims in any way)?
4 How would this right be exercised? *(Follow on: what is the process for victims to apply for ILR? What happens in court?*)
5 Should victims have the right to contact the Office of Commissioner for Victims' Rights for legal assistance and representation in certain criminal matters? Why/Why not?
6 How significant is this right for sexual assault victims?
7 In your view, what are the benefits that can arise for sexual assault victims (or victims more generally) from having access to this right? Can you provide an example?
8 In your experience, has this right produced problems for victims? In what ways? Are any of these problems specific to, or more evident for, sexual assault victims?
9 In your experience, have victims reported satisfaction with this right? Why/ Why not?

Provide context on Victoria, then ask:

10 Are you aware that Victoria has appointed a VoCC? What do you see as their primary role?
11 Should the Victorian VoCC have the same powers as the SACVR to offer ILR to victims? Why/Why not?
12 Do you see any benefits or problems if this right (ILR by the Commissioner) was introduced in other Australian jurisdictions?

Prospect for ILR for sexual assault victims:

13 In your view, is there potential for ILR for sexual assault victims in common law jurisdictions? Why/Why not?
14 If ILR was implemented for sexual assault victims, should the legal representative have a limited role? If so, what stages of the criminal prosecution process should their role be limited to? Can you provide some examples?
15 In your view, how important is ILR for sexual assault victims in an adversarial setting?

Explain the Irish reform:

Ireland has implemented a form of ILR for sexual assault victims through section 34 of the *Sex Offenders Act 2001* (Irl). Since 2001, this section allows a complainant to have ILR to oppose a defendant's application for the introduction of a victim's sexual history evidence in court.

16 Do you foresee any potential advantages or disadvantages associated with this form of ILR? Why/Why not? Can you provide any examples?
17 Do you think this form of ILR could be adopted in other common law jurisdictions? Why/Why not?
18 Does this form of ILR have the potential to conflict with traditional adversarial values? Is this an important consideration?

Explain the Victims' Right to Review reform:

Following the decision of the English High Court in Killick (*R v Killick [2011] EWCA Crim 1608*), in which the court considered the right of a victim of crime to seek a review of the CPS not to prosecute, victims in this jurisdiction now have the opportunity to challenge the prosecutor's decision not to proceed with a prosecution (CPS 2016). This process, referred to as the VRR, allows victims to challenge prosecutorial decisions not to proceed with a prosecution. The resulting outcome either includes the CPS providing a full explanation detailing the original decision to the victim, or in some cases, they may decide to overturn the original decision without going through the full review process.

19 Do you foresee any potential advantages or disadvantages associated with this scheme? Why/Why not? Can you provide an example?
20 There are some notable overlaps with what ILR entails and the VRR reform, particularly as it gives victims the opportunity to challenge decisions made by the prosecution. In your view, do you think the VRR is suggestive of a step towards ILR for victims in common law jurisdictions? Why/Why not?
21 In your view, which reform is more justified in an adversarial setting, the VRR or ILR? Why/Why not?
22 Do you think a VRR scheme could be adopted in Australian jurisdictions? Why/Why not?
23 Does the VRR have the potential to conflict with traditional adversarial values? Is this an important consideration?
24 Is one of the three reforms we have discussed more advantageous than the other in terms of the adversarial system incorporating victims' rights and ensuring a just outcome? Why/Why not?

Procedural justice:

25 How would you define procedural justice?

Notify interviewee: for the purpose of this research, procedural justice will mean that the process leading to a decision (the *how*) is as important as the outcome itself (the *what*) (Barsoux & Manzoni 1998: 2). In the context of this research, procedural justice is conceptualised as the actions and processes governing a criminal trial within adversarial legal systems and ensuring that the role and treatment of both parties (victim and offender) is fair and consistent, and that their rights are simultaneously upheld. Clark's (2010) study has found that four key elements are crucial in understanding sexual assault victims' procedural justice needs. These are:

Information – victims want to be informed about the progression of their case;
Validation – victims need justice system officials to acknowledge the seriousness of their victimisation experience and its impact on their life;
Voice – victims need a forum to narrate their story to a supportive and receptive audience; and,
Control – victims need representation and consultation, and decisions to be made within their interests, including having the capacity to challenge decisions.

26 Has this right impacted on victims' procedural justice needs? Why/Why not? In what ways?
27 In your experience, do victims feel like they experience procedural justice in criminal justice proceedings?
28 In which areas are they most likely to experience procedural justice?

29 In which areas are they most likely not to experience procedural justice?
30 In your experience, what do victims want most from the criminal justice process?
31 How much does the outcome of the case play a role in determining whether a victim feels they experience justice?

END INTERVIEW

Appendix D

Interview Schedule D (Victoria)

Introductory Statement – explain the aims of the research project, reiterate the interview timeframe, and respond to any questions the participant has about the research. Note to interviewees: my research is primarily focused on sexual assault victims. When answering the questions, where possible, can you please answer the questions in relation to sexual assault victims? If this is not possible in some circumstances, please respond to the questions in relation to victims more generally.

The prospect of ILR for sexual assault victims in Victoria:

1 Can you identify any aspects of the prosecution process that would be particularly challenging for sexual assault victims? Why/Why not? Can you provide an example?
2 In your view, is there prospect for ILR for sexual assault victims in common law jurisdictions? Why/Why not?
3 If ILR was implemented for sexual assault victims in Victoria, should the legal representative have a limited role? If so, at what stages of the prosecution process should their role be limited to? Why/Why not? Can you provide some examples?
4 In your view, how important is ILR for sexual assault victims?
5 In your view, do you foresee any benefits for sexual assault victims if they were to have ILR assist them with the prosecution process in Victoria?
6 In your view, do you foresee any disadvantages for sexual assault victims if they were to have ILR assist them with the prosecution process in Victoria?
7 Do you believe that ILR for sexual assault victims has the potential to conflict with the adversarial values that underpin the legal system? Why/Why not?

Explain the South Australian reform:

In South Australia, victims are entitled to apply to the SACVR for ILR in matters that involve 'consultation with prosecution, in criminal and civil proceedings and coronial inquests, as well as initiated legal matters that affect victims in general' (O'Connell 2012: 7). South Australia is the only Australian state or territory to have implemented this form of ILR for victims.

8 Are you aware that Victoria has appointed a VoCC? What do you see as their primary role?
9 Are you aware of the powers held by the SACVR and what their role entails? (*Briefly explain if need be).*
10 Can you identify any benefits of the SACVR's role?
11 Can you identify any limitations of the SACVR's role?
12 Should the Victorian VoCC have the same powers as the SACVR to offer ILR to victims? Why/Why not?
13 Do you see any benefits or problems if this right (ILR by the Commissioner) was introduced in other Australian jurisdictions?
14 Are you aware that the VLRC is currently undertaking a review into the role of victims of crime in Victoria's criminal trial?
15 What do you hope the outcome of the review and consultation will be?
16 If you were putting forward a submission, what would you suggest are the key issues that need addressing?

Explain the VRR reform:

Following the decision of the English High Court in Killick (*R v Killick [2011] EWCA Crim 1608*), in which the court considered the right of a victim of crime to seek a review of the CPS not to prosecute, victims in this jurisdiction now have the opportunity to challenge the prosecutor's decision not to proceed with a prosecution (CPS 2016). This process, referred to as the VRR, allows victims to challenge prosecutorial decisions not to proceed with a prosecution. The resulting outcome either includes the CPS providing a full explanation detailing the original decision to the victim, or in some cases, they may decide to overturn the original decision without going through the full review process.

17 Do you foresee any potential advantages or disadvantages associated with this reform? Why/Why not? Can you provide an example?
18 There are some notable overlaps with what ILR entails and the VRR reform, particularly as it gives victims the opportunity to challenge decisions made by the prosecution. In your view, do you think the VRR is suggestive of a step towards ILR for victims in common law jurisdictions? Why/Why not?
19 In your view, which reform is more justified in an adversarial setting, the VRR or ILR? Why?
20 Do you think a VRR scheme could be adopted in Australian jurisdictions? Why/Why not?
21 Does the VRR have the potential to conflict with traditional adversarial values? Is this an important consideration?

Explain the Irish reform:

Ireland has implemented a form of ILR for sexual assault victims through section 34 of the *Sex Offenders Act 2001* (Irl). Since 2001, this section allows a complainant to have ILR to oppose a defendant's application for the introduction of a victim's sexual history evidence in court.

22 What types of benefits do you think this form of ILR might offer victims? In what ways?
23 What types of limitations do you think may arise for victims from this form of ILR? Can you provide some examples?
24 Do you think this form of ILR could be adopted in other common law jurisdictions? Why/Why not?
25 Does this form of ILR have the potential to conflict with traditional adversarial values? Is this an important consideration?
26 From a discussion of the three victim-focused reforms, do you see one of the reforms as being more advantageous than the others in terms of the adversarial system incorporating victims' rights and ensuring a just outcome? Why/Why not?

Procedural justice:

27 How would you define procedural justice?

Notify interviewee: for the purpose of this research, procedural justice will mean that the process leading to a decision (the *how*) is as important as the outcome itself (the *what*) (Barsoux & Manzoni 1998: 2). In the context of this research, procedural justice is conceptualised as the actions and processes governing a criminal trial within adversarial legal systems and ensuring that the role and treatment of both parties (victim and offender) is fair and consistent, and that their rights are simultaneously upheld. Clark's (2010) study has found that four key elements are crucial in understanding sexual assault victims' procedural justice needs. These are:

Information – victims want to be informed about the progression of their case;
Validation – victims need justice system officials to acknowledge the seriousness of their victimisation experience and its impact on their life;
Voice – victims need a forum to narrate their story to a supportive and receptive audience; and,
Control – victims need representation and consultation, and decisions to be made within their interests, including having the capacity to challenge decisions.

28 Which of the three victim-focused reforms (England and Wales, Ireland, South Australia) do you see as having the greatest potential to meet victims' procedural justice needs? Why/Why not? In what ways?

29 In your experience, do victims feel like they experience procedural justice in criminal justice proceedings?
30 In which areas are they most likely to experience procedural justice?
31 In which areas are they most likely not to experience procedural justice?
32 In your experience, what do victims want most from the criminal justice process?
33 How much does the outcome of the case play a role in determining whether a victim feels they experience justice?

END INTERVIEW

Appendix E

Explanatory statement

EXPLANATORY STATEMENT

Interview Participants

Project: Adversarial justice and victims' rights: Reconceptualising the role of sexual assault victims

Mary Iliadis
Criminology, School of Social Sciences
Monash University
Email: mary.iliadis@monash.edu

You are invited to take part in this study. Please read this Explanatory Statement in full before deciding whether or not to participate in this research. If you would like further information regarding any aspect of this project, you are encouraged to contact the researchers via the phone numbers or email addresses listed above.

What does the research involve?

This research seeks to examine three victim-focused reforms operating across three adversarial jurisdictions – England and Wales, Ireland and South Australia. Each reform offers victims increased information and participation rights; for example, granting victims the right to challenge prosecutorial discretion (England and Wales) and affording victims independent legal representation within certain stages of the trial (Ireland and South Australia). The thesis considers the extent to which these reforms are meeting sexual assault victims' procedural justice needs and whether similar reforms, including the idea of independent legal representation for sexual assault victims, could operate in the Victorian adversarial justice system.

The research involves a semi-structured, one-on-one interview that will be conducted at an agreed time/date at a private study room within each participant's workplace. The interviews will be audio recorded, if you consent, and then transcribed verbatim at a later date. It is anticipated that the interview duration will be between 25–30 minutes. Interviews will take place in person, via phone or via Skype during regular business hours (9am–5pm), Monday to Friday.

Why were you chosen for this research?

Potential participants working within criminal justice systems (across England and Wales, Ireland, South Australia and Victoria), victim support organisations and prosecuting agencies were chosen for this research because they have the necessary expertise to assist in this research project concerning victim-focused reforms and will be able to provide well-informed responses to the questions asked of them, thus resulting in rich data analysis. In order for potential participants to be eligible for this research, they must be working within criminal justice sectors, victim support organisations or prosecuting agencies. Contact details were obtained from the relevant criminal justice, victim support or prosecuting agency websites, such as through Victim Support (UK); Victims' Rights Commissioners (UK; SA); Victims' Right to Review Unit (UK); Victims Support Agency (VIC); Crime Victims Support Association (VIC); Witness Assistance Service (VIC & SA); the Director of Public Prosecutions (Irl); and Cosc – the National Office for the Prevention of Domestic, Sexual and Gender-based Violence (Irl).

Consenting to participate in the project and withdrawing from the research

Participation in this research is voluntary. Should you agree to participate, you will be asked to read and sign the consent form (attached to the email containing this explanatory statement) and email this back to Mary Iliadis at mary.iliadis@monash.edu. Alternatively, Mary can collect the read and signed consent form from you directly prior to the interview commencing.

During the interview, you may choose not to answer a particular question(s) if for any reason you feel uncomfortable in doing so. Additionally, if you are experiencing any inconvenience or discomfort, you may withdraw yourself from the interview at any time.

Possible benefits and risks to participants

Your involvement in this project will contribute to an underdeveloped body of research supporting victims' rights, and particularly the role of sexual assault victims across three adversarial jurisdictions (England and Wales, Ireland and South Australia) that offer victims increased information and participation rights. This research considers the extent to which such reforms meet victims' procedural justice needs and expectations from the process, and whether similar reforms, including the idea of independent legal representation for sexual assault victims, would be viable within Victoria's legal system. This research will benefit the legal community, as it has the potential to influence social policy and legal reform. While there are no direct benefits for people who take part in this study, contributing to this project will help inform current debates around the very important public-interest topic of victims' rights.

Involvement in this research is highly unlikely to cause any stress, inconvenience or discomfort beyond the normal experience of everyday life, in either the short or long term. There is minimal possibility that you may experience some discomfort when reflecting on victim-focused reforms and victims' experiences with the reforms; that is, whether you have been involved in the criminal justice system or know someone who has experienced some form of victimisation. However, it is highly unlikely that this will occur, as the questions are not focused on any personal experiences, nor are you asked to discuss any experiences with victimisation. Instead, the questions focus on perceptions of victims' rights and victims' experiences with the criminal justice system from a purely professional viewpoint. Your participation in this project will be kept confidential; however there is a minimal possibility that someone may identify your involvement in the research through the agency that you work within. All measures will be made to ensure anonymity, including assigning all participants pseudonyms so that any data used in the research cannot be attributed to a particular participant.

Should you wish to withdraw your involvement in the project following the interview, this can be done up until 31 January 2017.

Services on offer if adversely affected

Participants in Australia: If in the unlikely scenario that you require them, the details of Beyond Blue are: 1300 359 467 or their online address is https://online.beyondblue.org.au/WebModules/Email/InitialInformation.aspx

Participants in the United Kingdom: If in the unlikely scenario that you require them, the details of NHS choices are www.nhs.uk/Pages/HomePage.aspx, and contact numbers to the appropriate services can be found on this webpage.

Participants in Ireland: If in the unlikely scenario that you require them, the details of Aware Support are: www.aware.ie/, and contact numbers to the appropriate services can be found on this webpage.

Confidentiality

Being in this study is voluntary and you are under no obligation to participate. All participants will remain anonymous through the use of codes. No names will appear in any data, transcripts or file notes. Pseudonyms will be used in draft copies and in the final thesis submissions to protect your privacy. This means that you involvement in the study will remain confidential.

Storage of data

All data collected will be stored in accordance with Monash University regulations, and kept on University premises, in a locked filing cabinet for five years. Only the chief investigator will have access to the data.

Use of data for other purposes

In addition to the Doctor of Philosophy (PhD) thesis, a report of the study may be submitted for publication in a journal(s) or through a conference paper(s), but individual participants will not be identifiable.

Results

If you would like to be informed of the aggregate research finding, please contact Mary Iliadis at mary.iliadis@monash.edu. The findings will be accessible for five years and may be made available through potential publications that could arise from this research project.

Complaints

Should you have any concerns or complaints about the conduct of the project, you are welcome to contact the Executive Officer, Monash University Human Research Ethics (MUHREC):
Room 111, Building 3e
Research Office
Monash University VIC 3800
Tel: +61 3 9905 2052
Fax: +61 3 9905 3831
Email: muhrec@monash.edu
Thank you,
Mary Iliadis

Appendix F

Consent form

CONSENT FORM
Interview Participants
Project: Adversarial justice and victims' rights: Reconceptualising the role of sexual assault victims
Chief Investigator: Mary Iliadis

I have been asked to take part in the Monash University research project specified above. I have read and understood the Explanatory Statement and I hereby consent to participate in this project.

I consent to the following:	*Yes*	*No*
I understand that I will be interviewed by the researcher	☐	☐
I understand that unless I otherwise inform the researcher before the interview, I agree to allow the interview to be audio-taped	☐	☐
I understand that my participation is voluntary and I can choose not to participate in part or all of the project, and I can withdraw at any stage of the project without being penalised or disadvantaged in any way.	☐	☐
I understand that any data that the researcher extracts from the interview for use in reports or published findings will not, under any circumstances, contain names or identifying characteristics without my signed consent below.	☐	☐
I understand that data from the interview will be kept in secure storage and accessible to the research team. I also understand that the data will be destroyed after a 5 year period.	☐	☐
I understand that no information I have provided that could lead to the identification of any other individual will be disclosed in any reports on the project, or to any other party.	☐	☐
I understand that I may ask at any time prior to 31 January 2016 for my data to be withdrawn from the project.	☐	☐

Name of Participant:

Participant Signature: Date:

References

Ames, A., Davis, S., Peckham, D., Boyle, E. & Micklewright, A. (2003), *Experiences of the criminal justice system: victims and witnesses of crime*, Audit Commission.

Armstrong, S. (2004), 'Is feminist law reform flawed? Abstentionists & sceptics', *Australian Feminist Law Journal*, 20/1, 43–63.

Australian Bureau of Statistics (2004), *Sexual assault in Australia: a statistical overview* (Cat. No. 4523.0), ABS, Melbourne.

Australian Institute of Family Studies (2014), *Victim/survivor-focused justice responses and reforms to criminal court practice: implementation, current practice and future directions*, research report, no. 27, March 2014, available online at https://aifs.gov.au/publications/victimsurvivor-focused-justice-responses-and-reforms-cri/executive-summary (last accessed 26 September 2017).

Australian Institute of Health and Welfare [AIHW] (2019), *Family, domestic and sexual violence in Australia: continuing the national story*, Cat. No. FDV 3, AIHW, Canberra.

Australian Law Reform Commission [ALRC] (2010), *Family violence: a national legal response*, Report 114, Sydney.

Babbie, E. (2010), *The practice of social research*, 13th edn, Cengage Learning, Wadsworth.

Bacik, I., Hanley, C., Murphy, J. & O'Driscoll, A. (2010), 'Separate legal representation in rape trials', paper presented at the *Rape Law: Victims on Trial? Conference*, 16 January 2010.

Bacik, I., Maunsell, C. & Gogan, S. (1998), *The legal process and victims of rape*, The Dublin Rape Crisis Centre, The School of Law, Trinity College, Dublin, available online at www.drcc.ie/wp-content/uploads/2011/03/rapevic.pdf (last accessed 10 August 2017).

Bankowski, Z. & Mugham, G. (2001), 'Appearing in courts and tribunals: a forensic degradation ceremony', in K. Laster (ed.), *Law as culture*, 2nd edn, The Federation Press, Sydney, pp. 331–4.

Barr, C. & Bowcott, O. (2019), 'Rape prosecutions in England and Wales at lowest level in a decade', *The Guardian*, 12 September, available online at www.theguardian.com/law/2019/sep/12/prosecutions-in-england-and-wales-at-lowest-level-in-a-decade.

Barsoux, J. L. & Manzoni, J. F. (1998), *Procedural justice in action: restructuring at Air France*, INSEAD, Fontainebleau, France.

Beloof, D. (2005), 'The third wave of crime victims' rights: standing remedy and review', *Brigham Young University Law Review*, 2/1, 255–370.

Blackstone, W. (1769, 1966), *Commentaries on the laws of England*, Clarendon Press, Oxford, reprinted, Dawsons of Pall Mall, London.

Bond, C., Holder, R., Jeffries, S. & Fleming, C. (2017), *Evaluation of the specialist domestic and family violence court trial in Southport*, Griffith Criminology Institute, available online at: www.courts.qld.gov.au/__data/assets/pdf_file/0018/515430/dfv-rpt-evaluation-dfv-court-southport-summary-report.pdf.

Booth, T. (2012), '"Cooling out" victims of crime: managing victim participation in the sentencing process in a superior sentencing court', *Australian and New Zealand Journal of Criminology*, 45/2, 214–30.

Booth, T. (2014a), 'The restorative capacities of victim impact statements: analysis of the victim–judge communication dyad in the sentencing of homicide offenders', *Restorative Justice*, 2/3, 253–77.

Booth, T. (2014b), 'Victim impact statements and the nature and incidence of offender remorse: findings from an observation study in a superior sentencing court', *Griffith Law Review*, 22/2, 430–55.

Booth, T. (2016), *Accommodating justice: victim impact statements in the sentencing process*, Federation Press, Sydney.

Booth, T. & Carrington, K. (2018), 'Victims' support in policy and legal process in Australia: still an ambivalent and contested space', in S. Walklate (ed.), *Handbook of victims and victimology*, Routledge, London. pp. 293–307.

Booth, T., Kaye, M. & Wangmann, J. (2019), 'Family violence, cross-examination and self-represented parties in the courtroom: the differences, gaps and deficiencies', *University of New South Wales Law Journal*, 42/3, 1106–42.

Bows, H. (2019), *Sexual violence against older people*, Routledge, London.

Bows, H. & Westmarland, N. (2016), 'Rape of older people in the United Kingdom: challenging the "real rape" stereotype', *British Journal of Criminology*, 57/1, 1–17.

Braithwaite, J. (1993), 'Juvenile offending: new theory and practice', in L. Atkinson & S. Gerull (eds), *National Conference on Juvenile Justice*, Australian Institute of Criminology, pp. 35–42.

Braun, K. (2014), 'Legal representation for sexual assault victims', *Current Issues in Criminal Justice*, 23/3, 819–37.

Braun, K. (2019), *Victim participation rights: variation across criminal justice systems*, Palgrave Macmillan, Switzerland.

Brienen, M. E. & Hoegen, E. H. (2001), *Victims of crime in 22 European criminal justice systems: the implementation of recommendations (85) 11 of the Council of Europe on the position of the victim in the framework of criminal law and procedure*, Wolf Legal Productions, Nijmegen, Netherlands.

Bronitt, S. (1998), 'The rules of recent complaint: rape myths and the legal construction of the "reasonable" rape victim', in P. Easteal (ed.), *Balancing the scales: rape, law reform and Australian culture*, The Federation Press, Leichhardt, Sydney, pp. 41–58.

Brown, J., Hamilton, C. & O'Neill, D. (2007), 'Characteristics associated with rape attrition and the role played by scepticism or legal rationality by investigators and prosecutors', *Psychology, Crime and Law*, 13/4, 355–70.

Brown, B., Burman, M. & Jamieson, L. (1992), *Sexual history and sexual character evidence in Scottish sexual offence trials*, Scottish Office, Central Research Unit Papers, Edinburgh.

Burgin, R. (2019), 'Persistent narratives of force and resistance: affirmative consent as law reform', *British Journal of Criminology*, 59/2, 296–314.

Burke, K. & Leben, S. (2007), 'Procedural fairness: a key ingredient in public satisfaction', *Court Review: The Journal of the American Judges Association*, 44, 4–25.

Burman, M., Jamieson, L., Nicholson, J. & Brooks, O. (2007), *Impact of aspects of the law of evidence in sexual offence trials: an evaluation study*, Scottish Government

Social Research, available online at: www.sccjr.ac.uk/wp-content/uploads/2009/01/Impact_of_Aspects_of_the_Law_of_Evidence_in_Sexual_Offence_Trials.pdf (last accessed 30 December 2019).

Campbell, R. (2006), 'Rape survivors' experiences with the legal and medical systems: do rape victim advocates make a difference?', *Violence Against Women*, 12/1, 30–45.

Canadian Department of Justice (2001), *Victims of crime research series: summary report on victim impact statement focus groups*, available online at www.justice.gc.ca/eng/rp-pr/cj-jp/victim/rr00_vic21/rr00_vic21.pdf (last accessed 6 January 2020).

Carrabine, E., Iganski, P., Lee, M., Plummer, K., & South, N. (2004), *Criminology: a sociological introduction*, Routledge, London.

CASA House (2010), *Our services*, Centre Against Sexual Assault, available online at www.casahouse.com.au/index.php?page_id=131 (last accessed 28 September 2017).

Cavadino, M. & Dignan, J. (1997), 'Reparation, retribution and rights', *International Review of Victimology*, 4/4, 233–53.

Centre for Innovative Justice (2014), *Innovative justice responses to sexual offending: pathways to better outcomes for victims, offenders and the community*, RMIT University, Melbourne.

Chan, J. (1997), *Changing police culture: policing in a multicultural society*, Cambridge University Press, Cambridge.

Chan, J. (2003), *Fair cop: learning the art of policing*, University of Toronto Press, Toronto.

Christie, N. (1986), 'The ideal victim', in E. Fattah (ed.), *From crime policy to victim policy*, MacMillan Press, UK, pp. 17–30.

Clark, H. (2010), 'What is the justice system willing to offer? Understanding sexual assault victim/survivors' criminal justice needs', *Family Matters*, 85, 28–37.

Clark, The Honourable Robert (2014), *Law Week Event 2014: victims of crime in the court process*, Victims Support Agency, Department of Justice.

Conley, J. & O'Barr, W. (1998), *Just words: law, language and power*, University of Chicago Press.

Cook, B., David, F. & Grant, A. (1999), *Victims' needs, victims' rights: policies and programs for victims of crime in Australia*, Research and Public Policy Series, no. 19, Australian Institute of Criminology, Canberra.

Crouch, M. & McKenzie, H. (2006), 'The logic of small samples in interview based qualitative research', *Social Science Information*, 45/4, 483–99.

Crown Prosecution Service [CPS] (2016), *Victims' right to review guidance*, CPS, available online at www.cps.gov.uk/sites/default/files/documents/publications/vrr_guidance_2016.pdf (last accessed 5 January 2020).

Currie, S. (1995), 'Validating women in the legal system: an analysis of the invisibility of women's perspectives in the law', *Social Alternatives*, 14/1, 14–17.

Dainow, J. (1966–67), 'The civil law and the common law: some points of comparison', *American Journal of Comparative Law*, *15/3*, 419–35.

Daly, K. (2002), 'Sexual assault and restorative justice', in Heather Strang & John Braithwaite (eds), *Restorative justice and family violence*, Cambridge University Press, Cambridge, pp. 62–88.

Daly, K. (2011), 'Conventional and innovative justice responses to sexual violence', *Australian Centre for the Study of Sexual Assault*, 12, 1–35.

Daly, K. (2017), 'Sexual violence and victims' justice needs', in Estelle Zinsstag & Marie Keenan (eds), *Sexual violence and restorative justice: legal, social and therapeutic dimensions*, Routledge, London.

Daly, K. & Bouhours, B. (2010), 'Rape and attrition in the legal process: a comparative analysis of five countries', in M. Tonry (ed.), *Crime and justice: a review of research*, vol. 39, University of Chicago Press, pp. 565–650.

Davis, C. K. (1969), 'Discretionary justice: a preliminary inquiry', *Case Western Law Review*, 21/1, 164–73.

Dean, C., Hardiman, A. & Draper, G. (1998), *National standards of practice manual for services against sexual violence*, National Association of Services Against Sexual Violence, CASA House, Melbourne.

Department of Justice and Equality (2018), 'Minister Flanagan publishes terms of reference for review of the investigation and prosecution of sexual offences', 7 September, available online at www.justice.ie/en/JELR/Pages/PR18000279 (last accessed 30 December 2019).

Deutsch, M. (1975), 'Equity, equality and need: what determines which value will be used as the basis of distributive justice?', *Journal of Social Issues*, 31/3, 137–49.

Dignan, J. (2005), *Understanding victims and restorative justice*, Open University Press, Maidenhead, UK.

Doak, J. (2005), 'Victims' rights in criminal trials: prospects for participation', *Journal of Law and Society*, 32/2, 294–316.

Doak, J. (2008), *Victims' rights, human rights and criminal justice: reconceiving the role of third parties*, Hart Publishing, Oxford and Portland, OR.

Doak, J., Henham, R. & Mitchell, B. (2009), 'Victims and the sentencing process: developing participatory rights?', *Legal Studies*, 29/4, 651–77.

Douglas, H. (2012), 'Battered women's experiences of the criminal justice system: decentring the law', *Feminist Legal Studies*, 20/2, 121–34.

Dowds, E. (2015), *Prosecuting rape in international criminal law: challenges and possibilities*, QUB Human Rights Centre.

Dowds, E. (2018), 'Conceptualizing the role of consent in the definition of rape at the international criminal court: a norm transfer perspective', *International Feminist Journal of Politics*, 20/4, 624–43.

Dussich, J. P. J. (2006), *Victimology: past, present and future*, available online at www.unafei.or.jp/publications/pdf/RS_No70/No70_12VE_Dussich.pdf (last accessed 26 August 2017).

Easteal, P. (1994), *Voices of the survivors*, Spinifex Press, Melbourne.

Easteal, P. (1998), *Balancing the scales: rape, law reform and Australian culture*, Federation Press, Leichhardt, NSW.

Easteal, P. & McOrmond-Plummer, L. (2006), *Real rape, real pain*, Hybrid Publishers, Melbourne.

Ehrlich, S. (2001), *Representing rape: language and sexual consent*, Routledge, New York.

Ellison, L. (2001), *The adversarial process and the vulnerable witness*, Oxford University Press, Oxford.

Ellison, L. (2007), 'Witness preparation and the prosecution of rape', *Legal Studies*, 27/2, 171–87.

Ellison, L. E. & Munro, V. E. (2009), 'Reacting to rape: exploring mock jurors' assessments of complainant credibility', *British Journal of Criminology*, 49/2, 202–19.

Engel, R. (2005), 'Citizens' perceptions of distributive and procedural injustice during traffic stops with police', *Journal of Research in Crime and Delinquency*, 42, 445–81.

Erez, E. (1989), 'The impact of victimology on criminal justice policy', *Criminal Justice Policy Review*, 3/3, 236–56.

Erez, E. (1990), 'Victim participation in sentencing: rhetoric and reality', *Journal of Criminal Justice*, 18/1, 19–31.

Erez, E. (1991), 'Victim impact statements', *Trends and Issues in Crime and Criminal Justice*, no. 2, Australian Institute of Criminology.

Erez, E. (2000), 'Integrating a victim perspective in criminal justice through victim impact statements', in A. Crawford & J. Goodey (eds), *Integrating a victim perspective within criminal justice*, Ashgate, Aldershot, UK, pp. 165–84.

Erez, E., Roeger, L. & O'Connell, M. (1996), 'Victim impact statements in South Australia', in C. Sumner (ed.), *International victimology: selected papers from the 8th International Symposium: Adelaide 21–26 August 1994*, Australian Institute of Criminology, Canberra, pp. 205–16.

Estrich, S. (1987), *Representing rape: language and sexual consent*, Routledge, London.

Fattah, A. (2000), 'Victimology: past, present and future', *Erudit*, 33/1, 17–46.

Feldthusen, B., Hankivsky, O. & Greaves, L. (2000), 'Therapeutic consequences of civil actions for damages and compensation claims by victims of sexual abuse', *Canadian Journal of Women and the Law*, 12, 66–116.

Fitzgerald, G. (1989), *Report of the commission of possible illegal activities and associated police misconduct*, Queensland Government Printer, Brisbane.

Fitz-Gibbon, K. (2014), *Homicide law reform, gender and the provocation defence: a comparative perspective*, Palgrave Macmillan, Basingstoke, UK.

Flood, M. & Pease, B. (2006), *The factors influencing community attitudes in relation to violence against women: a critical review of the literature*, Victorian Health Promotion Foundation, Melbourne.

Flynn, A. (2012), 'Bargaining with justice: victims, plea bargaining and the *Victims' Charter Act 2006* (Vic)', *Monash University Law Review*, 37/3, 73–96.

Flynn, A. (2016), 'Plea-negotiations, prosecutors and discretion: an argument for legal reform', *Australian and New Zealand Journal of Criminology*, 49/4, 564–82.

Flynn, A. & Freiberg, A. (2017), *Negotiating guilty pleas*, report to the Criminology Research Advisory Council, Australian Institute of Criminology, Canberra.

Flynn, A. & Henry, N. (2012), 'Disputing consent: the role of jury directions in Victoria', *Current Issues in Criminal Justice*, 24/2, 167–84.

Flynn, A. & Hodgson, J. (2017), 'Access to justice and legal aid cuts: a mismatch of concepts in the contemporary Australian and British legal landscapes', in A. Flynn & J. Hodgson (eds), *Access to justice and legal aid: comparative perspectives on unmet legal need*, Hart Publishing, Oxford, pp. 1–21.

Gans, J., Henning, T., Hunter, J. & Warner, K. (2011), *Criminal process and human rights*, The Federation Press, Annandale, NSW.

Garfinkel, H. (1956), 'Conditions of successful degradation ceremonies', *American Journal of Sociology*, 61/5, 420–4.

Garland, D. (2001), *The culture of control: crime and social order in contemporary society*, Oxford University Press, Oxford.

Sir John Gillen (2019), *The Gillen Review: Report into the law and procedures in serious sexual offences in Northern Ireland*, Final Report, available online at www.justice-ni.gov.uk/sites/default/files/publications/justice/gillen-report-may-2019.pdf (last accessed 30 December 2019).

Goffman, E. (1952), 'On cooling the mark out: some aspects of adaption to failure', *Psychiatry: Interpersonal and Biological Processes*, 15/4, 451–63.

Goldstein, A. S. (1984), 'The victim and prosecutorial discretion: the federal *Victim and Witness Protection Act* of 1982', *Law and Contemporary Problems*, 47/4, 225–48.

Gotell, L. (2007), 'The discursive disappearance of sexualized violence: feminist law reform, judicial resistance, and neo-liberal sexual citizenship', in D. E. Chunn, S. B. Boyd & H. Lessard (eds), *Reaction and resistance: feminism, law and social change*, UBC Press, Vancouver. pp. 127–63.

Gray, The Honourable Judge Ian (2014), *Law week event 2014: victims of crime in the court process*, Victim Support Agency, Department of Justice.

Hamilton, J. (2010), 'Rape law: victims on trial?' Dublin Rape Crisis Centre & the Law School Trinity College Conference 16 January 2010, available online at www.drcc.ie/2010/01/rape-law-victims-on-trial/ (last accessed 30 December 2019).

Hanly, C., Healy, D. & Scriver, S. (2009), *Rape and justice in Ireland*, Liffey Press, Dublin.

Hasday, E. J. (2000), 'Contest and consent: a legal history of marital rape', *California Law Review*, 88/5, 1373–505.

Heath, M. (2005), *The law and sexual offences against adults in Australia*, ACSSA no. 4, Australian Centre for the Study of Sexual Assault, Melbourne.

Heenan, M. (2003), 'Reconstituting the "relevance" of women's sexual histories in rape trials', *Women Against Violence: An Australian Feminist Journal*, 13, 4–17.

Heenan, M. (2014), *Law week event 2014: victims of crime in the court process*, Victim Support Agency, Department of Justice.

Heenan, M. & Murray, S. (2004), *Study of reported rapes in Victoria 2000–2003*, Statewide Steering Committee to Reduce Sexual Assault, Melbourne.

Heenan, M. & Murray, S. (2006), *Study of reported rapes in Victoria 2000–2003: summary research report*, Statewide Steering Committee to Reduce Sexual Assault, Office for Women's Policy, Melbourne.

Hellerstein, D. R. (1989), 'Victim impact statement: reform or reprisal?', *American Criminal Law Review*, 27, 391–430.

Henderson, E. (2015), 'Bigger fish to fry: should the reform of cross-examination be expanded beyond vulnerable witnesses?', *International Journal of Evidence and Proof*, 19/2, 83–99.

Henderson, L. N. (1985), 'The wrongs of victims' rights', *Stanford Law Review*, 37, 937–1021.

Herman, J. L. (1997), *Trauma and recovery: the aftermath of violence – from domestic abuse to political terror*, Basic Books, New York.

Herman, J. L. (2005), 'Justice from the victim's perspective', *Violence Against Women*, 11/5, 571–602.

Hilbery, M. (1946), *Duty and art in advocacy*, Stevens, London.

Hinds, L. & Murphy, K. (2007), 'Public satisfaction with police: using procedural justice to improve police legitimacy', *The Australian and New Zealand Journal of Criminology*, 40, 27–42.

Holder, R. (2018), *Just interests: victims, citizens and the potential for justice*, Edward Elgar Publishing Limited, Cheltenham, UK.

Holmstrom, J. A. & Burgess, A. W. (1978), *The victim of rape: institutional reactions*, Wiley, New York.

Houlihan, L. & Campbell, J. (2010), 'Sex assault victim "was denied fair hearing": magistrate scraps victim statement after going to wrong court and running out of time', available online at www.news.com.au/national/sex-assault-victim-claims-she-was-denied-fair-hearing/news-story/8f28244dd1d6d87a43c9591b1735ddf5.

Houses of the Oireachtas (2016), *Joint Committee on Justice and Equality*, available online at www.oireachtas.ie/parliament/oireachtasbusiness/committees_list/jde-committee/ (last accessed 27 October 2017).

Hoyano, L. (2014), 'What is balanced on the scales of justice? In search of the essence of the right to a fair trial', *Criminal Law Review*, 4(1), 4–29.

Htun, M. & Weldon, S. L. (2012), 'The civic origins of progressive policy change: combating violence against women in global perspective, 1975–2005', *American Political Science Review*, 106, 548–69.

Huxley-Binns, R. & Martin, J. (2014), *Unlocking the English legal system*, 4th edn, Routledge, London.

Iliadis, M. (2019), 'Victim representation for sexual history evidence in Ireland: a step towards or away from meeting victims' procedural justice needs?', *Criminology & Criminal Justice*, https://doi.org/10.1177/1748895819851848.

Iliadis, M., Fitz-Gibbon, K. & Walklate, S. (2019), 'Improving justice responses for victims of intimate partner violence: examining the merits of the provision of independent legal representation', *International Journal of Comparative and Applied Criminal Justice*, https://doi.org/10.1080/01924036.2019.1695639.

Iliadis, M. & Flynn, A. (2018), 'Providing a check on prosecutorial decision-making: an analysis of the Victims' Right to Review reform', *British Journal of Criminology*, 58/3, 550–68.

Iliadis, M. & Flynn, A. (2019), 'Victims deserve a right of review', *The Australian*, 17 May 2019.

International Criminal Court (2017), *International Criminal Court*, available online at www.icc-cpi.int/about/victims (last accessed 12 September 2017).

Irish Law Reform Commission [ILRC] (1987), *Rape consultation paper*, ILRC, available online at www.lawreform.ie/_fileupload/consultation%20papers/cpRape.htm (last accessed 28 September 2017).

Irish Law Reform Commission [ILRC] (1988), *Rape and allied offences*, ILRC, available online at www.lawreform.ie/_fileupload/Reports/rRape.htm (last accessed 28 September 2017).

Jehle, J. M. (2012), 'Attrition and conviction rates of sexual offences in Europe: definitions and criminal justice responses', *European Journal on Criminal Policy and Research*, 18, 145–61.

Johns, R. (2002), *Victims of crime: plea bargains, compensation, victim impact statements and support services briefing paper*, available online at www.parliament.nsw.gov.au/researchpapers/Documents/victims-of-crime-plea-bargains-compensation-vict/10-02.pdf (last accessed 26 October 2017).

Johnston, M. (2010), 'Attorney-General Rob Hulls weighs into magistrate row', *Herald Sun*, available online at www.heraldsun.com.au/news/lost-justice-for-sex-assault-victim/story-e6frf7jo-1225881777672 (last accessed 8 August 2017).

Jones, A. N., Parmentier, S. & Weitekamp, G. M. E. (2014), 'Transitional justice in Bosnia-Herzegovina: understanding accountability, reparation and justice for victims', in J. Wemmers (ed.), *Reparation for victims of crimes against humanity: the healing role of reparation*, Routledge, London, pp. 143–54.

Jordan, J. (1998), *Reporting rape: women's experiences with the police, doctors and support agencies*, Institute of Criminology, Wellington, NZ.

Jordan, J. (2001), 'Worlds apart? Women, rape and the police reporting process', *British Journal of Criminology*, 41/4, 679–706.

Jordan, J. (2004a), 'Beyond belief? Police, rape and women's credibility', *Criminal Justice*, 4/1, 29–53.

Jordan, J. (2004b), *The word of a woman? Police, rape and belief*, Palgrave Macmillan, Basingstoke, UK.

Jordan, J. (2008), *Serial survivors: women's narratives of surviving rape*, The Federation Press, Sydney.

Jordan, J. (2013), 'From victim to survivor – and from survivor to victim: reconceptualising the survivor journey', *Sexual Abuse in Australia and New Zealand*, 5/2, 48–56.

Karmen, A. (1992), 'Who's against victims' rights? The nature of the opposition to pro-victim initiatives in criminal justice', *St John's Journal of Legal Commentary*, 8/1, 157–75.

Karmen, A. (2013), *Crime victims: an introduction to victimology*, 8th edn, Wadsworth, Cengage Learning, Belmont, California.

Kelly, D. P. (1982), 'Victim's reaction to the criminal justice response', paper prepared for the Annual Meeting of the Law and Society Association, Toronto.

Kelly, L. (2002), *A research review on the reporting, investigation and prosecution of rape cases*, Her Majesty's Crown Prosecution Service Inspectorate, London.

Kelly, L., Lovett, J. & Regan, L. (2005), *A gap or chasm? Attrition in reported rape cases*, Home Office Research Study no. 293, Home Office, London.

Kelly, L., Temkin, J. & Griffiths, S. (2006), *Section 41: an evaluation of new legislation limiting sexual history evidence in rape trials*, Home Office Report, London, available online at http://citeseerx.ist.psu.edu/viewdoc/download?doi=10.1.1.628.3925&rep=rep1&type=pdf.

King, M. (2009), *Solution-focused judging bench book*, Australian Institute of Judicial Administration and the Legal Services Board of Victoria, Melbourne, available online at https://aija.org.au/wp-content/uploads/2017/07/Solution-Focused-Judging-Bench-Book.pdf (last accessed 30 December 2019).

Kirchengast, T. (2006), *The victim in criminal law and justice*, Palgrave MacMillan, Basingstoke, UK.

Kirchengast, T. (2010), *The criminal trial in law and discourse*, Palgrave Macmillan, Basingstoke, UK.

Kirchengast, T. (2013), 'Victim lawyers, victim advocates and the adversarial criminal trial', *New Criminal Law Review: An International and Interdisciplinary Journal*, 16/4, 568–94.

Kirchengast, T. (2016a), 'Victims' rights and the rights to review: a corollary of the victim's pre-trial rights to justice', *International Journal for Crime, Justice and Social Democracy*, 5/4, 103–15.

Kirchengast, T. (2016b), *Victims and the criminal trial*, Palgrave MacMillan, Basingstoke, UK.

Kirchengast, T. (2016c), *Victimology and victim rights: international comparative perspectives*, Routledge, Oxon, UK.

Kirchengast, K., Iliadis, M. & O'Connell, M. (2019), 'Development of the Office of Commissioner of Victims' Rights as an appropriate response to improving the experiences of victims in the criminal justice system: integrity, access and justice for victims of crime', *Monash University Law Review*, 45(1), 1–28.

Klug, F. (2004), 'Human rights and victims', in E. Cape (ed.), *Reconcilable rights? Analysing the tension between victims and defendants*, Legal Action Group, pp. 111–24.

Koss, M. P. (2006), 'Restoring rape survivors: justice, advocacy and a call to action', *Annals of the New York Academy of Sciences*, 1097, 206–34.

Larcombe, W. (2011), '*Worsnop v The Queen*: subjective belief in consent prevails (again) in Victoria's rape law', *Melbourne University Law Review*, 35/2, 697–716.

Larcombe, W., Fileborn, B., Powell, A., Hanley, N. & Henry, N. (2016), 'I think it's rape and I think he would be found not guilty', *Social and Legal Studies*, 25/5, 611–29.

Lees, S. (1993), 'Judicial rape', *Women's Studies International Forum*, 16/1, 11–36.

Lees, S. (1996), *Carnal knowledge: rape on trial*, Hamish Hamilton, London.

Lees, S. (2002), *Carnal knowledge: rape on trial*, The Women's Press, London.

Lees, S. & Gregory, J. (1993), *Rape and sexual assault: a study of attrition*, Islington Borough Council, London.

Legal Aid Board (2019), *Submission to the review of the investigation and prosecution of sexual offences*, accessed 16 January 2019.

Leventhal, G. S. (1976), 'The distribution of rewards and resources in groups and organizations', in L. Berkowitz & W. Walster (eds), *Advances in experimental social psychology*, Academic Press, New York, vol. 9, pp. 91–131.

Leventhal, G. S. (1980), 'What should be done with equity theory? New approaches to the study of fairness in social relationships', in K. J. Gergen, M. S. Greenberg & R. H. Willis (eds), *Social exchange: advances in theory and research*, Plenum, New York, pp. 27–55.

Lievore, D. (2003), *Non-reporting and hidden recording of sexual assault: an international literature review*, Office of the Status of Women, Canberra.

Lievore, D. (2005a), *No longer silent: a study of women's help-seeking decisions and service responses to sexual assault*, Office for Women, Canberra.

Lievore, D. (2005b), *Prosecutorial decisions in adult sexual assault cases: trends and issues in crime and criminal justice*, Australian Institute of Criminology, Canberra.

Lind, A. & Tyler, T. (1988), *The social psychology of procedural justice*, Plenum Press, New York.

Loftus, B. (2009), *Police culture in a changing world*, Oxford University Press, Oxford, UK.

Madigan, L. & Gamble, N. (1991), *The second rape: society's continued betrayal of the victim*, Lexington Books, New York.

Maguire, M. & Bennett, T. (1982), *Burglary in a dwelling: the offence, the offender and the victim*, Heinemann, London.

Mahoney, P., Williams, L. M. & West, C. M. (2001), 'Violence against women by intimate relationship partners', in C. M. Renzetti, J. L. Edleson & R. K. Bergen (eds), *Sourcebook on violence against women*, Sage Publications, Thousand Oaks, California, pp. 143–78.

Mason, M. (1995), 'Reforming the law of rape: incursions into the masculinist sanctum', in D. Kirby (ed.), *Sex, power and justice: historical perspectives of law in Australia*, Oxford University Press, Melbourne, pp. 50–67.

Mason, M. (2010), 'Sample size and saturation in PhD studies using qualitative interviews', *Forum: Qualitative Social Research*, 11/3, Article 8, available online at www.qualitative-research.net/index.php/fqs/article/view/1428/3027.

Mazengarb, O. (1964), *Advocacy in our time*, Sweet and Maxwell, London.

McAsey, B. (2011), 'Victim participation at the international criminal court and its impact on procedural fairness', *Australian International Law Journal*, 18, 105–25.

McBarnet, D. (1983), 'Victim in the witness box: confronting victimology's stereotype', *Contemporary Crises*, 7/3, 279–303.

McDonald, E. (2011), 'The views of complainants and the provision of information, support, and legal advice: how much should a prosecutor do?', *Canterbury Law Review*, 17, 66–87.

McGarry, R. & Walklate, S. (2015), *Victims: trauma, testimony and justice,* Routledge, London.

McGlynn C. (2017), 'Rape trials and sexual history evidence: reforming the law on third party evidence', *Journal of Criminal Law*, 81/5, 367–92.

McGlynn, C., Downes, J. & Westmarland, N. (2017), 'Seeking justice for survivors of sexual violence: recognition, voice and consequences', in E. Zinsstag & M. Keenan (eds), *Sexual violence and restorative justice: legal, social and therapeutic dimensions*, Routledge, London.

McGlynn, C., Westmarland, N. & Godden, N. (2012), '"I just wanted him to hear me": sexual violence and the possibilities of restorative justice', *Journal of Law and Society*, 39/2, 213–40.

McSherry, B. (1998), 'Constructing lack of consent', in P. Easteal (ed.), *Balancing the scales: rape, law reform and Australian culture*, Federation Press, Annandale, NSW. pp. 26–40.

Mendelsohn, B. (1940), 'Rape in criminology', translated and cited in S. Schafer (1968), *The victim and his criminal*, Random House, New York.

Mendelsohn, B. (1956), 'Une nouvelle branche de la science bio-psycho-sociale, la victimologie', *Etudes Internationales de Psycho-Sociologie Criminelle*, France, July-September.

Mendelsohn, B. (1963), 'The origin of the doctrine of victimology', *Excerpta Criminal*, 3, 239–44.

Miers, D. (1989), 'Positivist victimology: a critique', *International Review of Victimology*, 1/1, 3–22.

Mieth, D. T. (1985), 'The myth or reality of victim involvement in crime: a review and comment on victim-precipitation research', *Sociological Focus*, 18/3, 209–20.

Miller, L. S. & Hefner, M. K. (2013), 'Procedural justice for victims and offenders?: exploring restorative justice processes in Australia and the US', *Justice Quarterly*, 32/1, 142–67.

Ministry of Justice (2015), *Code of practice for victims of crime*, Ministry of Justice, UK.

Mohr, R. (2002), *Words are not enough: sexual assault – legislation, education and information*, Department of Justice, Ottawa, Canada, 16–17.

Morison, J. & Leith, P. (1992), *The barrister's world and the nature of law*, Open University Press, Milton Keynes, UK.

Nichols, M. (2001), 'No one can serve two masters: arguments against private prosecutors', *Capital Defence Journal*, 13/2, 279–305.

O'Connell, M. (2006), 'Evolving mechanisms for engaging victims in the sentencing process: should victims have a stronger voice in court?', in *Conference, Sentencing Principles, Perspectives & Possibilities*, Canberra.

O'Connell, M. (2008), 'Victimology: a social science in waiting?', *International Review of Victimology*, 15/2, 91–104.

O'Connell, M. (2012), *Victims' rights: integrating victims in criminal proceedings*, Commission for Victims' Rights, Government of South Australia.

O'Connell, M. (2015a), *Victimisation, justice and healing: challenging orthodoxies*, World Society of Victimology, 15th International Symposium, Perth Convention and Exhibition Centre, Perth, WA.

O'Connell, M. (2015b) 'The evolution of victims' rights and services in Australia', in D. Wilson and S. Ross (eds), *Crime, victims and policy: international contexts, local experiences*, Palgrave MacMillan, Basingstoke, UK. pp. 240–77.

Office for National Statistics (2013), *Focus on violent crime and sexual offences*, London, available online at www.ons.gov.uk/peoplepopulationandcommunity/crimeandjustice/compendium/focusonviolentcrimeandsexualoffences/2015-02-12.

Office for National Statistics (2018), *Sexual offences in England and Wales: year ending March 2017*, London, available online at www.ons.gov.uk/peoplepopulationandcommunity/crimeandjustice/articles/sexualoffencesinenglandandwales/yearendingmarch2017.

Office of Public Prosecutions [OPP] (2017), *Witnesses and victims*, Witness Assistance Service, OPP, Victoria, available online at https://victimsandwitnesses.opp.vic.gov.au/witnesses/witness-assistance-service (last accessed 2 January 2020).

Orth, U. (2002), 'Secondary victimization of crime victims by criminal proceedings', *Social Justice Research*, 15/4, 313–25.

Packer, H. (1968), *The limits of the criminal sanction*, Stanford University Press, California.

Papendick, M. & Bohner, G. (2017), '"Passive victim – strong survivor"? Perceived meaning of labels applied to women who were raped', *PLoS One*, 12/5, 1–21.

Paternoster, R., Brame, R., Bachman, R. & Sherman, W. L. (1997), 'Do fair procedures matter? The effect of procedural justice on spouse assault', *Law & Society Review*, 31/1, 163–204.

Payne, S. (2009), *Rape: the victim experience review*, Home Office, available online at https://webarchive.nationalarchives.gov.uk/+/http:/www.homeoffice.gov.uk/documents/vawg-rape-review/rape-victim-experience2835.pdf?view=Binary (last accessed 2 January 2020).

Pirro, J. (2004), *To punish and protect: a DA's fight against a system that coddles criminals*, 1st edn, Touchstone, New York.

Pizzi, W. T. & Perron, W. (1996), 'Crime victims in German courtrooms: a comparative perspective on American problems', *Stanford Journal of International* Law, 32/1, 37–64.

Plater, D. & Line, L. (2012), 'Has the "silver thread" of the criminal law lost its lustre? The modern prosecutor as a minister of justice', *University of Tasmania Law Review*, 31/2, 55–95.

Powell, A., Henry, N., Flynn, A. & Henderson, E. (2013), 'Meanings of sex and consent: the persistence of rape myths in Victorian rape law', *Griffith Law Review*, 22/2, 456–80.

Precel, N., Dexter, R. & Marsh, E. (2019), 'Are we failing victims of sexual violence?', *The Sydney Morning Herald*, 13 September, available online at www.smh.com.au/interactive/2019/are-we-failing-victims-of-sexual-violence-v-2/ (last accessed 6 January 2020).

Radford, J. (2006), 'Radical feminism', in E. McLaughlin & J. Muncie (eds), *The Sage dictionary of criminology*, 2nd edn, Sage, London.

Raitt, E. F. (2010), *Independent legal representation for complainers in sexual offence trials*, Research Report for Rape Crisis Scotland.

Rakoff, J. (2014), 'Why innocent people plead guilty', *The New York Review of Books*, 20 November, available online at www.nybooks.com/articles/2014/11/20/why-innocent-people-plead-guilty/ (last accessed 7 November 2016).

Rape Crisis Network Ireland [RCNI] (2010), *Rape and justice in Ireland*, available online at www.rcni.ie/wp-content/uploads/RAJIHandbook.pdf (last accessed 11 September 2017).

Rape Crisis Network Ireland [RCNI] (2012), *Previous sexual history evidence and separate legal representation: RCNI position paper on previous sexual history evidence in criminal trials*, May 2012, available online at www.rcni.ie/wp-content/uploads/RCNIPreviousSexualHistorySLRPositionPaperMay12.pdf (last accessed 10 August 2017).

Refshauge, Justice Richard (2013), 'Enhancing justice, empowering victims: victims in the criminal justice system – how creative can we be?', in proceedings of *National Victims of Crime Conference 2013*, Victim Support Service (SA), Office for Women (SA), Victims Support Australia Inc.

Reiner, R. (2010), *The politics of the police*, 4th edn, Oxford University Press, Oxford UK.

Resick, P. (1987), 'Psychological effects of victimization: implications for the criminal justice system', *Crime & Delinquency*, 33/4, 468–78.

Roberts, V. J. & Manikis, M. (2012), 'Victim personal statements in England and Wales: latest (and last) trends from the witness and victim experience survey', *Criminology and Criminal Justice*, 13/2, 245–61.

Rock, P. (1993), *The social world of an English crown court: witnesses and professionals in the crown court centre at wood green*, Clarendon Press, Oxford.

Rock, P. (1994), *Victimology*, Ashgate, Aldershot, UK.

Rock, P. (2007), 'New labour policies for victims', *Criminal Justice Matters*, 67/1, 38–9.

Royal Commission into Family Violence [RCFV] (2016), *Report and recommendations: volume III*, RCFV, Melbourne.

Royal Commission into Institutional Responses to Child Sexual Abuse [RCIRCSA] (2017), *Final report: recommendations*, Commonwealth of Australia.

Ryan, M. (2003), *Penal policy and political culture in England and Wales*, Waterside Press, Winchester, UK.

Sanders, A. & Jones, I. (2007), 'The victim in court', in S. Walklate (ed.), *Handbook of victims and victimology*, Willan Publishing, Cullompton, UK. pp. 282–308.

Sebba, L. (1996), *Third parties: victims and the criminal justice system*, Ohio State University Press, Columbus, OH.

Segrave, M., Wilson, W. & Fitz-Gibbon, K. (2018), 'Policing intimate partner violence in Victoria (Australia): Examining police attitudes and the potential of specialisation', *Australia and New Zealand Journal of Criminology*, 51/1, 99–116.

Shapland, J., Willmore, J. & Duff, P. (1985), *Victims in the criminal justice system*, Gower Publishing, Vermont, NH.

Shaw, D. (2014), 'Victims' Right of Review scheme sees 146 charged', *BBC News*, 19 July 2014, available online at www.bbc.com/news/uk-28377445, (last accessed 2 January 2020).

Skelton, A. & Frank, C. (2004), 'How does restorative justice address human rights and due process issues?', in H. Zehr & B. Toews (eds), *Critical issues in restorative justice*, Willan Publishing, Cullompton, UK. pp. 203–14.

Skolnik, J. & Fyfe, J. (1993), *Above the law: police and the excessive use of force*, Free Press, New York.

Smith, O. (2018), *Rape trials in England and Wales: observing justice and rethinking rape myths*, Palgrave, Basingstoke, UK.

Smith, O. & Skinner, T. (2017), 'How rape myths are used and challenged in rape and sexual assault trials', *Social & Legal Studies*, 26/4, 441–66.

Spencer, P. (2017), 'A view from the bench: a judicial perspective on legal representation, court excellence and therapeutic jurisprudence', in A. Flynn & J. Hodgson (eds), *Access to justice and legal aid: comparative perspectives on unmet legal need*, Hart Publishing, London.

Starkweather, D. A. (1992), 'The retributive theory of "just deserts" and victim participation in plea bargaining', *Indiana Law Journal*, 67/3, 853–78.

Stern Review (2010), *Rape reporting in England and Wales*, Home Office, London.

Stevenson, K. (2000), 'Unequivocal victims: the historical roots of the mystification of the female complainant in rape cases', *Feminist Legal Studies*, 8/3, 343–66.

Strang, H. (2002), *Repair or revenge: victims and restorative justice*, Clarendon Press, Oxford.

Strang, H. & Sherman, L. (2003), 'Repairing the harm: victims and restorative justice', *Utah Law Review*, 15/1, 15–42.

Stubbs, J. (2003), 'Sexual assault, criminal justice and law and order', *Women Against Violence: An Australian Feminist Journal*, 14, 14–26.

Stubbs, J. & Tolmie, J. (2008), 'Battered women charged with homicide: advancing the interests of indigenous women', *Australian and New Zealand Journal of Criminology*, 41, 138–61.

Sweeting, A., Owen, R., Turley, C., Rock, P., Garcia-Sanche, M., Wilson, L., Khan, U. (2008). (2008), *Evaluation of the victims' advocate scheme pilots*, Ministry of Justice Research Series 17/8, Ministry of Justice, London.

Talbert, P. A. (1988), 'The relevance of victim impact statements to the criminal sentencing decisions', *UCLA Law Review*, 36, 199–232.

Tankebe, J. (2013), 'Viewing things differently: the dimensions of public perceptions of police legitimacy', *The American Society of Criminology*, 51/1, 103–35.

Taylor, N. (2007), 'Juror attitudes and biases in sexual assault cases', *Trends & Issues in Crime and Criminal Justice*, Australian Institute of Criminology, 344, 1–6.

Taylor, S. C. (2004), *Court licensed abuse: patriarchal lore and the legal response to intrafamilial sexual abuse of children*, Peter Lang, New York.

Temkin, J. (2000), 'Prosecuting and defending rape: perspectives from the bar', *Journal of Law and Society*, 27/2, 219–48.

Temkin, J. & Krahé, B. (2008), *Sexual assault and the justice gap: a question of attitude*, Hart Publishing, Oxford.

Thibaut, J. W. & Walker, L. (1975), *Procedural justice: a psychological analysis*, Erlbaum, Mahwah, NJ.

Tuohy, W. (2017), 'Myths about how rape and sex assault victims "should" react will be busted by Victoria Police', *Herald Sun*, 23 June.

Tyler, T. (1988), 'What is procedural justice?: criteria used by citizens to assess the fairness of legal procedures', *Law and Society Review*, 22/1, 103–35.

Tyler, T. (1992), 'The psychological consequences of judicial procedures: implications for civil commitment hearings', *SMU Law Review*, 46, 433–48.

Tyler, T. (2006), *Why people obey the law*, Princeton University Press, Princeton, NJ.

Tyler, T. (2007), 'Procedural justice and the courts', *Court Review: The Journal of the American Judges Association*, 44/1–2, 25–31.

United Kingdom Judiciary (2017), *Judicial review*, Courts and Tribunals Judiciary, available online at www.judiciary.gov.uk/you-and-the-judiciary/judicial-review/ (last accessed 22 May 2017).

Van de Zandt, P. (1998), 'Heroines of fortitude', in P. Easteal, *Balancing the scales: rape, law reform and Australian culture*, The Federation Press, Sydney, pp. 124–42.

Victims of Crime Assistance Tribunal [VOCAT] (2016), Assistance available: primary victim, available online at www.vocat.vic.gov.au/assistance-available/types-victims/primary-victim (last accessed 3 January 2020).

Victims Support Agency (2009), *A victim's voice, victim impact statements in Victoria: executive summary*, Department of Justice, Victoria.

Victims Support Agency (2013), *Information and support needs of victims and witnesses in the Magistrates' Court of Victoria*, Department of Justice, Victoria.

Victorian Community Council Against Violence [VCCAV] (1997), *Community knowledge and perceptions of sentencing in Victoria: a report on the findings of the consultations*, VCCAV, Victoria.

Victorian Law Reform Commission [VLRC] (2001), *Sexual offences: law and procedure discussion paper*, VLRC, Melbourne.

Victorian Law Reform Commission [VLRC] (2003), *Sexual offences: interim report*, VLRC, Melbourne.

Victorian Law Reform Commission [VLRC] (2004), *Sexual offences: final report*, VLRC, Melbourne.

Victorian Law Reform Commission [VLRC] (2015), *The role of victims of crime in the criminal trial process*, consultation paper, available online at www.lawreform.vic.gov.au/sites/default/files/VLRC_Victims_of_Crime_consultation_paper_for_web_0.pdf (last accessed 30 December 2019).

Victorian Law Reform Commission [VLRC] (2016), *The role of victims of crime in the criminal trial process*, available online at www.parliament.vic.gov.au/file_uploads/VLRC_Victims_Of_Crime-Report_2016_sMw0x7nm.pdf (last accessed 30 December 2019).

Victorian Sentencing Advisory Council [VSAC] (2006), *Myths and misconceptions: public opinion versus public judgement about sentencing*, research paper, available online at www.sentencingcouncil.vic.gov.au/publications/myths-and-misconceptions-public-opinion-versus-public-judgment-about-sentencing (last accessed 30 December 2019).

Von Hentig, H. (1940), 'Remarks on the interaction of perpetrator and victim', *Journal of Criminal Law and Criminology*, 31, 303–9.

Von Hentig, H. (1948), *The criminal & his victim*, Yale University Press, New Haven, CT.

Walker, N. & Telford, M. (2000), *Designing criminal justice: the system in comparative perspective*, Report 14, Review of the Criminal Justice System in Northern Ireland, London, HMSO.

Walklate, S. (2005), *Criminology: the basics*, Routledge, New York.

Walklate, S. (2008), 'What is to be done about violence against women?' *British Journal of Criminology*, 48/1, 39–54.

Walster, E., Berscheid, E. & Walster, G. W. (1973), 'New directions in equity research', *Journal of Personality and Social Psychology*, 25/2, 151–76.

Wemmers, M. J. (2009), 'Where do they belong? Giving victims a place in the criminal justice process', *Criminal Law Forum*, 20, 395–416.

Wemmers, M. J. (2013), 'Victims' rights are human rights: the importance of recognizing victims as persons', *Temida*, June 2012, ISSN: 1450–6637, available at SSRN: https://ssrn.com/abstract=2364886.

Wemmers, M. J. (2014), *Reparation for victims of crimes against humanity: the healing role of reparation*, Routledge, London and New York.

Wexler, D. & Winick, B. (1996), *Law in a therapeutic key*, Academic Press, Durham, NC.

Wiebe, R. P. (1996), 'The mental health implications of crime victims' rights', in D. Wexler & B. Winick (eds), *Law in a therapeutic key*, Carolina Academic Press, Durham, NC, pp. 213–41.

Wilcox, P. (2010), 'Victimisation, theories of', in B. Fisher & S. Lab (eds), *Encyclopedia of victimology and crime prevention*, SAGE Publications, Thousand Oaks, CA. pp. 978–86.

Wolfgang, M. E. (1957), 'Victim precipitated criminal homicide', *Journal of Criminal Law and Criminology and Political Science*, 48, 1–11.

Wood, J. (1996), *Royal commission into the New South Wales police service: interim report*, New South Wales Government Printer, Sydney.

Woodhouse, Sir Owen (1967), *Royal Commission of Inquiry: Compensation for Personal Injury in New Zealand*, Government Printer, Wellington, NZ.

Wright, M. (2004), 'The rights and needs of victims in the criminal justice process', in H. Kaptein & M. Malsch (eds), *Crime, victims and justice: essays on principles and practice*, Ashgate, Aldershot, UK.

Zehr, H. (2003), 'Retributive justice, restorative justice', in G. Johnstone (ed.), *A restorative justice reader: text, sources, context*, Willan Publishing, Cullompton, UK.

Legislation, treaties and declarations

An Garda Síochána *Victims' Charter* (Irl)

Charter of Human Rights and Responsibilities Act 2006 (Vic)

Children's Protection Act 1993 (SA)

Civil Legal Aid Act 1995 (Irl)

Code of Practice for Victims of Crime 2015 (UK)

Constitution Act 1934 (SA)

Convention on Preventing and Combating Violence Against Women and Domestic Violence. (2011), opened for signature 11 May 2011, entered into force 1 August 2014.

Convention on the Rights of the Child. (1989), (resolution 44/25), opened for signature 20 November 1989, entered into force 2 September 1990.

Crimes Act 1958 (Vic)

Crimes Act 1914 (Cth)

Crimes Amendment (Rape) Act 2007 (Vic)

Crimes Amendment (Rape) Bill 2007 (Vic)

Criminal Code 1985 (RSC)

Criminal Code Act 1899 (QLD)

Criminal Code Act 1995 (Cth)

Criminal Code Act Compilation Act 1913 (WA)

Criminal Evidence Act 1992 (Irl)

Criminal Justice Act 2003 (UK)

Criminal Justice (Sexual Offences) Act 2017 (Irl)

Criminal Law Consolidation Act 1935 (SA)

Criminal Law (Rape) Act 1981 (Irl)

Criminal Law (Sentencing) Act 1988 (SA)

Criminal Practice Directions [2013] EWCA Crim 1631

Criminal Procedure Act 2009 (Vic)

Criminal Procedure Act 1986 (NSW)

Criminal Procedure Act 1995 (Scot)

Declaration of Basic Principles of Justice for Victims of Crime and Abuse of Power 1985

Directive 2012/29/EU of the European Parliament and of the Council of 25 October 2012, Establishing Minimum Standards on the Rights, Support and Protection of Victims of Crime, and Replacing Council Framework Decision 2001/220/JHA.

Evidence Act 1929 (SA)

Evidence Act 2008 (Vic)

German Code s397a(1), 395(1)

Jury Directions Act 2015 (Vic)

Legal Aid, Sentencing and Punishment of Offenders Act 2012 (UK)

Privacy and Data Protection Act 2014 (Vic)

Public Prosecutions Act 1994 (Vic)

Sentencing Act 2017 (SA)

Sentencing Act 1991 (Vic)

Sex Offenders Act 2001 (Irl)

Sexual Offences Act 2003 (UK)

Sexual Offences (Criminal Procedure) Act 2002 (Scot)

Sexual Offences (Procedure and Evidence) Act 2002 (Scot)

The Code for Crown Prosecutors 2013 (UK)

The Victims' Bill of Rights 2001 (Manitoba)

Universal Declaration of Human Rights 1948 (resolution 217 A), adopted 10 December 1948
United Nations Declaration of Basic Principles of Justice for Victims of Crime and Abuse of Power 1985 (resolution 40/34), adopted 29 November 1985.
Victims' Charter Act 2006 (Vic)
Victims' Charter and Guide to the Criminal Justice System 2010 (Irl)
Victims of Crime Act 1996 (RSBC)
Victims of Crime Act 2001 (SA)
Victims of Crime Commissioner Act 2015 (Vic)
Victorian Criminal Charge Book
Victims Rights and Support Act 2013 (NSW)
Youth Justice and Criminal Evidence Act 1999 (UK)

Cases

Attorney-General's Reference (No 3 of 1999) [2001] 2 AC 91 [118]) cited with approval by the House of Lords in R v H [2004] 2 AC 134, 145–6.
Crampton v The Queen (2000) 206 CLR 161, 173, (Gleeson CJ).
Dix v Attorney-General [2002] AJ No 784.
Doggett v The Queen (2001) 208 CLR 343, 246 (Gleeson CJ) cited in David Ross, Ross on Crime (Lawbook Co, 2nd edn, 2004), 231 [20.1405].
Jago v District Court of New South Wales (1989) 168 CLR 23.
Judge v UK, Application No 35863/10, 2011 SCCR 241 at 28.
Lord Steyn cited in R v H [2004] 2 AC 134, 145–6.
R v A (No 2) [2002] 1 AC 45.
R v Carroll [2002] HCA 55; 213 CLR 635 at 643 [21].
R v H [2004] 2 AC 134, 145–6.
R v Killick [2011] EWCA Crim 1608, [2012] 1 Cr. App. R. 10 [48].
R v Milton Keynes Magistrates' Court; ex parte Roberts [1995] Crim LR 225.
Worsnop v The Queen [2010] 28 VR 187.

Index

Page numbers in **bold** denote tables.

accountability: of the Victims' Right to Review (VRR) (*see* Victims' Right to Review (VRR), accountability of); of the accused 58, 62, 103; of the criminal justice system 79, 80–1 (*see* Victims' Right to Review (VRR)); of police and prosecutors 37; of victims 31
accused: and consent 46, 47; due process rights of 6, 42, 136–7, 150; fairness to 42, 62–3, 164; and harsher sentences 58; interests of 4, 42; and legal aid 138–9; rights of 2, 4, 11, 15, 128, 163; and sexual history evidence 106; status of, within adversarial system 2, 5, 11; status of, within inquisitorial systems 14
adversarial justice 2, 5–6, 8, 16, 42, 112, 116, 122, 127, 134, 157, 166; adversarial criminal trial 38, 126; and victims 3, 17, 24, 28, 30, 43, 70, 152, 154, 155, 162, 165
adversarial system *see* adversarial justice
An Garda Síochána *Victims' Charter* (Irl) 101
appeals 50; Appeals and Review Unit (CPS) 12, 74, 76, 85
attrition 32, 102, 106, 134; improper 41, 68, 153
Australian Institute of Family Studies (AIFS) 59–60, 63–4

Blackstone, William 6, 43
Braun, Dr Kerstin 3, 8, 9, 12, 13, 14, 15, 16, 27, 28, 36, 45, 51, 53, 128
burden of proof of state prosecutor 5, 26n7, 85

Centre for Innovative Justice 58
Centres Against Sexual Assault 141, 151n3
charging 12, 73, 75, 82–3, 90, 91
Charter of Human Rights and Responsibilities Act 2006 (Vic) 7
Children's Protection Act 1993 (SA) 118
Child Witness Service 141, 151n3
Clark, Haley 10, 40, 58–9, 63, 66, 67–71, 80, 170, 174, 177, 181
Code of Practice for Victims of Crime 2015 (UK) 75
commissioners for victims' rights 28, 123, 147; *see also* South Australian Commissioner for Victims' Rights (SACVR); Victims of Crime Commissioner (VoCC)
compensation for victims 4, 61, 65, 78, 113
complainants *see* victims; witnesses
compliance with the law 62–3
control, by victims over criminal justice process 10, 13, 39, 40, 57, 60, 62, 63, 64, 70–2, 77–9, 81–3, 86, 87, 100, 101, 118, 119, 128, 130, 158; *see also* victims, procedural justice needs of
Convention on Preventing and Combating Violence Against Women and Domestic Violence, Council of Europe 3, 45
Convention on the Rights of the Child 1990 118
convictions 6, 23, 32, 35, 58, 59, 60, 61–2, 67, 77, 78, 82, 84, 102, 107, 117, 119; conviction rates 9, 32, 45, 51, 82
Crimes Act 1958 (Vic) 46
Crimes Amendment (Rape) Act 2007 (Vic) 47
criminal justice system: accountability of *see* accountability, of criminal justice system; agencies 33; confidence in 3, 6, 10; transparency of (*see* transparency);

victims' experiences of (*see* victims, experiences of criminal justice system); and victims' needs (*see* victims, needs of); victims' rights within (*see* victims, rights of); victims' role within 4, 6, 7, 8, 15, 24, 27–8, 30; victims' satisfaction with (*see* victims, satisfaction of); *see also* adversarial justice
Criminal Law (Rape) Act 1981 (Irl) 47, 97, 100, 106; *see also Sex Offenders Act 2001* (Irl)
Criminal Law (Sentencing) Act 1988 (SA) 48, 114, 115
Criminal Law Consolidation Act 1935 (SA) 47
criminal procedure 2, 99, 100; *see also* criminal proceedings
criminal proceedings 3, 7, 25, 45, 48, 98, 112, 114, 116, 117, 149; *see also* criminal procedure
criminology 30, 62
cross-examination: of accused 35–6; of victims 6–7, 9, 36, 38, 39–40, 41, 68, 97, 98, 99, 100, 102, 105–8, 130, 133, 137, 157
Crown Prosecution Service (CPS), England and Wales 12, 21, 32, 38, 74, 75, 82–3, 142–6, 161; Ch 4

decision-making 23, 34, 52, 91, 95, 105, 142, 144, 157, 161; and control 71–2; Crown Prosecution Service 21, 83, 90 (*see* Victims' Right to Review (VRR)); overturning 12, 21, 73, 76, 77, 83, 86, 87, 90, 92, 94, 95, 157, **158**; and procedural justice 61, 64; prosecutorial 75, 80, 82, 87, 88, 94, 144, 161, 162; reviews of 74; South Australian Director of Public Prosecutions 123; transparency of (*see* transparency); unfettered 34, 74, 80, 121; and victims 13, 48, 87, 145, 149; and voice 69
Declaration of Basic Principles of Justice for Victims of Crime and Abuse of Power (1985) 45, 52, 113
defence counsel 6, 14, 16, 36, 38, 39, 40, 82, 100, 101, 102, 103–6, 109, 116, 118–19, 120, 121, 123, 137, 146–7, 155, 160, 161
defendant *see* accused; perpetrator
degradation ceremony 38–41, 54
deterrence 58
Director of Public Prosecutions, Australia 144, 154
Director of Public Prosecutions, UK 83, 145
distributive justice 60
Doak, Professor Jonathan 4, 8, 15, 16–17, 35, 37–8, 53, 69, 127
Dublin Rape Crisis Centre 99
due process rights, of the accused *see* accused, due process rights of

England and Wales 2–3, 12, 17, 21–2, 32, 47, 48, 49, 71, 74, 75, 79, 82, 108, 138, 143, 144, 156, 157, **158**, 160; *see also* Victims' Right to Review (VRR)
equality 2, 5, 36, 43, 60, 74; *see also* 'equality of arms'
'equality of arms' 5, 6, 7, 134–5, 138, 150
evidence 3, 5, 74, 75–7, 81–2, 84–6, 93, 94, 113, 116, 137; forensic 9; omission of 80; physical 9; probative 6, 40; sexual history 9, 13, 25, 40–1, 45, 63, 97, 99, 100–2, 103–10, 123, 138, 147, 150, 155, 161; video 26n8, 45

fairness 2, 4, 5–6, 7, 10–11, 36, 42, 44, 57, 60, 61–4, 74, 79, 106, 118, 129, 140, 164; fair processes 10–11, 12, 24, 26, 57–8, 60, 61–4, 69, 72, 98, 128, 136, 162, 164n1; *see also* procedural justice
false complaints 45, 68
feminist activism 6, 43–4; *see also* women's movements
Fitz-Gibbon, Dr Kate 32, 34, 44, 154, 155
Flynn, Asher, Associate Professor 5, 10, 36–8, 46, 49, 51, 55n9, 63, 73, 80, 83, 92, 138–9, 144

Glidewell Review, UK 75, 83
guilty pleas 12, 36, 51, 126, 144, 154

Hodgson, Professor Jacqueline 5, 138–9

ideal victim 6, 30–3, 34, 40, 41, 43, 45, 53, 82, 91, 95; *see also* myths and misconceptions about rape and sexuality
Iliadis, Dr Mary 10, 63, 144, 155
independent legal representation (ILR) for sexual assault victims in Victoria 28–9; Ch 7; duplicating role of prosecutor 137–8; funding of 138–40; impact on due process rights of accused 136–7; limitations of 134–42; potential benefits of 128–31; problems with a 'third player' 135–6; stages of process 131–4; and withdrawal of state support services 140–2

independent legal representation (ILR) for victims 13–14, 15–16, 38, 127; *see also* independent legal representation (ILR) for sexual assault victims in Ireland; independent legal representation (ILR) for sexual assault victims in Victoria; South Australian Commissioner for Victims' Rights (SACVR)
independent legal representation (ILR) for victims in Ireland 12–14, 157; Ch 5; background to 97–9; initial proposals for 97–9; introduction of 99–100; problems with application of 103–9; and victims' procedural justice needs 100–3; *see also Sex Offenders Act 2001* (IRL)
information, for victims about criminal justice process 2–3, 10, 16, 36, 45, 50–1, 57, 64, 65–7, 77, 87, 89–90, 100, 118, 119, 128, 130, 155, **158**, 161, 163; *see also* victims, procedural justice needs of
inquisitorial systems 14–17, 28, 53, 136
intimate partner violence 7, 28, 34, 106
Ireland 13–14, 17, 41, 47, 70, 155, 157, **158**, 161; Ch 5; *see also* independent legal representation (ILR) for victims in Ireland
Irish Law Reform Commission 98–9
Istanbul Convention *see Convention on Preventing and Combating Violence Against Women and Domestic Violence*, Council of Europe

Joint Oireachtas Committee, Ireland 97, 98, 99
Jordan, Adjunct Professor Jan 33, 40, 58, 67
judges 5, 14, 49, 63, 99, 104, 106, 120, 160, 161
jury 5, 36, 78, 82, 105, 106; deliberations 107; directions 47
'just deserts' 42, 55n6, 58, 60; *see also* punishment
justice *see* distributive justice; procedural justice

Kirchengast, Associate Professor Tyrone 2, 8, 14, 15, 52, 53, 162, 163

law: case 22; common 26n6, 41, 45, 48, 143–4; compliance with (*see* compliance); criminal 32, 34, 152–3; domestic 118; impacts of 99, 115; international 16; interpretations of 117; rape 46, 153; reform 11, 22, 43, 45, 46, 47, 48, 100, 120, 127, 155, 166; rule of 6
legal aid 98, 99, 104, 106, 136, 138–9, 140, 150
Legal Aid Board, Ireland 104
Legal Aid, Sentencing and Punishment of Offenders Act 2012 (LASPO), UK 138–9
legal culture 88
legal representation 6, 98, 101; for victims 13–14, 15, 146–50; *see also* independent legal representation (ILR) for victims
Lord Steyn 2, 44, 132, 152; *see also* 'triangulation of interests'

myths and misconceptions about rape and sexuality 6, 9, 32, 45, 46, 81, 82, 90, 91, 95, 106–9, 146, 153, 155, 156, 160, 161; *see also* stereotypes about sexual violence

O'Connell, Michael James 2, 8, 16, 49–50, 52, 114, 115, 124n6
Office of Public Prosecutions (OPP) 37, 138
Office of the Commissioner for Victims' Rights, Australia 112–13, 149
outcomes 46, 50, 57, 60–2, 64, 65, 88, 107, 139, 149, 157; just 57, 61, 72, 103, 121, 164; procedural 149; punitive 58, 60, 72; of reviews 20, 21, 156; sentencing (*see* sentencing, outcomes); substantive 3, 9, 12, 66, 68, 94, 106, 131, 155; therapeutic 10, 48; unjust 41, 57

patriarchy 6, 33, 43, 146
perpetrators 9, 23, 31, 32, 40, 46, 58, 71, 103, 106–7, 108, 109, 153; *see also* accused
plea bargaining *see* plea negotiations
plea deals 88
plea hearing 16
plea negotiations 36–7, 49, 67, 75, 80, 88, 90, 92, 115, 116, 117, 133
police 22, 32–4, 37, 68, 71, 75, 83, 117, 120, 133, 138, 144, 157; England and Wales 75, 78, 82–3, 90; legitimacy 62; treatment of sexual assault victims 32–4, 45, 54, 67, 68, 153; *see also* Victoria Police
presumption of innocence 6
procedural justice 10–11, 103, 119, 120; Ch 3; *see also* control, by victims over criminal justice process; information,

for victims about criminal justice process; validation, of victims' experiences; victims, experiences of procedural justice; victims, procedural justice needs of; voice, of victims within criminal justice process
procedural justice theory 24, 57, 60, 61–72, 102, 129; key elements of 64
prosecutions 5, 32, 34, 45, 76, 80, 82, 83, 86, 87, 126, 144, 153, 154, 155, 160
prosecutorial decisions 73–4, 90; accountability of 80; *see also* Victims' Right to Review (VRR)
prosecutors 34–8, 42, 73–4, 88, 91, 133, 138; decision-making (*see* prosecutorial decisions); role of 82, 98, 101, 103, 121–2, 123, 137, 141, 147
punishment 8, 48, 55n6, 56–8, 60, 78; *see also* 'just deserts'

R v Killick 74
rape 9, 23, 31–4, 39–41, 45–7, 59, 80, 82, 90–1, 98–9, 101, 102, 105, 106–9, 153, 155, 161; 'real' 32, 33–4, 45, 46, 107; cases 98–9, 107; consent 45, 46–7, 107; convictions 82, 102; *see also* myths and misconceptions about rape and sexuality; sexual assault; sexual offences
rape crisis centres 97
Rape Crisis Network Ireland (RCNI) 33, 66, 104, 107
reporting of crime 2, 9, 23, 27, 32–4, 45, 51, 58, 68, 70, 71, 78, 86, 91, 102, 103, 107, 153; fear of 32, 46, 80, 81, 160
restorative justice 27, 52–3, 63
retribution *see* punishment
rights of victims *see* victims, rights of
Royal Commission into Family Violence (RCFV) 7, 28, 34, 38, 53, 65, 112, 126–7, 153, 154, 166
Royal Commission into Institutional Responses to Child Sexual Abuse (Cth) (RCIRCSA) 7, 29, 38, 53, 71–2, 112, 126–7, 144, 151, 153, 154, 163, 165

secondary harm *see* secondary victimisation
secondary victimisation 2, 4, 7, 11, 13, 27, 38, 41, 70, 100, 102, 120, 128, 153, 154
sentencing 48, 49, 58, 115, 116; mandatory minimum 58; outcomes 48; severity of 41, 58; uniformity of 58
Sex Offenders Act 2001 (Irl) 12–13, 157, 161; Ch 5; background to introduction of independent legal representation 99–100; limited role of legal representative 105–6; and myths and misconceptions about rape and sexuality 106–9; notice of intention to cross-examine 103–5; problems with application 103–9; section 34, 2, 12–13; Ch 5; and victims' procedural justice needs 100–3; *see also* independent legal representation for victims in Ireland
sexual assault 31, 68, 117, 118; *see also* rape; sexual offences
sexual assault victims 8–10, 51–3; belief in 33–4, 68–9, 81; expectations of 56–7; experiences of 46, 51–3, 59; independent legal representation for (*see* independent legal representation (ILR) for victims); needs of 8, 63; rights of 8–10, 28–9, 43–4, 98; and secondary victimisation (*see* secondary victimisation); treatment of 8, 44, 58–60, 98
sexual offences 9, 23, 32, 58, 78, 80, 90, 91–2, 98, 119, 146, 153; *see also* rape; sexual assault
Sexual Offences (Criminal Procedure) Act 2002 (Scot) 105
Sexual Offences Act 2003 (UK) 47
socio-legal scholarship 24, 25, 30, 62
South Australia 13, 17, 24, 47, 48, 70, 147–9, 157–8, **158**, 161; Ch 6
South Australian Commissioner for Victims' Rights (SACVR) 13; Ch 6, 147–50; and accountability 121, 161; benefits of 116, 120; emergence of 113–14; involvement prolonging criminal justice process 122–3; legislative limits 121–2; limitations of 120–3; limited resources 120–1; powers and functions of 114–17
specialist family violence courts 7, 38, 53, 154, 166
state: interests of 2, 4, 35, 37, 48, 92, 123, 150, 155–6 (*see also* 'triangulation of interests'); represented by the prosecution 98; rights of 2, 155, 163; role within adversarial system 5, 123, 130, 139; role within inquisitorial system 14; as the wronged party 34–5, 43, 58, 130
state support services 140–2
statutory charging process 75
statutory definition 46
statutory limitations 35–6

statutory obligations 92, 121, 138
statutory powers 112, 125n10
statutory requirements 37, 121, 122
statutory right 54n1
stereotypes about sexual violence 9, 31–3, 34, 40, 82, 90–2, 109, 146, 153, 155, 156, 157, 161

The Role of Victims of Crime in the Criminal Trial Process 28, 126, 127
transparency 12, 64, 83–7, 88–9, 91, 95, 142, 143, 157, 160; *see also* accountability; Victims' Right to Review (VRR)
'triangulation of interests' 2, 11, 16, 24, 29, 38, 41–2, 44, 48, 54, 97–8, 132, 140, 152, 155, 156, 163–4; *see also* Lord Steyn
truth 6, 14, 56, 69–70
Tyler, Tom 10, 61–2, 64

Universal Declaration of Human Rights 1948 118

validation, of victims' experiences 10, 34, 39, 57, 58–9, 63, 64, 67–9, 77–9, 86, 101, 128, 130, 131, **158**, 166; *see also* victims, procedural justice needs of
vengeance 42, 58; vengeful victims 57–60; *see also* punishment
verdicts 5, 38, 42, 103, 107, 117; guilty 12, 22–3, 41, 59, 67, 68, 78, 101, 109, 118, 119
victim advocates 4, 36, 137, 145
Victim Impact Statement (VIS) 45, 48–50, 63, 70, 113–14, 115, 162; inconsistent implementation 49; and victim satisfaction 48; *see also* Victim Personal Statement (VPS)
Victim Personal Statement (VPS) 49; *see also* Victim Impact Statement (VIS)
victim support organisations 45, 50, 78, 79, 98, 135, 141, 150; workers 17, 23, 156, 164
victim-focused reform 2–3, 28; emergence and development 44–6; key reforms 46–51
victimology 10, 30, 31, 53
victims of crime: at-risk 2; belief in 32; coaching of 99; definition of 'victim' 23, 30; dissatisfaction of 33, 41, 46, 49, 61, 79, 93–4, 106, 128, 132, 154, 159; emerging interest in 30; expectations of 12, 17, 39, 40, 44–5, 56–7, 92–3, 135–6; experiences of criminal justice system 4, 6, 23, 27–30, 57, 59, 61, 63, 64, 80, 101, 112; experiences of procedural justice 41, 46, 51, 54, 63, 70, 101, 104, 109, 118, 128, 142, 151, 155–61; interests of 2, 4, 7, 8, 11, 14, 24, 33–8, 42, 44, 92, 97–8, 115–17, 123, 130, 155–6 (*see* 'triangulation of interests');1 needs of 2, 40–1, 44–5, 57, 63–5, 128, 150, 165; participation of 41–2, 48, 58, 61, 100–2, 109–10, 116, 126, 131 (*see* independent legal representation (ILR) for victims); procedural justice needs of 10–11, 63, 67, 69, 71, 74, 77–8, 81, 83, 86, 87, 88, 90, 94, 100, 114, 128, 141–2; recovery of 94; rights of 27–9, 43–4, 52, 53, 79, 100, 109, 112, 115–16, 123, 126; satisfaction of 10, 12, 48, 57, 60, 63, 68, 79, 84, 93–5, 102–3; of sexual assault (*see* sexual assault victims); treatment of 6, 8, 30, 35, 45, 61, 64, 114, 121 (*see* sexual assault victims, treatment of); vengeful 24, 57–60, 72, 136; victim-blaming 30–2; vulnerable 15, 140; as witnesses 6, 7, 35, 67, 70; *see also* compensation for; control, by victims over criminal justice process; cross-examination of victims; ideal victim; information, for victims about criminal justice process; validation, of victims' experiences; voice, of victims within criminal justice process
Victims Assistance Program 141
Victims' Charter Act 2006 (Vic) 7, 22, 36–7, 45, 49, 50–1, 54, 67, 92, 122, 126, 127, 148, 154
Victims of Crime Act 2001 (SA) 13, 114–17, 121, 123, 157, 159
Victims of Crime Commissioner (VoCC) 7, 28, 127, 147–50, 154, 163; enhancing powers of 147–50
Victims' Right to Review (VRR), England and Wales 12, 144–6; Ch 4; accountability of 87–90, 95, 142, 157, 160; benefits of 79; data on 89–92; eligibility for 75–6; independence of 88–9; limitations of 81–3, 87–8; process 75–7; style reform 144–6, 151; transparency 83–7; and victim expectations 92–3; victim satisfaction with 93–5; and victims' procedural justice needs 77–8; victims' satisfaction in 79

Victims' Rights and Support Act 2013 (NSW) 113
Victims' Rights Charter 113
victims' rights groups 4, 43–4; *see also* feminist activism
victims' rights movement 6, 53, 113; *see also* feminist activism
Victims Support Agency, Victoria 65
Victoria 3, 7, 17, 24, 28–9, 36–8, 46, 48, 50, 51, 52, 53, 58, 65, 92, 108, 124, 153, 154–5, 156, 162, 163, 165, 166; Ch 7
Victoria Police 65, 91, 141, 148
Victorian Law Reform Commission (VLRC) 28, 52, 65, 126–7, 141, 148
video testimony *see* evidence, video
voice, of victims within criminal justice process 3, 8, 10, 19, 48, 58, 61, 63, 64, 69–70, 77, 79, 81–3, 100–1, 118, 120, 128, 129, 130, **158**, 166; *see also* victims, procedural justice needs of

Walklate, Professor Sandra 6, 7, 9, 23, 28, 31, 38, 39, 40, 43, 80, 127, 128, 140, 154, 155, 163
Wemmers, Professor Jo-Anne 10, 12, 27, 60, 61, 69, 71
Witness Assistance Service (WAS) 141
witnesses 5, 6, 9, 15, 42, 44, 82, 99, 137; victims as (*see* victims, as witnesses)
women's movements 43–4; *see also* feminist activism
women's organisations 97
Worsnop v The Queen 47

Youth Justice and Criminal Evidence Act 1999 (UK) 108

www.ingramcontent.com/pod-product-compliance
Lightning Source LLC
LaVergne TN
LVHW011129300926
849160LV00008B/568
* 9 7 8 0 3 6 7 4 9 1 5 2 9 *